MySocialWorkLab offers:

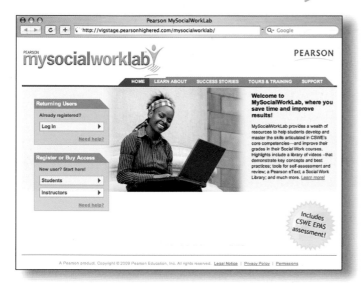

- A complete **Pearson eText** of the book
- A wealth of engaging **videos**
  - **Brand-new videos**—organized around the competencies and accompanied by interactive assessment—that demonstrate key concepts and practices
  - **Career Exploration videos** that contain interviews with a wide range of social workers
- Tools for **self-assessment and review**—chapter specific quizzes tied to the core competencies, many written in the same format students will find on the licensing exam
- A **Gradebook** that reports progress of students and the class as a whole
- **MySocialWorkLibrary**—a compendium of articles and case studies in social work, searchable by course, topic, author, and title
- **MySearchLab**—a collection of tools that aid students in mastering research assignments and papers
- **And much more!**

Save time and improve results!

MySocialWorkLab is a dynamic website that provides a wealth of resources geared to help students develop and master the skills articulated in CSWE's core competencies—and improve their grades in their social work courses.

MySocialWorkLab is available at no extra cost when bundled with any text in the **Connecting Core Competencies Series.** Visit **www.mysocialworklab.com** to learn more.

> **"I would require [MySocialWorkLab]—especially if there were a way to harvest the results for program assessment."**
>
> —Jane Peller, *Northeastern Illinois University*

In recent years, many Social Work departments have been focusing on the CSWE Educational Policy and Accreditation Standards (EPAS) to guide their accreditation process. The current standards, issued in 2008, focus on mastery of the CSWE's ten core competencies and practice behaviors. Each of the ten core competencies now contains specific knowledge, values, skills, and the resulting practice behaviors as guidance for the curriculum and assessment methods of Social Work programs.

In writing this text, we have used the CSWE core competency standards and assessment recommendations as guidelines for structuring content and integrating the pedagogy. For details on the CSWE core competencies, please see www.cswe.org.

For the core competencies highlighted in this text, see page iv.

CSWE EPAS 2008 Core Competencies

Professional Identity

2.1.1 Identify as a professional social worker and conduct oneself accordingly.

Necessary Knowledge, Values, Skills

- Social workers serve as representatives of the profession, its mission, and its core values.
- Social workers know the profession's history.
- Social workers commit themselves to the profession's enhancement and to their own professional conduct and growth.

Operational Practice Behaviors

- Social workers advocate for client access to the services of social work;
- Social workers practice personal reflection and self-correction to assure continual professional development;
- Social workers attend to professional roles and boundaries;
- Social workers demonstrate professional demeanor in behavior, appearance, and communication;
- Social workers engage in career-long learning; and
- Social workers use supervision and consultation.

Ethical Practice

2.1.2 Apply social work ethical principles to guide professional practice.

Necessary Knowledge, Values, Skills

- Social workers have an obligation to conduct themselves ethically and engage in ethical decision-making.
- Social workers are knowledgeable about the value base of the profession, its ethical standards, and relevant law.

Operational Practice Behaviors

- Social workers recognize and manage personal values in a way that allows professional values to guide practice;
- Social workers make ethical decisions by applying standards of the National Association of Social Workers Code of Ethics and, as applicable, of the International Federation of Social Workers/International Association of Schools of Social Work Ethics in Social Work, Statement of Principles;
- Social workers tolerate ambiguity in resolving ethical conflicts; and
- Social workers apply strategies of ethical reasoning to arrive at principled decisions.

Critical Thinking

2.1.3 Apply critical thinking to inform and communicate professional judgments.

Necessary Knowledge, Values, Skills

- Social workers are knowledgeable about the principles of logic, scientific inquiry, and reasoned discernment.
- They use critical thinking augmented by creativity and curiosity.
- Critical thinking also requires the synthesis and communication of relevant information.

Operational Practice Behaviors

- Social workers distinguish, appraise, and integrate multiple sources of knowledge, including research-based knowledge, and practice wisdom;
- Social workers analyze models of assessment, prevention, intervention, and evaluation; and
- Social workers demonstrate effective oral and written communication in working with individuals, families, groups, organizations, communities, and colleagues.

Adapted with the permission of Council on Social Work Education

Diversity in Practice

2.1.4 Engage diversity and difference in practice.

Necessary Knowledge, Values, Skills

- Social workers understand how diversity characterizes and shapes the human experience and is critical to the formation of identity.
- The dimensions of diversity are understood as the intersectionality of multiple factors including age, class, color, culture, disability, ethnicity, gender, gender identity and expression, immigration status, political ideology, race, religion, sex, and sexual orientation.
- Social workers appreciate that, as a consequence of difference, a person's life experiences may include oppression, poverty, marginalization, and alienation as well as privilege, power, and acclaim.

Operational Practice Behaviors

- Social workers recognize the extent to which a culture's structures and values may oppress, marginalize, alienate, or create or enhance privilege and power;
- Social workers gain sufficient self-awareness to eliminate the influence of personal biases and values in working with diverse groups;
- Social workers recognize and communicate their understanding of the importance of difference in shaping life experiences; and
- Social workers view themselves as learners and engage those with whom they work as informants.

Human Rights & Justice

2.1.5 Advance human rights and social and economic justice.

Necessary Knowledge, Values, Skills

- Each person, regardless of position in society, has basic human rights, such as freedom, safety, privacy, an adequate standard of living, health care, and education.
- Social workers recognize the global interconnections of oppression and are knowledgeable about theories of justice and strategies to promote human and civil rights.
- Social work incorporates social justice practices in organizations, institutions, and society to ensure that these basic human rights are distributed equitably and without prejudice.

Operational Practice Behaviors

- Social workers understand the forms and mechanisms of oppression and discrimination;
- Social workers advocate for human rights and social and economic justice; and
- Social workers engage in practices that advance social and economic justice.

Research Based Practice

2.1.6 Engage in research-informed practice and practice-informed research.

Necessary Knowledge, Values, Skills

- Social workers use practice experience to inform research, employ evidence-based interventions, evaluate their own practice, and use research findings to improve practice, policy, and social service delivery.
- Social workers comprehend quantitative and qualitative research and understand scientific and ethical approaches to building knowledge.

Operational Practice Behaviors

- Social workers use practice experience to inform scientific inquiry; and
- Social workers use research evidence to inform practice.

Human Behavior

2.1.7 Apply knowledge of human behavior and the social environment.

Necessary Knowledge, Values, Skills

- Social workers are knowledgeable about human behavior across the life course; the range of social systems in which people live; and the ways social systems promote or deter people in maintaining or achieving health and well-being.
- Social workers apply theories and knowledge from the liberal arts to understand biological, social, cultural, psychological, and spiritual development.

Operational Practice Behaviors

- Social workers utilize conceptual frameworks to guide the processes of assessment, intervention, and evaluation; and
- Social workers critique and apply knowledge to understand person and environment.

Policy Practice   2.1.8 Engage in policy practice to advance social and economic well-being and to deliver effective social work services.

Necessary Knowledge, Values, Skills

- Social work practitioners understand that policy affects service delivery and they actively engage in policy practice.
- Social workers know the history and current structures of social policies and services; the role of policy in service delivery; and the role of practice in policy development.

Operational Practice Behaviors

- Social workers analyze, formulate, and advocate for policies that advance social well-being; and
- Social workers collaborate with colleagues and clients for effective policy action.

Practice Contexts

2.1.9 Respond to contexts that shape practice.

Necessary Knowledge, Values, Skills

- Social workers are informed, resourceful, and proactive in responding to evolving organizational, community, and societal contexts at all levels of practice.
- Social workers recognize that the context of practice is dynamic, and use knowledge and skill to respond proactively.

Operational Practice Behaviors

- Social workers continuously discover, appraise, and attend to changing locales, populations, scientific and technological developments, and emerging societal trends to provide relevant services; and
- Social workers provide leadership in promoting sustainable changes in service delivery and practice to improve the quality of social services.

Engage, Assess, Intervene, Evaluate   2.1.10 Engage, assess, intervene, and evaluate with individuals, families, groups, organizations, and communities.

Necessary Knowledge, Values, Skills

- Professional practice involves the dynamic and interactive processes of engagement, assessment, intervention, and evaluation at multiple levels.
- Social workers have the knowledge and skills to practice with individuals, families, groups, organizations, and communities.
- Practice knowledge includes
  - identifying, analyzing, and implementing evidence-based interventions designed to achieve client goals;
  - using research and technological advances;
  - evaluating program outcomes and practice effectiveness;
  - developing, analyzing, advocating, and providing leadership for policies and services; and
  - promoting social and economic justice.

Operational Practice Behaviors

(a) Engagement

- Social workers substantively and effectively prepare for action with individuals, families, groups, organizations, and communities;
- Social workers use empathy and other interpersonal skills; and
- Social workers develop a mutually agreed-on focus of work and desired outcomes.

(b) Assessment

- Social workers collect, organize, and interpret client data;
- Social workers assess client strengths and limitations;
- Social workers develop mutually agreed-on intervention goals and objectives; and
- Social workers select appropriate intervention strategies.

(c) Intervention

- Social workers initiate actions to achieve organizational goals;
- Social workers implement prevention interventions that enhance client capacities;
- Social workers help clients resolve problems;
- Social workers negotiate, mediate, and advocate for clients; and
- Social workers facilitate transitions and endings.

(d) Evaluation

- Social workers critically analyze, monitor, and evaluate interventions.

FIFTH EDITION

The Social Work Practicum

A Guide and Workbook for Students

Cynthia L. Garthwait
The University of Montana

Allyn & Bacon

Boston Columbus Indianapolis New York San Francisco Upper Saddle River
Amsterdam Cape Town Dubai London Madrid Milan Munich Paris Montreal Toronto
Delhi Mexico City Sao Paulo Sydney Hong Kong Seoul Singapore Taipei Tokyo

To the social work practicum students, both BSW and MSW levels, who inspire and teach me daily as they prepare to join the social work profession, and to the social work field instructors and faculty supervisors who give so generously of their time to the education and mentoring of future social workers

To my family,
Gary, Nathan, and Benjamin

Editor in Chief: Dickson Musslewhite
Executive Editor: Ashley Dodge
Editorial Assistant: Carly Czech
Director of Development: Sharon Geary
Development Editor: Deb Hanlon
Director of Marketing: Brandy Dawson
Senior Marketing Manager: Wendy Albert
Marketing Assistant: Kyle VanNatter
Advertising Director: Kate Conway
Advertising Manager: Sara Sherlock

Design Specialist: Robert Farrar-Wagner
Copywriter: Jonathan Andrew
Senior Media Editor: Melanie MacFarlane
Senior Production Project Manager: Pat Torelli
Editorial Production and Composition Service: Laserwords, Maine
Manager of Design Development: John Christiana
Interior Design: Joyce Weston Design
Cover Design: Joel Gendron; Kristina Mose-Libon
Manufacturing Buyer: Debbie Rossi

Credits appear on page 226, which constitutes an extension of the copyright page.

Library of Congress Cataloging-in-Publication Data

Garthwait, Cynthia L.
  The social work practicum : a guide and workbook for students / Cynthia L. Garthwait. — 5th ed.
    p. cm.
  ISBN-13: 978-0-205-76944-5
  ISBN-10: 0-205-76944-6
  1. Social work education—United States—Outlines, syllabi, etc. 2. Social work education—United States—Examinations, questions, etc. I. Title.
  HV11.7.H67 2011
  361.3076—dc22

                    2009045499

10 9 8 7 6 5   BRR 14 13 12 11

Allyn & Bacon
is an imprint of

www.pearsonhighered.com

ISBN-10:   0-205-76944-6
ISBN-13: 978-0-205-76944-5

Contents

Foreword

Welcome to the exciting and challenging world of social work practice. The practicum learning experience is the centerpiece of social work education where the integration of professional knowledge, skills, and values comes to life. Many students describe the practicum as the most meaningful and powerful component of their educational experience. In the context of the practicum, students actively contribute to fulfilling the core purpose of social work—the promotion of human and community well-being. The practicum is key to formation of professional identity; preparation for ethical practice; and development of direct practice, advocacy, and community-building skills. Through the practicum experience students gain confidence in fulfilling multiple social work roles; competence in the application and evaluation of conceptual frameworks and practice models; and critical self awareness and respect for difference. It is in practicum settings that students experience first-hand the process of engagement, power of bearing witness to human pain and resilience, and possibilities of people coming together to create change.

The Social Work Practicum: A Guide and Workbook for Students provides students with a user-friendly guide to make connections between theories and concepts learned in the classroom and the dynamic world of practice. The text presents learning goals, background and context, guidance and direction, food for thought, activities, and selected bibliographies for a comprehensive range of themes that are central to the practicum experience. Cynthia Garthwait has drawn from her rich and varied professional experience as a social work practitioner, educator, scholar, and practicum coordinator in crafting this text. Garthwait does not offer her readers a "cookbook" approach, but rather a thoughtful guide to ethical and empowering social work practice. Her commitment to and enthusiasm for the social work profession shines through as she invites readers to honor their strengths and hone their skills as they launch into hands-on practice.

According to the Council on Social Work Education (CSWE) (2008), field education constitutes the "signature pedagogy" of the social work learning experience. It is the "central form of instruction that socializes the learner to the role of practitioner" (Shulman, 2005). It is through the practicum that the abstract concept of "generalist social work" is translated into concrete actions. Garthwait encourages students to embrace a strengths-based approach to their professional socialization, and she provides opportunities for them to identify their own strengths as well as those of the individuals, families, and communities with whom they work.

The text provides students with specific learning opportunities to link course-based understanding of the ten core social work competencies (CSWE, 2008) with their integration and application in the context of the practicum experience. It offers a comprehensive range of activities designed to encourage critical thinking and deepen self awareness as students develop their professional identity, ethical judgment, and practical skills. Utilizing the text as their guide, students enhance their understanding of and ability to work within diverse contexts of practice; strengthen their skills of assessment, intervention, and evaluation at multiple levels; and gain deeper insight into the effects of social problems and policy responses on social work organizations and on the lives of those we serve. Further, the text provides tools and exercises to help students honor diversity and difference in practice; advance human rights and social and economic justice; advocate for policies that promote social and economic well-being; engage in research-informed practice and practice-informed research; and apply knowledge of social policy and human behavior in the social environment to practice.

The Social Work Practicum offers a well planned approach for maximizing field education that serves as a model for effective practice. Garthwait provides clear guidance for students, agency field instructors, and faculty supervisors to anticipate the practicum experience; engage in dialogue about teaching and learning; clarify expectations; and develop clear goals, objectives, and learning activities to ensure a productive and positive experience for all. Particular attention is paid to strategies for effective supervision and communication that are keys to a successful practicum experience and future professional practice.

The text concludes with a challenge and a charge that fuel social workers' passions for a lifetime—become the person you want to be and the social worker you want to be. Become a leader and seeker of social justice. Let the practicum begin.

Janet L. Finn, Ph.D.
Professor and MSW Program Director
School of Social Work, The University of Montana

References:

Council on Social Work Education (2008). Educational Policy and Accreditation Standards. Alexandria, VA: CSWE.

Shulman, L. (2005). Signature pedagogies in the professions. *Daedelus,* Summer, 52–59.

Preface

Having taught social work at the BSW and MSW levels, including administering a social work program and serving as Practicum Coordinator, I have 22 years of experience with and observations about the importance of the practicum experience in social work education. It is in the practicum that conceptual frameworks such as professional perspectives, orienting theories, practice theories, and practice models come to life. The practicum affords the opportunity to provide services to real individuals, families, groups, and communities, and it also requires that students bring their academic learning with them to the practicum. It is in the practicum that theory translates into practice, that assessing real clients leads to real interventions, that ethical issues are no longer hypothetical, and that students move from learners to professionals. They now have the chance to try out the skills and techniques they previously rehearsed in role plays and simulations.

This book was written to support the vital purpose of the practicum, helping students make the transition from student to social worker through a planned revisiting of the curriculum with an eye to applying it all to real people in real situations. The book will help students link theory and practice, and build competency at every step. Each chapter focuses on a discrete topic of great importance to practicum and to practice. Each chapter builds on previous chapters, and there are notations throughout the book tying content both to previous and subsequent chapters.

Connecting Core Competencies Series

The new edition of this text is now a part of Pearson Education's new *Connecting Core Competencies* series, which consists of five foundation-level texts that make it easier than ever to ensure students' success in learning the ten core competencies as stated in 2008 by the Council on Social Work Education. Because of the demands on social work practitioners, it is important that schools of social work, including practicum programs, devise strategies that help students acquire these competencies over time. This text contains:

- **Core Competency Icons** throughout the chapters, directly linking the CSWE core competencies to the content of the text. **Critical thinking questions** are also included to further students' mastery of the CSWE's standards. For easy reference, page iv and the beginning of each chapter also display which icons are used in each chapter.
- **An end-of-chapter Practice Test**, with reflection questions for chapters 1-4 and multiple-choice questions for chapters 5-19, that tests students' knowledge of the chapter content and mastery of the competencies. These questions are constructed in a format that will help prepare students for the **ASWB Licensing exam.**
- **Additional questions pertaining to the videos found on the new MySocialWorkLab** at the end of each chapter to encourage students to access the site and explore the wealth of available materials. If this text did not come with an access code for MySocialWorkLab, you can purchase access at: **www.mysocialworklab.com**.

Acknowledgments

I am grateful to many individuals who helped shape my ideas and offered encouragement on the completion of the fifth edition of this book. This includes faculty colleagues, staff members, agency field instructors, and both BSW and MSW students. All of their points of view, individual experiences, and commitment to the profession have made me a better teacher and also enhanced my understanding of the ways in which students integrate theory and practice.

Thanks go to Tondy Baumgartner, Randy Wood, Janet Finn, Kerrie Ghenie, Catherine O'Day, Tammy Tolleson Knee, Charlie Wellenstein, Heidi Holzer, and Judy Pfaff. A special thanks goes to my colleague and friend Charles Horejsi, whose enthusiasm for preparing competent and caring social workers led to our collaboration on the first two editions of this text. Acknowledgments also go to the Allyn and Bacon staff, including Ashley Dodge, Executive Editor, and Deb Hanlon, Development Editor, and Patricia Quinlin, the editor who conceived of and initiated the Connecting Core Competencies series of which this book is a part.

The Purpose of a Practicum

LEARNING GOALS FOR THIS CHAPTER

▶ To understand the purpose of a social work practicum

▶ To complete a self-assessment of your readiness for practicum

CONNECTING CORE COMPETENCIES *in this chapter*

| Professional Identity | Ethical Practice | Critical Thinking | Diversity in Practice | Human Rights & Justice | Research Based Practice | Human Behavior | Policy Practice | Practice Contexts | Engage Assess Intervene Evaluate |

Congratulations for embarking on your exciting social work practicum experience. You are to be applauded for reaching this stage in your professional education and for being selected and approved for a practicum based on your academic achievements and your readiness for professional experience. The practicum offers a unique opportunity to apply what you have learned in the classroom, to expand your knowledge, and to develop your skills. It is time for you to move from the role of a student to the role of a professional social worker.

BACKGROUND AND CONTEXT

Critical Thinking

Building on what you have learned about social policy in your previous classes, what social policy analysis model can you use to assess the effectiveness of social policies in your agency?

A **practicum** is an experience that requires the practical application of theory or conceptual knowledge. Most types of professional education—whether in medicine, nursing, law, pharmacy, speech therapy, or social work—wisely employ some form of practicum, internship, or preceptorship to help the student learn how to apply knowledge and general principles to real situations, problems, and concerns. Many social workers, agency supervisors, and social work educators use the terms *practicum, field work, field education, field practicum,* and *internship* somewhat interchangeably. This book will use the term *practicum.*

The Council on Social Work Education's (CSWE) Educational Policies, and Academic Standards (2008) states:

> In social work, the signature pedagogy is field education. The intent of field education is to connect the theoretical and conceptual contribution of the classroom with the practical world of the practice setting. It is a basic precept of social work education that the two interrelated components of curriculum—classroom and field—are of equal importance within the curriculum, and each contributes to the development of the requisite competencies of professional practice. Field education is systematically designed, supervised, coordinated, and evaluated based on criteria by which students demonstrate the achievement of program competencies. (8)

Almost universally, students of social work at both the BSW and MSW levels describe their practicum as the single most useful, significant, and powerful learning experience of their formal social work education. It is during the practicum that the concepts, principles, and theories discussed in the classroom come to life. During the practicum, students work with real clients and have the opportunity to try out the skills and techniques they previously rehearsed in classroom role playing and simulations. It is also during the practicum that students make considerable progress in developing self-awareness and come to a better understanding of their particular strengths and limitations as well as the influence of their personal values, attitudes, and life experiences on their practice. The practicum can and should be a time when classroom theory is integrated with social work practice and when students merge with the values and fundamental principles of their chosen profession.

Professional Identity

Although you are just beginning your practicum, you have some of the strengths a social worker will need. As you complete this self-assessment, identify the strengths you already have.

For many students, the practicum is a very positive and meaningful experience, but for some the practicum can fall short of expectations. The quality of every practicum experience can be enhanced if students are provided with guidance in identifying and making use of learning opportunities. A structure that helps students to examine and analyze their settings in ways that build on prior classroom learning is of critical importance. Some of the most meaningful learning occurs as a result of having to deal with unexpected events and frustrations during the practicum.

HOW TO USE THIS BOOK

This book is designed to provide you with guidance and structure during the social work practicum. If used in a thoughtful manner throughout the practicum, it will help you make the best of whatever your practicum setting has to offer. Needless to say, this will not happen without effort. It requires a real commitment and a willingness to invest time in the learning process.

HOW THE CHAPTERS ARE STRUCTURED

Although the chapters are numbered in the conventional manner, this is not to suggest that you are to necessarily move through the book sequentially, one chapter after another. Rather, it is expected that you will be gathering information to complete the workbook activities in several of the chapters at the same time. It is expected that you will move back and forth between sections and will also revisit the same section several times as you gain experience in the practicum and begin to look at various questions and issues from a new perspective.

Each chapter begins with a section titled ***Goals for Learning***. It lists possible goals or desired outcomes related to the knowledge, values, and skills that you can expect to learn and develop during the practicum.

The next major section, ***Background and Context***, presents selected concepts and principles related to the topic addressed by the chapter. The box titled Food for Thought will contain several relevant quotations. The concepts and definitions presented in these two sections are not a substitute for a textbook or assigned readings, but rather should act as a review of key ideas that set the stage for what follows, stimulate creative thinking, and raise important questions.

In each of the sections labeled ***Guidance and Direction***, you are offered general suggestions, guidance, and advice, and sometimes a few specific do's and don'ts intended to encourage and facilitate learning in relation to the chapter's objectives and its particular focus.

In most of the chapters, several pages have been cast into a workbook format and titled ***A Workbook Activity***. You will be asked to use your critical thinking skills to seek answers to each of the questions and record the answers or related comments in the spaces provided.

A section titled ***Suggested Learning Activities*** lists several specific tasks and activities that provide additional opportunities and experiences for learning as well as a few additional ideas, words of encouragement, and specific cautions that may be important to you and the practicum experience.

Each chapter ends with a ***Selected Bibliography*** that lists several books or articles related to the topics addressed in the chapter. The sources listed should be fairly easy for you to locate in a college or agency library. Frequent reference will be made to the *Encyclopedia of Social Work* and to commonly used social work textbooks. Because the book *Techniques and Guidelines for Social Work Practice* by Sheafor and Horejsi (2008) is frequently used in social work practice courses and practicum seminars, the list will usually include a reference to specific sections in that book.

Food for Thought

Experience, both intellectual and emotional, is the raw material of the internship (Sweitzer and King, 2009, 8).

We are bound together by the task that lies before us.
—*Martin Luther King*

The transition between the skills class and your practice/internship is a critical time in which you prepare yourself for applying what you have learned to the real world. If you have been doing your work all along, we still cannot in good faith reassure you that you will be ready. In truth, you will *never* be ready (Brew and Kottler, 2008, 382).

Practicum-Related Strengths: A Workbook Activity

No doubt you have heard about the importance of taking a strengths perspective on your clients, helping them to address their problems by building on their strengths. This exercise will help you do the same thing for yourself. Because you may be wondering if you have the knowledge and ability to succeed in your practicum, following is a self-assessment tool designed to help you identify the resources you bring to this experience.

Below is a list of strengths that are important to a successful practicum experience. Depending on the nature of the setting, some will be of more importance and relevance than others will. This list can also be used to assess the appropriateness of a match between you and your practicum setting.

Place a check mark by all items that apply to you. Acknowledge your strengths, identify the areas in which you lack experience, and begin to set goals for professional development in both areas. Later in this book you will be asked to complete this self-assessment again, which will show you what you have learned over time.

Strengths for a Successful Practicum (Pre-and-Post Test)

Attitudes and Values

_____ 1. Empathetic, caring, and concerned for clients served by the practicum agency

_____ 2. Personal values, beliefs, and perspectives that are compatible with the agency's mission, goals, and philosophy

_____ 3. Personal values, beliefs, and perspectives that are compatible with the National Association of Social Workers (NASW) *Code of Ethics*

_____ 4. Committed to achieving social justice

_____ 5. Respectful of a broad range of diversity among clients and communities

Motivation and Desire to Learn

_____ 6. Eager and open to new learning experiences

_____ 7. Self-discipline and motivation to do what needs to be done, even when you may not feel like doing it

_____ 8. Willingness to take on new responsibilities and perform tasks and activities within your range of abilities

_____ 9. Open to building self-awareness

_____ 10. Adequate time and energy to devote to the practicum

_____ 11. A sense of "calling" to the social work profession

_____ 12. Excitement about helping people improve the quality of their lives

Abilities and Skills

_____ 13. Writing skills (selecting and organizing content, drafting reports, preparing letters, keeping professional records, and utilizing technological communication tools)

_____ 14. Verbal communication skills (explaining, describing, and informing)

_____ 15. Ability to listen (understand what others are saying and respectfully consider their views, perspectives, and opinions)

_____ 16. Ability to quickly process information, understand new concepts, and learn new skills

_____ 17. Ability to read rapidly, grasp ideas quickly, and pull meaning and information from the written word

_____ 18. Ability to organize and plan work to be done and effectively manage and use available time

_____ 19. Ability to meet deadlines and work under pressure

_____ **20.** Ability to follow through on planned actions and complete tasks and assignments

_____ **21.** Ability to make thoughtful and ethical decisions under stressful conditions

_____ **22.** Assertiveness and self-confidence in professional relationships and group discussion

_____ **23.** Committed to self-awareness and professional competence, including a desire to evaluate your own effectiveness

_____ **24.** Ability to build relationships with the agency's clients

_____ **25.** Thoughtful, organized, confident, and comfortable when meeting with a wide variety of people

_____ **26.** Thoughtful, organized, confident, and comfortable when working in groups

_____ **27.** Ability to identify a need and formulate a course of action to address that need

_____ **28.** Ability to solve problems creatively and effectively

Knowledge and Experience

_____ **29.** High level of self-awareness (an understanding of how your own values, beliefs, attitudes, family background, lifestyle, appearance, and life experiences might be perceived by others)

_____ **30.** Familiarity with communication methods and equipment used in the practicum agency (word processor, e-mail, computer software)

_____ **31.** Prior successful experience in adapting to change, new situations, and new work environments

_____ **32.** Prior successful employment or volunteer experience with services or programs similar to those provided by the practicum agency

_____ **33.** Prior successful employment or volunteer experience in working with types of consumers or clients served by the practicum agency

_____ **34.** Working knowledge of the state and federal laws, rules, regulations, and policies relevant to the practicum agency

_____ **35.** Knowledge of the assessment and planning tools, methods, and techniques used by the practicum agency

_____ **36.** Knowledge of the intervention methods and techniques used by the practicum agency

_____ **37.** Knowledge of the research and evaluation tools, methods, and techniques used by the practicum agency

_____ **38.** Understanding of the process of planned change

_____ **39.** Understanding of the generalist perspective in social work practice and other practice perspectives, theories, and models relevant to the practicum setting

1. What are the most significant strengths that you bring to the practicum based on the preceding checklist?

_____

_____

_____

2. What other strengths not on this list do you bring to your practicum experience?

_____

_____

_____

3. What can you do to secure learning experiences that will build on your strengths?

_____

_____

_____

4. What are the most significant limitations that you bring to the practicum experience?

_____

_____

_____

5. What practicum-related learning experiences will help you to address or overcome your limitations?

_____

_____

_____

How Do We Learn? A Workbook Activity

The social work practicum is a unique opportunity to learn. You are being offered the chance to prepare for professional social work practice by integrating your classroom knowledge and skills into a real social work setting with real clients. Your experience will be enhanced if you are aware of how you learn.

Learning is a type of change, which can be exciting and exhilarating or difficult and painful. Basically, we learn when we take risks—when we begin to think in a different way, when we view the familiar from a different angle, or when we try out new behavior. Openness to this type of learning can bring unexpected insights and unanticipated growth. Learning to face our fears, take risks, challenge ourselves beyond our current competencies, and then be open to supervision and feedback will always result in an enriching learning experience. This new learning will excite and inspire you. It will create some discomfort, but that is the price of learning. When the learning is about ourselves—our biases, prejudices, and emotional hang-ups—the experience can be especially challenging. However, this can free us from attitudes and behaviors that limit personal growth and effectiveness. Because clients deserve the highest quality of services possible, the profession of social work is committed to identifying competencies needed for practice, developing best practice standards, and adhering to evidence-based practice that measures the effectiveness of interventions. Answer the following questions about your learning style and learning goals, and think ahead about how you can maximize your learning experience. Your practicum will stretch your thinking. Open yourself up to this experience so that you do not miss a significant learning opportunity?

1. What learning experiences do you hope will help you acquire knowledge and develop social work practice skills?

_____

_____

_____

2. What are you most excited and enthusiastic about?

_____

_____

_____

3. What are your greatest fears or worries?

_____

_____

_____

4. Given what you know about yourself and how you learn, what types of assistance, guidance, or structure would help you lower your defenses and be more open to learning in the areas that cause you some level of anxiety or worry (e.g., demonstrations, shadowing, reading client records, watching videos)?

_____

_____

_____

5. If you have a learning disability, what accommodations will you request in your practicum agency?

_____

_____

_____

SUGGESTED LEARNING ACTIVITIES

- Conduct a cursory examination of each chapter in this book. Note the topics addressed and how the content is organized. Try to identify the links between chapters, since they are designed to build on each other.
- Keep this book with you while at your practicum agency and try to answer all of the workbook questions.
- If you write about a client, make sure to follow agency rules of confidentiality.

Log onto **www.mysocialworklab.com** and select the **Career Exploration** videos from the left-hand menu. Answer the questions below. (*If you did not receive an access code to **MySocialWorkLab** with this text and wish to purchase access online, please visit* www.mysocialworklab.com.)

1. Watch the interview with social worker Sue Dowling. Listen to her response to question 12 about why she chose social work. How does this compare with the reasons you chose social work?

2. Watch the interview with Beth Harmon, social work supervisor. Listen to her response to question 17 about her advice for students. How does this fit with the purpose of a practicum?

PRACTICE TEST

Critical Thinking

1. After taking the self-assessment in this chapter of your strengths going into practicum, identify and prioritize the strengths you wish you acquire in terms of (1) attitudes and values, (2) motivation and desire to learn, (3) abilities and skills, and (4) knowledge and experience.

_____

_____

_____

_____

_____

_____

_____

Professional Identity

2. Devise a plan for building on your strengths and acquiring the ones listed in question 1 above.

_____

_____

_____

_____

_____

_____

_____

2

School, Agency, and Student Expectations

LEARNING GOALS FOR THIS CHAPTER

▶ To understand what you can and should expect of your school's practicum program

▶ To understand what you can and should expect of your practicum agency

▶ To understand what will be expected of you by your school program and your practicum agency

CONNECTING CORE COMPETENCIES *in this chapter*

| Professional Identity | Ethical Practice | Critical Thinking | Diversity in Practice | Human Rights & Justice | Research Based Practice | Human Behavior | Policy Practice | **Practice Contexts** | Engage Assess Intervene Evaluate |

A key to making your social work practicum a quality learning experience is the clarification of expectations. What do you really expect? What does the agency expect of you? What does your school expect of you and your practicum agency? Identifying and clarifying expectations will ensure a smooth and positive practicum experience, and not doing so may lead to problems. The purpose of this chapter is to encourage and facilitate a clarification of expectations.

BACKGROUND AND CONTEXT

Practice Contexts

What characteristics of organizations and communities might serve to make clients distrustful of social workers?

Standards issued by the Commission on Accreditation of the Council on Social Work Education (CSWE) require a minimum of 400 social work practicum hours at the baccalaureate level (BSW) and a minimum of 900 hours at the master's (MSW) level. Some programs of social work education require additional hours because of the importance they place on professional readiness for practice

Schools may use slightly different terms to describe the personnel associated with a practicum program. In this book the term *field instructor* is used when referring to the agency-based person who is responsible for the day-to-day supervision of a practicum student. This person is usually an agency employee. The faculty member who is responsible for organizing and guiding the practicum program is here termed the *practicum coordinator.*

Most schools assign a faculty member as a liaison to individual practicum agencies and organizations. In this book this individual is referred to as the *faculty supervisor.* This individual maintains regular contact with an agency's field instructor and with the student. He or she monitors practicum, serves as a troubleshooter when problems arise, and is involved with the field instructor in the evaluation of student performance.

Programs of social work education typically use a *practicum seminar* to help students connect or integrate what they have learned in the classroom with the real-world experiences in their practicum setting. These seminars are usually under the direction of a faculty member who may or may not also be the student's faculty supervisor.

The specific objectives associated with a practicum can be found in your school's practicum manual, in official descriptions of your social work curriculum, and in other documents issued by the social work program. All parties to the practicum are expected to adhere to the National Association of Social Workers (NASW) *Code of Ethics.* Below are listed general expectations of all the parties that will be involved in your practicum. Please note that the expectations described by your school's practicum program may differ somewhat from the general expectations listed here.

The **practicum coordinator** is expected to:

▶ Coordinate the overall practicum program
▶ Select practicum agencies and train field instructors
▶ Place students in appropriate practicum settings
▶ Assign faculty supervisors to practicum students
▶ Provide consultation on practicum issues and problems

The **social work practicum student** is expected to:

▶ Be familiar with the expectations of practicum students, including policies in practicum manuals
▶ Comply with all requirements for documentation of the practicum
▶ Develop a learning agreement in conjunction with field instructor and faculty supervisor

- Seek and use supervision by the field instructor and faculty supervisor
- Integrate classroom learning with practicum experiences
- Adhere to the NASW Code of Ethics, abide by agency policy, and exhibit professional behavior
- Bring to the attention of the faculty supervisor any questionable professional practices within the agency

The **field instructor and/or practicum agency** are expected to:

- Participate in school sponsored training for field instructors
- Orient practicum students to agency structure, function, policies and procedures, and student responsibilities
- Assist students in developing a learning agreement to structure the practicum experience
- Assign duties and responsibilities of increasing difficulty and challenge as appropriate
- Follow policies and procedures outlined in the school's practicum manual
- Monitor student performance, providing ongoing feedback to the student
- Complete a formal evaluation of the practicum experience
- Provide reasonable accommodations for students with disabilities

The school's **faculty supervisor** is expected to:

- Assist student in developing a learning agreement
- Meet with students and field instructors as required by the program
- Assist students in integrating classroom learning with practicum experiences
- Participate in evaluations of student performance
- Serve as a liaison between the practicum agency and the school

The **practicum seminar** will:

- Bring together students from various practicum settings to give them an opportunity to learn about different types of agency settings from each other's experiences
- Arrange or structure learning activities that will help students integrate social work theory with practice (e.g., discussions, student presentations, guest speakers, summative papers, or professional portfolios)
- Provide a forum for student discussion and problem solving regarding practicum

Your Responsibilities to Agency Clients

Professional
Identity

Although you are a student, how can you provide the level of service clients expect and deserve?

Given the fact that you are in the process of learning to become a social worker and you generally lack experience, you must consider how this lack of skill and experience might affect clients and the quality of the services provided to them. Even though you are a student, you will have a great deal to offer your clients, and when the work expected of you is beyond your level of knowledge and skill, consult with your field instructor for guidance and suggestions. Review your classroom learning, drawing upon theory and any skill-building exercises in which you have participated. The clients served by a student social worker are to be made aware that they are being served or assisted by a student. However, most clients will see you as a developing professional and will be cooperative and trusting of you, your knowledge, and your skills.

GUIDANCE AND DIRECTION

Practicum placements that are most beneficial are those in which there is a good match between the student's learning needs and the learning opportunities available within the practicum setting. In contrast, the source of many problems in the practicum is a mismatch between what the student needs to learn and what the setting has to offer. For this reason, the careful assessment of your abilities and needs prior to the selection of a practicum setting is of critical importance. This is not to imply that you need to know everything about your agency or possess the skills that social workers in the agency display. It is only to suggest that your practicum experience will be more satisfying if your learning needs and career goals match the learning experiences your practicum agency can offer.

Three major factors will determine the overall quality of your social work practicum experience, including your motivation to learn, your capacity to learn, and your opportunity to learn. In order for those who will be assisting you during the practicum to be truly helpful, they need information about your motivation. What do you really want and expect from the practicum? What are you willing to do to obtain the learning experiences you seek? What do you already know? What skills do you possess? Be sure to communicate your hopes and expectations to your field instructor, faculty supervisor, and practicum coordinator. Be honest and open in describing your expectations and motivation.

Similarly, in order for others to help you make the practicum a good learning experience, they need to know about your capacity to learn. They need to know about your strengths so they can help you build on them. They need to know your limitations so they can help you find ways to work around them or enhance your knowledge and skills. When your field instructor accurately understands your expectations, strengths, and limitations, he or she will be in a better position to select and arrange those learning opportunities, activities, and work assignments that will advance your learning. Acknowledge, confront, and honestly work to address any special limitations that may affect your practicum learning. Your clients deserve the best services possible, and thus any limitations you have should be acknowledged and remedied. You can expect to have significant difficulties during the practicum if you:

- Have poor writing skills
- Have difficulty managing time, meeting deadlines, organizing work, and staying on task

Food for Thought

Life is a journey that we take only one time. As a social worker makes that one journey through life, it is important that he or she is truly comfortable with social work as a traveling companion (Sheafor and Horejsi, 2006, 18).

• • •

What one hears, one forgets. What one sees, one remembers. What one does, one understands.
—*Chinese Proverb*

• • •

Because the practicum is an interactive and structured learning process, numerous expectations will be placed on you. The social work program will communicate educational expectations for students, agencies, and field instructors. However, as an adult learner, you, too, must develop expectations for your agency and your field instructor. Establishing a clear understanding of mutual expectations will enhance your ability to determine your goals, role, and performance standards (Birkenmaier and Berg-Weger, 2007, 8).

- ‣ Are unusually shy and lack assertiveness
- ‣ Are unusually aggressive, dominating, or opinionated
- ‣ Are unable or unwilling to conform with agency policy and procedures
- ‣ Are unable to maintain boundaries between your personal life and your professional responsibilities
- ‣ Disagree or do not comply with the NASW *Code of Ethics*

Clarifying Expectations: A Workbook Activity

1. You will be spending hundreds of hours in your practicum setting. What do you expect from this investment of your time? What do you really hope to gain?

_____

_____

2. Knowing that what you are willing to invest in the practicum determines what you will get out of it, list the key things you expect of yourself during the practicum.

_____

_____

3. Are there any expectations that you are concernted about meeting? What can you do to successfully meet those objectives?

_____

_____

4. If you were a client of your practicum agency, what would you expect of your social worker? Of your practicum student?

_____

_____

SUGGESTED LEARNING ACTIVITIES

▸ Most schools make use of a signed agreement to clarify expectations for the practicum. Read this document to understand what will be expected of all parties.

▸ Read your school's practicum manual. Pay special attention to descriptions of what is expected of the practicum student.

▸ Ask your field instructor if there is a job description for social work practicum students. If there is, read it carefully to understand what your agency expects of its students.

▸ Carefully examine the practicum evaluation form and specific criteria that will be used to evaluate your performance. What do these documents tell you about what is expected of you? (See Chapter 17 for additional information on evaluation.)

▸ Talk to former students who have completed a practicum in your agency. Ask them for advice and guidance on what to expect. Ask about any problems they experienced and about learning opportunities available.

▸ Listen carefully to other students in your practicum seminar. Are their concerns similar to or different from yours? What are they doing in their practicum settings that might work for you?

Succeed with PEARSON mysocialworklab

Log onto **www.mysocialworklab.com** and select the **Career Exploration** videos from the left-hand menu. Answer the questions below. (*If you did not receive an access code to* **MySocialWorkLab** *with this text and wish to purchase access online, please visit* www.mysocialworklab.com.)

1. **Watch the interview with Christine Mitchell, clinical and medical social worker.** Listen to her response to question 3 about how much school prepared her for her work. Like her, what can you learn on the job and from your clients that will help you get the most out of your practicum?

2. **Watch the interview with administrator Karen Cowan.** Listen to her response to question 6 about what she expects in an employee. How does this help you understand what employers expect?

PRACTICE TEST

Engage Assess Intervene Evaluate

1. Expectations are placed on practicum by students, agencies, and schools of social work. Although they overlap and resemble each other, they are also distinct because of the unique nature of each interested party. How might this be like the variety of expectations a client and social work have at the beginning of an intervention? What can you learn from this comparison?

_____

_____

_____

_____

_____

_____

_____

Ethical Practice

2. Reflect on Section 3.02(C) of the NASW Code of Ethics which provides guidelines for practicum students. Although you are still a student, clients have the right to expect quality services. What is your plan for addressing this expectation?

_____

_____

_____

_____

_____

_____

_____

3

Developing a Learning Plan

LEARNING GOALS FOR THIS CHAPTER

▸ To become familiar with the terms *learning goal, learning objective, learning activity,* and *learning outcome*

▸ To identify learning goals, objectives, and activities relevant to your social work practicum setting

▸ To write a learning contract outlining your proposed practicum experience in collaboration with your field instructor and faculty supervisor

CONNECTING CORE COMPETENCIES *in this chapter*

| Professional Identity | Ethical Practice | Critical Thinking | Diversity in Practice | Human Rights & Justice | Research Based Practice | Human Behavior | Policy Practice | Practice Contexts | Engage Assess Intervene Evaluate |

17

Good learning experiences in practicum are usually the result of a well-planned learning agreement. For the most part, a good practicum experience is usually one that has been well conceived and outlined. In addition, however, you may have some very good unplanned learning experiences. Overall, you will increase your chances of success if you design a clear learning plan, but will also do well if you watch for opportunities to participate in learning opportunities that present themselves along the way. Although most students avoid negative learning experiences, they may very well be the best teachers.

As you begin your practicum, it is important to list your desired outcomes for learning and then identify and arrange activities and experiences that will help you reach those goals. A *learning outcome* is what you gain, achieve, get exposed to, or master as you work toward professional competency. A *learning goal* is a broad description of what you plan to learn, and is not usually measurable. A *learning objective* is what you hope you will know or be able to do following your practicum and is usually measurable. *Learning activities* are the actual steps you take to help you achieve the outcomes you desire.

This chapter provides basic information, guidance, and a workbook activity that can assist you in developing an effective plan for learning. This plan will be extremely useful, but it is also important to recognize that not everything will go as planned. Unexpected experiences may also provide you with insightful and valuable learning.

BACKGROUND AND CONTEXT

Professional Identity

A professional social worker possesses knowledge, skills, and values. What do you see as the relationship between them?

A plan for learning during the practicum is like a road map, identifying destinations and possible routes for getting where you want to go. The development of this plan is important, but it is not a simple or easy task. However, it is always better to have a plan—even if it is a rather general one—than to have no plan at all.

A plan for learning will incorporate educational goals and anticipated outcomes from three sources: the school's curriculum, the field instructor, and the student. These goals will usually fall into three categories: knowledge, skills, and values, all of which contribute to your competency as a social worker.

Social work *knowledge* is an understanding of professional terminology, facts, principles, concepts, theories, and perspectives. No doubt you have spent many hours learning about individuals and families, communities, and social policy. This knowledge will be used in the practicum as you apply it in real-life situations.

Social work *skills* are the behaviors of practice. They are the techniques and procedures used by social workers to bring about desired change in the social functioning of clients or in social systems with which clients interact. For the most part, skills are learned by watching and following the lead of skilled practitioners. You can learn about skills from a textbook, but you cannot acquire skills simply by reading about them. Your practicum experience will afford you the opportunity to acquire and enhance your social work skills.

A *value* is a strong preference that affects one's choices, decisions, and actions and that is rooted in one's deepest beliefs and commitments. Values determine what a person considers important, worthwhile, right, or wrong. Social work values (e.g., service, social justice, integrity) can be learned or "caught" from others, but it is doubtful that they can be taught by others in a systematic and deliberate way. Typically, our values arise from our deepest beliefs about the way the world ought to be. Your practicum will undoubtedly be a time for you to more clearly understand what your values are, and you will also begin to see how your values may at times be in conflict with the values of others, including your clients.

It is possible to separate social work knowledge, skills, and values for purposes of discussion and analysis, but in the actual practice of social work, they are interwoven. For example, one's skill grows out of one's knowledge and values. Likewise, the possession of social work knowledge and values is of little use unless they both are expressed in action. Finally, knowledge and skills can be used to harm or manipulate clients unless guided by an ethical value base of services to clients.

PREPARING A PLAN FOR LEARNING

The most common approach to the formulation and writing of a plan for practicum learning is described next. It involves the development of a learning agreement that includes learning goals, objectives, activities, and criteria for monitoring and evaluating your learning.

A form for preparing a written learning plan using this approach can be found in the Appendix. This sample form, and the ideas behind it, can be modified to fit the requirements of a particular school of social work. This form lists the school's general goals for the practicum in the left-hand column. The field instructor and student select additional goals specific to the practicum setting and add them to the form.

A **learning goal** is a rather broad and general statement of intended outcome. For example, a learning goal might be "to become familiar with the history of a social agency." Another would be "to develop the skills of interviewing." The following verbs often appear in goal statements:

to acquire	to comprehend	to learn
to analyze	to develop	to perceive
to become familiar with	to discover	to synthesize
to know	to explore	to understand

Once the goals have been specified, various learning activities are listed in the second column. A **learning objective** is a statement of desired outcome that is written in a way that allows measurement. An objective is a precisely worded, specific, and concrete statement of activities to be undertaken to reach a goal. It stipulates what the learner will do, and how and when he or she will do it.

Writing an objective can be a challenging task. Such writing requires the use of behavioral language. A behavior is an activity that can be observed. The use of completion dates and counting completed tasks and activities can often transform an unmeasurable goal into a measurable objective. The learning objectives you put into your learning agreement should be measurable so you know whether you complete them, and so they can be monitored and evaluated.

The words and phrases used in writing objectives describe specific actions and activities. For example:

to answer	to decide	to obtain
to arrange	to define	to participate in
to circulate	to demonstrate	to revise
to summarize	to direct	to schedule
to collect	to discuss	to select
to compile	to give examples	to supervise
to conduct	to write	to verify

When selecting and writing learning objectives, it is important to remain focused on outcomes that are truly important and relevant to the learning of social work practice. Although being able to measure progress is desirable, one must avoid becoming so preoccupied with trying to achieve measurability that the focus shifts to outcomes that are most easily measured rather than the ones that are most important.

Finally, this sample form has a third column for statements that describe the ***method and criteria for evaluating progress*** toward the learning goal. Two common methods of documenting and evaluating progress are listing proposed dates for completing the task or assignment and stating that the work is to be reviewed and critiqued by the field instructor. Other forms of measurement could include direct observation of your work by your field instructor, review of your written documentation, or the use of video or audio taping. Whatever method of evaluation you use to measure your learning and performance, remember that there may be facets of your learning that are hard to measure in behavioral terms, but that can be areas of significant professional growth for you.

THE GENERALIST PERSPECTIVE AND THE PLAN FOR LEARNING

Although generalist social workers practice at various levels, they understand the connections between these levels of practice. How do you see them as connected?

The responsibility of a social worker is to enhance social functioning. What theories do you think might explain the social functioning issues addressed by your agency?

The curricula for BSW programs and the first year of MSW programs are built around the concept of generalist social work practice. Thus, the practicum experiences of many students are expected to reflect a generalist perspective.

The ***generalist perspective*** is a way of viewing and thinking about the process and activities of social work practice. It is a set of ideas and principles that guide the process of planned change at all levels of practice, in a wide variety of settings, and as you practice a number of social work roles. Keeping that definition in mind, The University of Montana School of Social Work BSW Competency Catalogue (2008, 8–9) lists the following ***generalist competencies***:

1. The generalist social worker practices at multiple levels (micro, mezzo, macro) and moves between systems and levels of practice based on client/client system needs and resources to enhance social functioning and facilitate social change.

2. The generalist social worker plays a variety of social work roles (advocate, broker, networker, counselor, educator, case manager, facilitator, planner, researcher, mediator, administrator) and moves between roles, matching them to client/client system need and resources.

3. The generalist social worker uses a variety of lenses and conceptual frameworks to guide practice, including the strengths perspective, ecological perspective, and diversity perspective.

4. The generalist social worker uses a variety of orienting theories to guide practice, including social systems theory, human development theory, group theory, organizational theory, community development, and societal development theory.

5. The generalist social worker uses a variety of practice theories and models to guide practice, including task-centered casework, crisis intervention, client-centered casework, empowerment model, cognitive behavioral model, mutual aid model, structural model, organizational development model, community development model, and social change model.

Engage Assess Intervene Evaluate

Which of the practice theories that you learned in class will you use with your clients?

Ethical Practice

Which social work ethical principles seem to be most central to the work of your agency?

6. The generalist social worker, in partnership with client systems, uses the planned change process of assessment, planning, intervention, termination, and evaluation.

7. The generalist social worker is guided by the National Association of Social Workers' Code of Ethics, incorporates social work values into intervention at all levels, and uses a process for examining and dealing with ethical situations and dilemmas.

The Educational Policy and Accreditation Standards of the Council on Social Work Education (2008, 3–7) also identify **core competencies** for social workers and write that social workers:

1. Identify as a professional social worker and conduct oneself accordingly.

2. Apply social work ethical principles to guide professional practice.

3. Apply critical thinking to inform and communicate professional judgments.

4. Engage diversity and difference in practice.

5. Advance human rights and social and economic justice.

6. Engage in research-informed practice and practice-informed research.

7. Apply knowledge of human behavior and the social environment.

8. Engage in policy practice to advance social and economic well-being and to deliver effective social work services.

9. Respond to contexts that shape practice.

10. Engage, assess, intervene, and evaluate with individuals, families, groups, organizations, and communities.

All of these core competencies are highlighted throughout this text to help you see how your classroom learning and practicum experiences are being integrated as you develop into a professional.

These two ways of describing generalist social work practice can guide the structure of your practicum, so identify ways in which you can acquire those competencies vital to the practice of social work. The core competencies identified by the Council on Social Work's *Educational Policy and Accreditation Standards* are integrated throughout this book in multiple ways, showing you how they are acquired over time and in a variety of ways. Watch for reference to these core competencies and work to integrate them into your professional repertoire.

Food for Thought

Teachers open the doors. Students must enter by themselves.
—*Chinese Proverb*

• • •

If acknowledging what you do not know is a first step toward learning, being willing to take some risks and extend yourself is a key second step. Internships allow you to try new skills that you may have only read about before. To develop these skills, you have to test them and learn from both your successes and your mistakes.

A concept that is useful to interns, and that will later be useful in treatment, is the idea of a "learning edge." This term refers to the point just beyond one's present level of knowledge or skill. It is not so far ahead that we are in danger of making mistakes that could be calamitous for ourselves or others, but it is beyond our habitual level of functioning and comfort (Baird, 2008, 22).

• • •

The classroom remains the most radical space of possibility (hooks, 1994, 12).

One of the unique characteristics of the generalist social worker is commitment and ability to adapt his or her approach to the needs and circumstances of the client or client system, rather than expecting the client to conform to the methods of the professional or the agency. The generalist avoids selecting an intervention method or approach until after he or she and the client or client system have worked together to complete a careful assessment of the client's concern or problem and have considered various ways in which the client's problem or concern can be defined, conceptualized, and approached. Finally, the generalist is prepared to draw on and use a wide range of intervention techniques and procedures, and is not bound to a single theory or model.

GUIDANCE AND DIRECTION

As you prepare your learning agreement in light of generalist competencies and core competencies of the social work profession, incorporate learning experiences that will help you develop these competencies. Your learning contract is negotiated between you, your field instructor, and your faculty supervisor. They understand what you must learn to become a competent generalist social worker. Most learning agreements are working documents that are modified throughout the practicum as additional learning needs are identified and new learning opportunities arise. Your plan should be exciting and ambitious to stretch and expand your knowledge and skills. It must also be realistic given your practicum setting, your abilities, your prior experience, and the time available to you.

Each of us has a unique approach to learning or a particular learning style. As you develop your plan, consider your preferred method of learning. For example, you may be inclined to jump into the middle of an activity or opportunity because you learn best by doing. Perhaps you learn best by first observing others and then later trying your hand at the activity. Maybe you need to first understand the theory or rationale behind an activity before you feel ready to take action. No one learning style is best or most effective in all situations. You may want to use a learning styles inventory or assessment instrument to better understand your preferred method of learning. (See, for example, Kolb, 1981.) Give your field instructor as much information as possible about how you learn. That information will help him or her select assignments and responsibilities as well as determine your readiness for certain experiences.

If you have a learning disability or a condition that, without accommodation, may in some way limit your learning or performance, be sure to share this information with your field instructor and faculty supervisor. Such conditions need to be considered in developing a plan for practicum learning. If you suspect you may have a learning disability, consult with a learning specialist who can assess the nature of the disability, recommend ways of compensating for the limitation, and guide you toward a program of remediation and accommodation. Your university may also have services available to students with disabilities, and may have professionals skilled in adapting practicum experiences to meet individual needs as well as advocating for reasonable accommodations in practicum settings.

Include in your plan experiences and activities that will help you to integrate theory and practice. Classroom learning should come alive during the practicum. Strive to identify the beliefs, values, and theories behind your decisions and your selection of an intervention. Seek exposure to social work

Practice Contexts

Ask other practicum students what they are learning in their practicum settings so that you can anticipate what you might learn in other agencies that could be used as you move into a different position.

practice and programs based on various beliefs about how, when, and why people and social systems are able to change.

Even though your practicum learning experience will be specific to your practicum agency, remember that you are developing knowledge and skills that can be generalized to other social work settings. Secure a breadth of experience while also finding ways to go into depth in your particular area of interest. By doing so, you will prepare yourself for work in another setting while immersing yourself in practice issues about which you care deeply.

Describe your desired outcomes for learning in ways that permit the monitoring and the measurement of progress. However, also recognize that many important outcomes such as developing a commitment to social work values, growing in self-awareness and self-confidence, and using a variety of perspectives and theories are inherently difficult to quantify and measure. Describe your desired outcomes as precisely as possible, but do not get hung up on measurability. It is better to describe outcomes in only general and imperfect ways than to not mention them at all, even if you have a hard time showing how you will measure them. Consider how your attempts to measure your learning parallel your clients' attempts to demonstrate their growth. Your struggle to grow and to measure that growth will hopefully increase your sensitivity to your clients' hard work.

If your school requires you to complete a professional portfolio or final professional paper as part of the practicum experience, build into your learning plan as many of the elements of the portfolio or paper as are possible and appropriate. Because a portfolio is usually focused on the demonstration of your knowledge and skills in a variety of areas, the practicum is an ideal opportunity to structure your learning and then to showcase the ways in which you integrated academic classroom learning with practicum activities. If your school requires a summative paper, project, or presentation based on your practicum experiences, plan now to acquire the learning experiences that will help you successfully complete that assignment and demonstrate your competence.

Once you have completed your plan and it has been approved by your field instructor and faculty supervisor, follow it. Review it often and modify it as needed, but resist the temptation to abandon a part of the plan simply because it calls for a learning opportunity that is difficult to arrange. Do everything possible to obtain the experiences you need to advance your learning. Become assertive in asking for meaningful learning experiences. If you need help to arrange these because of agency reluctance to offer them to you, ask your faculty supervisor to advocate on your behalf. In addition, be alert to learning experiences that become available to you unexpectedly during your practicum, and find ways to integrate these experiences into your learning plan. You will be asked to perform tasks and take on responsibilities for which you feel unprepared. That may cause anxiety, fear, and embarrassment, which are understandable and normal reactions. You must be willing to take on tasks and responsibilities even when you do not feel ready. If you wait until you feel confident and certain that you would not make mistakes, you might miss opportunities to learn something new.

As you formulate your learning plan, give careful thought to your personal plans for the next five years. For example, if you are a BSW student hoping to go on to graduate school, what can you do during the practicum to prepare yourself for graduate study or to increase your chances of being accepted into graduate school? If you expect to enter the job market immediately after graduation, what can you build into your plan that will prepare you for the job you seek? What specific licensing or certification may be required for you to practice social work in your state or to become certified in a specialty area? If you are an MSW student, what learning goals can you set for yourself that will adequately prepare you for advanced practice?

During your practicum, you may learn some things that are surprising or even discouraging. For example, you will probably discover that not all clients are motivated, that some are difficult to like and respect, and that some will not make use of needed and available services. You will probably learn that client, agency, or social changes can be slow, that social problems are more complex than you realized, that you must be skillful in the art of politics, and that not all professionals are competent and ethical. Your faculty supervisor can help you gain perspective on such matters, so be sure to share these experiences and observations with him or her.

In addition to the formal learning plans you develop, consider using a professional journal. This exercise can help you in many ways. A journal can document your progress in learning, show your professional growth over time, allow you to express your doubts and questions without sharing them with your supervisors, and offer you the chance to reflect on the very personal nature of your work. Many students report that journal keeping is very useful because it serves as a written record of growth that is encouraging and reinforcing.

Do not be surprised if much of what you actually learn during your practicum was not anticipated and could not have been written into your plan. Expect some surprises. Perhaps your agency's funding will be drastically cut, and you may end up working in a different unit or service area. Your field instructor may take another job and you will have to adjust to a successor with a different supervisory style. Although such experiences can be stressful, they can be valuable learning opportunities. They will certainly teach you to be flexible and open to new experiences. You can also gain invaluable perspective on how agencies and the social workers in them cope with change and stress, capitalize on funding or policy shifts, and turn problems into opportunities.

Planning to Learn: A Workbook Activity

Your responses below will help you identify desired outcomes and prepare a plan that can guide and enhance your practicum. Respond honestly and with as much precision as possible.

What learning objectives or activities will deepen your understanding of the following key components of social work practice?

1. The core values and mission of the social work profession

_____

_____

2. The major social work roles (e.g., broker, case manager, organizer, educator, facilitator, counselor, advocate)

_____

_____

3. The organizational context of your practicum (e.g., history, agency purpose, structure, function, funding)

_____

_____

4. The social problems addressed by your agency

_____

_____

5. The skills needed for practice with individuals (assessment, planning, intervention, evaluation)

_____

_____

6. The skills needed for practice with families (assessment, planning, intervention, evaluation)

_____

_____

7. The skills needed for practice with groups and organizations (assessment, planning, intervention, evaluation)

_____

_____

8. The skills needed for practice with communities (assessment, planning, intervention, evaluation)

_____

_____

9. The skills needed for practice at the social policy level (analysis, advocacy, planning, organizing)

_____

_____

10. The legal and ethical dimensions of practice

_____

_____

11. The impact of human diversity on the clients served by your agency

_____

_____

12. What type of orientation or initial training do social workers in your agency receive soon after they are hired? Can you take advantage of this training?

_____

_____

13. How do you plan to learn about yourself (e.g., strengths and gifts, core values, biases)?

_____

_____

14. How do you plan to remain open to constructive criticism?

_____

_____

SUGGESTED LEARNING ACTIVITIES

- Consult your school practicum manual and various descriptions of the curriculum in search of specific learning goals and objectives for the practicum.
- Work with a group of other students to brainstorm possible tasks, activities, and projects that might be pursued in your practicum agency as a way of expanding learning opportunities.
- If your practicum agency cannot provide the learning experience that you need, ask your field instructor to help you gain that experience by working a few hours each week in another agency.
- Read your school practicum evaluation form or rating instrument to better understand what you are expected to learn during the practicum and how you are expected to demonstrate that you have acquired specific knowledge and skills
- If you have a specific career goal such as chemical dependency certification, school social work certification, social work licensing, or graduate school, identify the requirements for this goal and seek practicum experiences related to that goal.
- Ask social workers in your agency what they wish they had known or were able to do when they started their social work position. Find ways to learn this for yourself while in practicum.
- If at any time you feel disappointed with your field experience, discuss this concern with your field instructor. Do not delay or avoid this discussion and let your negative feelings build up inside.

1. **Watch the interview with Karen Cowan.** Listen to her response to question 21 and begin to think about how you can use her advice in evaluating your learning.

2. **Watch the interview with Beth Harmon.** Listen to her response to question 15 about the most rewarding aspect of her work. How does that compare with what you are planning to learn and gain?

PRACTICE TEST

**Engage
Assess
Intervene
Evaluate**

1. As a practicum student, you will be asked to design a learning agreement for practicum. In what ways is this document similar to a client intervention plan in terms of (1) the need for a baseline of skill or knowledge, (2) the need for measurable objectives, (3) the need for guidance, and (4) the need for evaluation of growth?

_____

_____

_____

_____

_____

_____

_____

**Professional
Identity**

2. You will need to prepare yourself for generalist practice even if at some point in your career you specialize in one area. Refer ahead to Chapter 13 (Professional Social Work) where generalist competencies are listed. How can you make sure you have the learning experiences you will need to function as a generalist?

_____

_____

_____

_____

_____

_____

_____

4

Getting Started

LEARNING GOALS FOR THIS CHAPTER

▶ To become familiar with the professional staff and other personnel within your agency

▶ To become familiar with the various units, departments, and divisions within your agency

▶ To become familiar with the basic routines and procedures of your agency

▶ To prepare yourself for a positive entry into your agency

CONNECTING CORE COMPETENCIES *in this chapter*

| Professional Identity | Ethical Practice | Critical Thinking | Diversity in Practice | Human Rights & Justice | Research Based Practice | Human Behavior | Policy Practice | Practice Contexts | Engage Assess Intervene Evaluate |

28

Previous chapters have asked you to learn about what will be expected of you in the practicum and what you can expect of the practicum. They have underscored the importance of formulating learning goals and identifying activities that can facilitate your learning and help you reach those desired outcomes. This chapter focuses on questions and concerns that are common during the first days and weeks of the practicum.

Beginning a practicum is similar to starting a new job. It is a time of excitement and confusion. There are many new people to meet and much to learn, so the first few weeks can feel overwhelming. Entering an unfamiliar organization is something like entering an unfamiliar culture where you encounter a new set of norms, rules, and customs, but will be unsure what they are until you have become familiar with what is expected of you. You will probably feel some anxiety about your knowledge and skills, and you will wonder if you will be able to perform competently. However, within a matter of weeks you will be familiar with the setting and will be much more comfortable.

BACKGROUND AND CONTEXT

First experiences are pattern setting. If the first days and weeks of contact with a new student are positive for the field instructor and other agency staff, the field instructor will likely conclude that the student can be trusted and given responsibilities. If, on the other hand, these first contacts give the field instructor cause to doubt whether the student is capable and responsible, he or she may hesitate to assign meaningful work to the student.

In order to get the practicum off to a good start, you must anticipate how you might be perceived by the field instructor and what he or she might be thinking and feeling about your presence in the agency. Among the field instructor's thoughts about supervising students might be the following:

Human Behavior

On what assumptions or understandings of student behavior in practicum settings might your agency field instructor be operating?

- ▶ I look forward to having a student. Practicum students usually have a lot of enthusiasm, and they tend to look at the work of this agency from a fresh perspective.
- ▶ I'm glad that we have a practicum student because we're understaffed and have too much work to do. The student can do some of my work.
- ▶ I hope this student works out. I remember one student who did not do well in this agency because she was too insecure and immature.
- ▶ I wonder if I can find the time necessary to properly supervise this student. I hope he or she catches on quickly, because I am too busy to baby-sit.
- ▶ I worry about students overstepping the bounds of their assignments and responsibilities and dislike having to clean up messes made by others.
- ▶ I don't think this student has much experience in the real world. I hope he is ready for a taste of harsh reality.
- ▶ I like having students here because their questions encourage me to think critically about what I do and why.

Some of the challenges encountered in a practicum are related to the need for a social work student to shift from the university's focus on education to the agency's focus on training. The faculty members of a social work program emphasize the learning of general knowledge, theory, and broad principles that can be applied in many practice settings. By contrast, agency administrators and supervisors are concerned mostly with training that emphasizes the learning of policies, procedures, and skills specific to their agency. Education encourages discussion, debate, and the consideration of alternative ways of assessing and responding to a problem or situation. By contrast, training is designed to teach what the agency has established as the standard or typical responses to given situations. Because these responses reflect the agency's purpose, policy, and procedures, they are generally to be followed rather then challenged and debated. Hopefully you will integrate the broad knowledge obtained from the academic world with the specific training provided within the agency.

How might the office culture of your agency impact clients?

All social agencies have what is often called an ***office culture.*** This term refers to the general ways of operating that are based in history, agency values, theoretical underpinnings of services provided, morale, policies and procedures, and staff interaction. Hopefully the office culture is positive and optimistic, as this will allow you to see an organization at its best and learn how a healthy and functional agency operates.

All organizations, including human services agencies, have a political dimension. For example, an agency's managers must make difficult and unpopular decisions, and thus must use their power and authority to accomplish the agency's goals. Some conflict and power struggles are inevitable in organizational life, and these will soon become apparent to you. You need to be aware that aligning yourself with one side or another in these conflicts can undermine the success of your practicum.

The term ***office politics*** refers to the undercurrent of power struggles created by factors such as conflict between various factions within an organization, personal ambition, jockeying for greater power, and efforts to lobby on behalf of a certain opinion. The larger the organization, the more complex its internal politics. Even though office politics are normal and difficult to avoid, if you become caught up in these power struggles and conflicts, learning opportunities may be closed and some agency staff may withdraw their support.

As a general rule, the larger and more political an organization, the more active the office grapevine. Rumors, gossip, and speculations are common within organizations having many bureaucratic layers, and are especially frequent during times of uncertainty, conflict, and rapid change. Participating in agency gossip can be another major pitfall for you.

GUIDANCE AND DIRECTION

What behavior will you exhibit that will demonstrate your wish to move from student to professional?

First impressions have a powerful impact on personal and professional relationships. Because of that, it is vital that you make a favorable first impression on your field instructor and the other staff members in your practicum agency. Make a deliberate effort to get the practicum off to a good start.

As suggested previously, there are a number of reasons why a field instructor will feel confident about assigning challenging responsibilities to a student. To make these assignments, the field instructor must trust the student and believe that he or she is capable of doing the work and not likely to make significant mistakes. Very often, the field instructor makes this decision on the basis of patterns he or she sees in the student's ordinary behavior (i.e., on the basis of the little things he or she notices about the student). Thus, you should strive to display behaviors that can assure your field instructor that you can and will perform in a responsible manner. For example, do your best to develop the following ***attitudes toward learning*** and ***work habits.***

Attitudes toward Learning

‣ Demonstrate your enthusiasm for learning and applying your knowledge in the agency.

‣ Inform your field instructor of your prior work and volunteer experiences to help him or her better understand your abilities.

‣ Demonstrate initiative and a willingness to take on responsibilities and assignments.

‣ Take all assignments seriously, no matter how trivial and unimportant they may seem.

‣ Keep your field instructor informed about what you are doing, why you are doing it, and what you plan to do next.

‣ Consult with your field instructor immediately if you encounter an unusual or unanticipated problem or difficulty, especially one that has legal ramifications or one that might create a public relations problem for the agency.

‣ Be a good listener and be attentive to your field instructor and to other staff members during supervisory conferences and staff meetings.

‣ Demonstrate the ability to accept and use constructive criticism of your work, skills, and attitudes.

‣ Ask questions that reveal a desire to learn and to understand the work of the agency and its policies and procedures, but avoid asking in a manner that appears to challenge or criticize the agency.

‣ Volunteer to take on tasks that are not attractive to regular agency staff.

‣ Make friendly overtures to others in the agency. Demonstrate a capacity to build relationships and get along with a variety of different people.

Work Habits

‣ Prepare all letters, reports, and client records with great care, according to the agency's prescribed format, and in a timely manner.

‣ Meet all deadlines. Be on time for all scheduled appointments and meetings. Remain on the job for all the hours you are expected to be in the practicum agency.

‣ If you must make a change in your work schedule, or if you discover that you will not be able to keep an appointment, contact your field instructor immediately and work out an alternative plan.

‣ Be well prepared for all meetings with your field instructor and for agency staff meetings.

‣ Demonstrate that you have read agency manuals and other materials and are therefore familiar with your agency's mission, programs, policies, and procedures.

‣ Do your best to understand a new assignment or responsibility the first time it is explained to you. If you are unclear about something, ask for clarification rather than pretending you understand.

‣ Keep your desk and work space neat and organized.

‣ Pay attention to your personal grooming, and dress appropriately for the practicum.

‣ Do not engage in gossip, spread rumors concerning other agencies or professionals, or criticize other students, agency staff, clients, or other agencies in the community.

‣ Be extremely careful to protect your clients' rights to privacy and the confidentiality of agency records.

Ethical Practice

On what ethical principles of practice are these attitudes and work habits based?

The . . . difference between internships and class-room study is that it is never clear beforehand just what you will have to know. One of the truest statements I know about life applies well to internships: "Live gives the test first, then the lesson." At an internship, at any given moment you may be called on to use any knowledge or skills you have and possibly some you do not have. Therefore, your study approach must prepare you with the skills of understanding people and interactions in general. It must also teach you to be flexible, think on your feet, expect the unexpected, and understand that the grades are not at all what you are accustomed to (Baird, 2008, 20).

• • •

Take time to deliberate, but when the time for action has arrived, stop thinking and go in.
—*Napoleon Bonaparte*

• • •

There is no shortcut to acquiring competence and confidence in professional work (Royse, Dhooper, and Rompf, 2007, 31).

As you enter your agency, recognize that there are both formal and informal aspects to the structure and function of your setting. There are the official policies and procedures, the formal organizational chart, and the chain of command, all of which serve to describe the work of your agency, show who is responsible for what, and provide written guidelines for employees. There are also the informal workings of the agency, and they may differ greatly from what is shown in organizational charts or policy manuals. You may discover that official titles and actual job descriptions do not match, that those with official power may not be the ones to whom others look for guidance, and that exceptions may be made to official policies under certain circumstances.

As you encounter office politics, make very thoughtful decisions about how you can respond in ways that will protect your practicum experience and avoid offending others. Although it is difficult to offer guidance on how to handle office politics because every situation is different, here are some general guidelines for you to consider:

- Use the first several weeks and months in the practicum to carefully observe how staff members interact, maneuver, and use their power and influence.
- Be cognizant of and sensitive to the official lines of authority and to the power relationships inherent in the chain of command as described by the agency's organizational chart. Follow the chain of command. To disregard those established power relationships will cause confusion and may put your practicum in jeopardy.
- Do not jump to conclusions concerning who is most valued and respected within the agency and who has the most power and influence. Power relationships are often more subtle and complex than they appear at first. Consequently, your first impressions may be erroneous.
- Cultivate relationships with those in the agency who command the respect of most fellow professionals and the support staff and who are respected and valued by their administrative superiors. Longtime office staff are often very powerful in an organization.
- Do not align yourself with someone in the agency who has a reputation for being a complainer, a loose cannon, a troublemaker, a back stabber, or who has little loyalty to the agency.

Deciding how to respond to office gossip and rumors is also difficult for a practicum student. In general, there are two types of office gossip and rumors: people gossip and professional banter. ***People gossip*** has to do with purely personal matters about other staff members (e.g., who is dating whom, who is getting a divorce, who is deeply in debt). ***Professional banter*** focuses on matters related to the work of the agency (e.g., who is getting promoted, who is getting hired, what is being said by top administrators, what new policies are being discussed).

Here is some general guidance on dealing with the gossip and rumors you may hear in your practicum agency:

- Avoid becoming a party to people gossip. It is not relevant to your work as a practicum student. Engaging in gossip may cause others to view you as unprofessional and untrustworthy.
- In some situations, you may have no choice but to passively listen to someone engaging in people gossip. Say nothing that would further encourage their gossip. Never repeat what you have heard.
- Pay attention to professional banter. It may reveal important information about the informal structure of your agency, but do not assume that what you are hearing is necessarily true. This banter may be inaccurate or only partially true. Do not base a decision on rumor. If it is an important matter, get accurate information before making a decision.

Every organization has many unwritten rules. It is likely that no one will think to tell you about them until after you ask about or have broken one. For example, you might be breaking a rule if you bring food or drink to a staff meeting, or if a certain report is submitted late even though it is permissible to be a little late on other types of reports. The best way to learn about these informal rules and procedures is to observe the work of others in the agency and ask why things are done a certain way.

Remember that there is no such thing as a stupid question. Your field instructor expects you to ask many questions, especially in the beginning, but he or she also expects you to remember the answers that you are given. Thus, record the answers so you do not ask the same questions over and over. Your field instructor expects that you will make some mistakes, but he or she expects you to learn from each mistake and not make it a second time.

Also remember that your actions and your behavior always speak louder and more clearly than do your words. In the professional world, you will be judged primarily on the basis of your performance. Judgments about your potential will likely be based on your past and current performance, so take your practicum as seriously as you would a professional social work position.

Practicum Agency Information: A Workbook Activity

The following questions are designed to assist you in securing the information and orientation needed to get your practicum experience off to a good start. Some can be answered by your field instructor and others will need to be answered by the practicum coordinator of your school.

1. Who are the social workers who will supervise your work during the practicum?

    Name   Phone Number   E-Mail Address

    _____

    _____

    _____

2. Which faculty member will serve as your faculty supervisor and primary contact to your practicum agency?

    Name   Phone Number   E-Mail Address

    _____

3. How many hours each week are you to be at your practicum agency? What days and times are you to be there?

    _____

4. How are you to document the number of hours you devote to your practicum? To whom is this documentation to be submitted? How often are you to report?

    _____

    _____

5. What regularly scheduled agency meetings are you expected to attend?

    _____

    _____

6. What are you to do if you are sick or for some other good reason cannot be at the practicum agency when scheduled and expected to be there? Whom do you contact? Who will fill in for you when you are absent? How much notice are you required to give?

    _____

    _____

7. How are you expected to dress when at the agency? Is there a dress code? What types of clothing, jewelry, or attire are considered inappropriate?

    _____

    _____

8. How do the regular staff members want to be addressed? Do they prefer to be called Ms., Mrs., Mr., or Dr.? Is it appropriate to use first names?

    _____

    _____

9. What term is used to refer to the people who make use of your agency's programs and services (e.g., clients, consumers, members, patients, customers, recipients)? How are they to be addressed (e.g., Mr., Mrs., or Ms.)? Is the use of first names permitted?

_____

_____

10. Are you expected to sign an agreement to protect the confidentiality of your clients?

_____

11. Do you need to obtain an agency staff identification card, name badge, keys, cell phone, or security code? If so, how is this to be done?

_____

_____

12. Is there a specific support staff person assigned to work with you? If yes, what is his or her name?

_____

13. Are you permitted to send a letter or complete written documentation without approval or a countersignature? If not, who must approve or countersign your letters and reports?

_____

_____

14. Are there personal safety concerns that you need to understand and keep in mind while in this agency, neighborhood, and community? (See Chapter 6, "Personal Safety.") What policies and procedures are in place to ensure your safety and that of the staff?

_____

_____

_____

15. Are you permitted to make personal phone calls, use the Internet, or send and receive personal e-mail while in your practicum agency? What rules apply?

_____

_____

SUGGESTED LEARNING ACTIVITIES

- Read agency manuals and websites that describe agency policy and procedures.
- Request opportunities to be introduced to a variety of staff members. Write down their names and job titles so you will learn their names quickly.
- Attend any staff or committee meetings open to you to observe employee interaction.
- Maintain an up-to-date appointment book or PDA in which you enter the times and dates of all staff meetings, appointments, and other obligations.
- Carry a notebook in which you can record important information and instructions.
- Walk around the agency building. Locate potentially critical features such as emergency exits, fire alarms, and fire extinguishers.

Succeed with **PEARSON** **mysocialworklab**

Log onto **www.mysocialworklab.com** and select the **Career Exploration** videos from the left-hand margin. Answer the questions below. (*If you did not receive an access code to* **MySocialWorkLab** *with this text and wish to purchase access online, please visit* www.mysocialworklab.com.)

1. **Watch the interview with Christine Mitchell.** Listen to her response to question 4 about a typical day.

How can her description help you visualize a typical day in practicum?

2. **Watch the interview with Beth Harmon about her daily routine.** Is this what you would have expected?

PRACTICE TEST

Critical Thinking

1. Reflect on what was written in this chapter about the contrasts between university education and agency training. How can your education form the basis for your training, and how can agency training build on what you have learned in the classroom?

_____

_____

_____

_____

_____

_____

Professional Identity

2. Practicum students and professional social workers need to grow professionally, and one important method for promoting growth is learning to seek, accept, and use constructive feedback from clients, colleagues, and supervisors. What is your usual reaction to receiving feedback, and how can you use such feedback to learn and grow?

_____

_____

_____

_____

_____

_____

Learning from Supervision

LEARNING GOALS FOR THIS CHAPTER

▶ To understand the nature and purpose of practicum supervision

▶ To understand the types of supervision, including individual, group, and peer supervision

▶ To use supervision for practicum learning and professional growth

▶ To identify styles of supervision

CONNECTING CORE COMPETENCIES *in this chapter*

| Professional Identity | Ethical Practice | Critical Thinking | Diversity in Practice | Human Rights & Justice | Research Based Practice | Human Behavior | Policy Practice | Practice Contexts | Engage Assess Intervene Evaluate |

The quality of your practicum is closely tied to the nature and quality of the teacher–student relationship you develop with your field instructor. Learning from a skilled and caring supervisor can enrich a practicum experience and provide a positive model of staff interaction. Every supervisor or field instructor, like every student and every client, has both strengths and limitations. You will need to identify your field instructor's strengths and plan your practicum to take advantage of them.

BACKGROUND AND CONTEXT

In order to understand practicum supervision and how to make good use of it, it is necessary to examine the purpose and functions of supervision within an organization. Although the word ***supervision*** has its roots in a Latin word that means "to look over" or "to watch over," modern supervisory practice places less emphasis on the supervisor being an overseer of work and more emphasis on the supervisor being a skilled master of the work to be done, a leader, a mentor, and a teacher.

There are few jobs more challenging than that of a supervisor in a human services agency. It is a job that takes sensitivity, skill, common sense, commitment, good humor, and intelligence. Supervisors are mediators between line-level social workers and higher-level agency administrators. They frequently represent the agency in its interactions with other agencies and the community. In addition, they are often faced with the challenging tasks of responding to the concerns and complaints of clients who are dissatisfied with the agency's programs or with the performance of a social worker or other staff member.

Although being a supervisor can be demanding, it can also be a satisfying job, especially for those who understand and appreciate the teaching aspect of supervision. Watching a new social worker or social work student learn and develop on the job can be a satisfying and inspiring experience. That is one reason why many busy agency supervisors volunteer to serve as field instructors to social work students. Hopefully your field instructor is highly motivated to teach you about social work practice because he or she wants to give back to the profession.

Kadushin (2002) identifies three functions of agency-based supervisory practice: the administrative function, the supportive function, and the educational function. The ***administrative function*** of supervision includes such responsibilities as recruiting, selecting, and orienting new staff; assigning and coordinating work; monitoring and evaluating staff performance; facilitating communication up and down within the organization; advocating for staff; serving as a buffer between staff and administration; representing the agency to the public; and encouraging needed agency change.

The ***educational function*** of supervision focuses on providing informal training and orientation and arranging for formal in-service staff training. Basically, the supervisor is responsible for ensuring that staff members receive all of the initial training needed to perform well in their positions. In addition, the supervisor is responsible for recognizing training needs and providing ongoing in-service training.

The ***supportive function*** of supervision has to do with sustaining staff morale, cultivating a sense of teamwork, building commitment to the agency's goals and mission, encouraging workers by providing support, and dealing with work-related problems of conflict and frustration. This aspect of supervision is extremely important in human services agencies in which stress and burnout can be common risks. The supervisor must strive to create a work environment that is conducive to the provision of quality services to clients, while also supporting staff who may at times feel stressed and unappreciated.

A field instructor will be concerned with these three functions as they relate to practicum students. He or she will pay attention to whether you are performing the work of the agency in an appropriate manner and in keeping with agency policy and procedure. He or she will be sensitive to your fears and insecurities, and to the fact that you have personal responsibilities in addition to those related to the practicum. Your field instructor will want to do everything possible to facilitate your learning but, in the final analysis, his or her primary obligation must be to the agency's clients or consumers and to the agency that serves those clients.

Practice Contexts

How will the issues facing your practicum agency influence your supervisor?

There are many types of supervision, all of which serve an important purpose, and all of which are valuable in specific ways. Each type of supervision is able to meet a certain need or situation, and it is recommended that you expose yourself whenever possible to as many forms of supervision as you can. You may receive several of the following types of supervision.

- *Individual supervision* entails regularly planned, one-to-one meetings between the field instructor and the student.
- *Group supervision* consists of regularly scheduled meetings between the field instructor and a small group of students.
- *Peer supervision* involves regularly scheduled meetings attended by a small group of social workers who assume responsibility for providing guidance and suggestions to each other and to the agency's practicum students.
- *Formal case presentations* are regularly scheduled meetings at which one or more social workers describe their work on a specific case and invite advice and guidance on how it should be handled.
- *Ad hoc supervision* refers to brief, unscheduled meetings to discuss a specific question or issue.
- *Virtual supervision* is computer, e-mail, or web supervision.

Ethical Practice

What ethical behavior are you expecting from your supervisor?

A social worker who assumes the role of field instructor has special ethical obligations. Supervisors assume responsibility for the quality of work done by those they supervise. Ethically, they must have knowledge and skill in the areas in which they provide supervision. They are expected to evaluate the performance of those they supervise, use helpful and fair methods, and help supervisees gain knowledge and skills. They must also take care to manage the supervisory relationship, maintaining professional boundaries and avoiding dual relationships, both of which can complicate and undermine the supervisory relationship.

Your field instructor will no doubt take these obligations seriously; thus you can expect that he or she will treat the supervisory relationship in an ethical and professional manner. Certain behaviors by a field instructor may prompt your school's faculty supervisor or practicum coordinator to reevaluate the suitability and appropriateness of using a particular field instructor as a supervisor for students. This may include:

- The field instructor is not readily available to the student or often misses scheduled appointments.
- The field instructor shows little interest in teaching and helping the student learn social work knowledge and skills.
- The field instructor's behavior or practice is discovered to be unethical or incompetent.

Food for Thought

If practitioners are to treat their clients with the deepest possible integrity, they must have a place to go where they can carefully and honestly examine their own behavior. That place, ideally, is the supervisory relationship (Kaiser, 1997, 7).

• • •

Supervisors are apt to forget the steps they followed to deepen their own insights into the content. Ideas that have become obvious to them in their current practice may not be simple or obvious to their staffs. . . . Unless supervisors work at it, they can forget how they had to construct, element by element, their understanding of a complex construct such as contracting. They believe they can hand over the years of learning and are surprised to discover that a student or staff member is having great difficulty constructing even a simple version of the idea. . . . [Because they] have discovered some of the shortcuts, and are aware of some of the pitfalls, supervisors can guide their staff members and make their journey more certain and quicker, but they cannot take the journey for them (Shulman, 1993, 159).

• • •

One of the greatest joys in any manager's work is to foster the skills and talents of others, to see people achieving their full potential and flourishing over time and to assist them in giving a good professional service to others. Sometimes all it takes to do this is a listening ear, a few questions to draw them out, some words of praise or guidance, and ensuring that you yourself keep on top of what is happening in the wider agency and, preferably, in the profession as a whole (Coulshed, Mullender, Jones, and Thompson, 2006, 162).

• • •

The supervisor should not apologize for corrective feedback. This discounts its importance and attenuates its impact. The supervisee needs feedback to help overcome performance deficiencies so that he or she can do better work. Feedback helps make learning explicit and conscious. The supervisor has the perspective, the objectivity, and the knowledge of what good performance is supposed to look like—a *super vision,* so to speak (Kadushin and Harkness, 2002, 160).

• • •

Vicarious liability may be charged when . . . errors of commission or omission were those of the supervisee. In addition to mistreatment of clients or patients by a practitioner, some claims may implicate supervisors. These claims are made under the legal doctrine of *respondeat superior,* that is "let the master respond." This doctrine means a supervisor is responsible for the actions of a supervisee that were conducted during the course of employment, training, or field instruction (Dolgoff, 2005, 84).

If your field instructor exhibits any of these behaviors or attitudes, consult with your faculty supervisor or practicum coordinator to determine a course of action in order to ensure the quality of supervision available to you.

Supervisors have a variety of styles or preferred ways of doing their jobs, all of which will affect the student's experiences in the agency. No one style or approach is necessarily more right or better than others. Different supervisory styles are more or less effective depending on the nature of the work to be done and the level of training and experience of those being supervised. The following examples illustrate the variety of approaches to supervision to which the student will generally need to adapt.

- Some supervisors are task oriented, while others are process oriented.
- Some prefer to make decisions alone, while others prefer to involve many people in making decisions.
- Some make decisions quickly, while others take more time to do so.
- Some strive to retain authority and power, whereas others share power and try to empower others.
- Some are reluctant to share information with others, whereas others share information with staff and students.

- Some prefer routines and clear procedures, while others are flexible and function well on an ad hoc basis.
- Some want decisions and agreements in writing, while others are comfortable with verbal agreements.
- Some pay great attention to detail, while others deal with only the "big picture" and leave details to others.
- Some closely monitor the work of others, assuming that things can and will go wrong, while others assume that everything is fine unless someone says there is a problem.
- Some do not see the personal needs, concerns, and problems of colleagues and those they supervise as their responsibility, while others pay close attention to such matters.
- Some are quick to delegate work to others, while others are cautious about making new work assignments.
- Some emphasize organizing, planning, and directing the work assigned to those they supervise, while others assume that they will know what to do and can figure out how to do the work.

GUIDANCE AND DIRECTION

Professional Identity

As you read the following expectations for you, consider how each of them contributes to the delivery of effective and ethical social work services to clients.

Learning to use supervision is of central importance to the success of a practicum. Because social work is challenging and sometimes stressful, and also because your work directly affects clients' lives, you will need guidance, direction, support, and feedback from your field instructor. Social workers use supervision to help them deal with challenging situations, to provide performance feedback, and to give support. Learning to use supervision for professional development is an important part of your practicum.

Strive to use supervision in a purposeful and responsible manner. Having a regularly scheduled supervisory meeting time each week will help you avoid the difficulties of constantly having to arrange a suitable meeting time. Prepare for each meeting and do not expect your field instructor to do all of the talking. Bring questions, observations, and requests for input and feedback to the meeting. Use this time to examine your performance and explore new ideas.

Your field instructor will have expectations of you and it will be important for you to understand these expectations. In general, you will be expected to exhibit:

- Dependability and follow-through on assigned work
- Attention to detail and proper procedures
- Initiative in work-related assignments
- A cooperative attitude toward the field instructor and other staff
- Willingness to learn from whatever tasks are assigned
- Ability to assume assignments of increasing complexity and challenge
- Openness to supervision, including asking for, and learning from, constructive criticism
- Willingness to seek help when needed

Expect your field instructor to ask some very pointed, thorough, and thoughtful questions in order to learn about and monitor your work in the agency. Supervisors ask these questions in order to be of support to you and to ensure that clients are well served. They will help you analyze your performance, understand why an intervention was successful or not, and develop your critical thinking skills. Possible supervisory questions about an intervention in which you have been involved may include the following:

- What specific problem or issue were you addressing?
- What information did you gather?
- What assessment tools did you use?
- What meaning did you assign to this information?
- What were your goals and objectives?
- What were your client's goals and objectives?
- What were you trying to accomplish?
- Why did you choose that specific intervention?
- How did you build on the work of other professionals inside and outside the agency?
- What ethical and legal concerns affected your decision?
- Was the intervention successful? If not, what are the ramifications for the client and agency?
- How do you know whether the intervention was or was not successful?
- What other interventions might have worked better?
- What needs to be done next?
- What did you learn from this experience?
- What would you do differently next time?
- What did you learn about yourself?
- Would your client agree with your assessment of the intervention?

The role of a supervisor is to give both instruction and feedback, and you will increase your chances of success if you seek and are open to this input about yourself and your work. You may be anxious because your field instructor will be evaluating your performance. However, that is his or her responsibility. He or she has been asked by your school to guide your learning and offer constructive criticism in order that you might learn about yourself and develop your knowledge and skills.

In order for you to develop your knowledge and skills over time, your field instructor should evaluate your performance in an ongoing and continuous manner. You should receive feedback, suggestions, and constructive criticism during all phases of your practicum so that you can continue to grow professionally. If this is not happening, discuss the matter with your field instructor and ask for an ongoing critique of your performance.

Your field instructor is responsible for conducting a comprehensive evaluation of your learning and performance at the end of the academic term, and this will likely translate into a final grade in your practicum. You can expect that this evaluation will be based on:

- Direct observation of your work by your field instructor or other social workers in the agency
- Your verbal descriptions of what you are doing and learning
- Your written documentation, reports, and case notes
- Feedback received from clients regarding your work
- Observations and input from social workers in the community who have worked with you

As you begin your practicum and take on new responsibilities, you may be afraid of making a serious mistake or in some way hurting your clients. Such worries are to be expected. In fact, your field instructor will become concerned if you do not have these concerns, because that could mean that you are overconfident or that you do not understand the seriousness of your situation. Do not hesitate to express your fears. Your field instructor can help you with these issues and help prepare you for any tasks assigned to you. Take heart in the knowledge that most student errors tend to be those related to not doing enough because students are tentative, rather than actually doing harm to clients.

Supervision is an interactional process that in many ways parallels the social worker–client relationship and the helping process (Shulman, 1992). In order to help you improve your performance, your field instructor will employ many of the helping skills and techniques that you and other social workers use in working with clients such as offering guidance and support, providing feedback, recognizing strengths, and confronting when necessary. However, supervision is not counseling or therapy. If the supervision you receive feels too much like therapy, consult with your faculty supervisor. If you need counseling for personal issues or those related to your practicum, seek counseling from a professional rather than from your field instructor.

Field instructors use a variety of techniques to help students examine and process their experiences and deepen their learning. For example, your field instructor may use didactic instruction such as lecture or presentation, role playing, technique rehearsal, demonstration, modeling, and case consultation. View these techniques as valuable learning opportunities, although you may feel threatened or put on the spot.

Students tend to move through several stages during their practicum experience, including orientation, exploration and skill building, and beginning competency. Your field instructor will provide specific types of help at each stage, helping you move forward as a professional.

When you begin your practicum, you are in what is called an ***orientation stage.*** At this stage, you may feel anxious, overwhelmed, unsure, and even incompetent. It is your field instructor's job to provide orientation and training so that you know what the agency is all about and what is expected of you. He or she will offer guidance, provide encouragement, assist you in selecting learning activities that build skills, and help you develop confidence so you are willing to take on additional tasks and responsibilities.

After becoming familiar and comfortable with your practicum setting and what is expected, you will enter the ***exploration and skill building stage.*** During this stage, you will gain knowledge, skills, and confidence as you participate in various interventions and projects and take on added responsibilities. You will feel less anxious than when you first began the practicum, and although you will still make mistakes, you can analyze them and learn from them. Your field instructor will help you build on prior experiences and become comfortable taking risks and working with more difficult and challenging situations. He or she will help you learn general principles of practice, as well as the theory underlying interventions. You will be able to function more independently at this stage.

As the end of the practicum approaches, you will enter the ***beginning competency stage.*** At this stage, you will have developed a variety of skills and acquired considerable knowledge about your agency, its clients, and its specific programs and approaches. You will have identified your strengths, your limitations, and your interests. Your field instructor will reinforce your successes, encourage you to refine your skills, and expect you to work with an even wider variety of clients and projects. Hopefully you will need less supervision and will be gaining knowledge and skills that can be generalized to other similar client situations and other agency settings. Pay attention to your journey through these stages, including how you learn and grow. Try to plan

Engage Assess
Intervene Evaluate

What parallels do you see between students being evaluated by their supervisors and clients being assessed by their social workers?

Engage Assess
Intervene Evaluate

How are these stages of learning and developing competency similar to those that clients experience when they participate in interventions?

your learning experiences so that you feel ready for social work practice at the end of your practicum.

Some students begin the practicum with the hope that their field instructor will become a true mentor. When this happens, it is a great experience for a practicum student. Mentors can be role models and can inspire students to achieve higher levels of competence. However, this may not happen for a number of reasons. Even if your field instructor does not become a mentor, he or she can teach you what you need to know to be effective. When seeking a mentor, you may need to look to persons outside your practicum agency.

Conflicts may arise in the supervisory relationship. For example, you may feel that your field instructor does not devote enough time to you and your learning needs. You may feel that your field instructor is either too controlling or not structured enough. The two of you may have very different personalities. Perhaps you and your field instructor differ in terms of gender, race, ethnic background, or age, and at times these differences affect your relationship. Whatever the conflict is about, talk about it. Do not avoid the problem. You will be expected to find ways to deal with these issues. If the problem cannot be worked out with your field instructor, consult with your faculty supervisor.

Rothman (2000, 167–168) stresses the importance of optimizing your relationship with your field instructor when problems arise and describes a variety of approaches often used by practicum students. ***Confronting*** your supervisor directly helps clarify the problem so you can work to resolve it effectively. ***Circumventing*** your supervisor may be necessary if your relationship with your supervisor is only a formal one or if he or she does not have time to supervise you. ***Denying*** the conflict and choosing to accept your supervisor's perspective on the problem may be necessary and even helpful at times. ***Adapting*** to your supervisor's style, perspective, and policies may help you learn to work flexibly with others very different from you. ***Avoiding*** the problem by not discussing it will limit the amount of guidance you receive from your supervisor. ***Withdrawing*** from the conflict may be necessary if you cannot resolve the problem, and you may choose to leave your practicum site.

Exercise caution on developing a dual relationship with your field instructor. He or she is to be a supervisor, not a friend or a counselor. Although there can be an element of friendship between students and supervisors, this can be problematic when supervisors need to provide feedback and students need to be able to accept it. If personal problems arise during your practicum, do not ask or expect your field instructor to provide counseling. If you need such services, arrange to receive them in another way.

Hopefully you will never experience negative treatment by your supervisor, but should some negative behavior occur, seek the help of your faculty supervisor. For example, sexual harassment of a student by a field instructor is a very serious matter that should be immediately reported to your faculty supervisor or practicum coordinator. An allegation of sexual harassment is a complex legal concern. Should this problem arise in your practicum, immediately seek consultation on how to proceed.

If you observe that your field instructor violates the NASW *Code of Ethics,* consult with your school's practicum coordinator or your faculty supervisor.

Using Supervision for Learning: A Workbook Activity

1. Does your field instructor also supervise other social workers or agency staff? If so, who?

   _____

   _____

2. Who supervises your field instructor?

   _____

3. Has your field instructor previously supervised practicum students? If yes, about how many students?

   _____

4. Has your field instructor received agency-based training on staff supervision?

   _____

5. Has your field instructor attended training on practicum supervision and instruction provided by your school's practicum program? If yes, what was the nature of this training?

   _____

   _____

6. What specific types of knowledge and skills can you learn from your field instructor? Is your field instructor known to possess some special knowledge, experience, and skills?

   _____

   _____

7. In what areas of your learning do you want and welcome feedback from your field instructor?

   _____

   _____

8. In what areas of performance are you overly sensitive or fearful about receiving feedback from your field instructor? What might these feelings be telling you?

   _____

   _____

9. Are you afraid of anything related to your practicum? What is a positive way of dealing with these fears?

   _____

   _____

10. It has been said that people often avoid the experiences they need most in order to learn and grow personally. Are you avoiding any practicum-related experiences? How can you gain this experience in spite of your reservations?

    _____

    _____

11. Is it possible for you to observe and receive supervision from other social workers in your agency?

_____

_____

12. What teaching techniques does your field instructor use (lecture, presentation, demonstration, case consultation, role playing, or direct observation)?

_____

_____

13. Which of the following learning experiences can you use to enhance your practicum?

_____ Discussing possible decisions and actions with your supervisor before you have met with your client

_____ Discussing possible decisions and actions with your supervisor after you have met with your client

_____ Discussing how your interventions fit with various perspectives, theories, or models

_____ Using role-play and simulations to rehearse the techniques, skills, or approaches you want to learn

_____ Observing others modeling the skill or technique you wish to learn

_____ Brainstorming various ways in which a situation might be handled

_____ Watching a video or listening to an audiotape of an experienced worker's session with a client

_____ Reading and discussing an article related to the skills you wish to learn

_____ Reviewing and discussing the case notes and the written record of others' work with their clients

14. How can you work with your field instructor in order to have as many of these learning experiences as possible?

_____

_____

SUGGESTED LEARNING ACTIVITIES

▶ Read your university practicum manual so you understand what is expected of both your faculty supervisor and your field instructor.

▶ Attend group or peer supervisory sessions offered in your agency in order to learn about the various modes of providing and receiving supervision.

▶ Present a case you are working on at a peer supervisory session, asking for input from other social workers.

▶ If appropriate and feasible, work with a variety of social workers, supervisors, and managers in your agency so that you can observe differing supervisory styles.

▶ Ask your field instructor how your agency provides support to its employees, such as through an employee assistance program or continuing education.

▶ In Sheafor and Horejsi (2008), read the sections entitled "Giving and Receiving Supervision" (596–600) and "Developing Self Awareness" (576–580).

Succeed with **mysocialworklab**

Log onto **www.mysocialworklab.com** and select the **Interactive Skill Module** videos from the left-hand menu. Answer the questions below. (*If you did not receive an access code to* **MySocialWorkLab** *with this text and wish to purchase access online, please visit* www.mysocialworklab.com.)

1. Watch page 19 (Clarification of the Role of Agency) in the child welfare module. Supervision is essential in child welfare practice considering the seriousness of most cases. In what serious practice situations will you seek supervision?

2. Watch page 16 (Focusing the Group on Problem-Solving and Mutual Aid) in the group work module. Given the number of clients in most groups, why would supervision be important for the facilitator?

PRACTICE TEST

The following questions are similar in phrasing and content to those asked in social work licensing examinations. They should help you prepare to take the licensing examination in your state.

1. In addition to state licensing requirements for social work supervision, _____ provides additional expectations for supervisors:
   a. universities
   b. NASW Code of Ethics
   c. Labor unions
   d. Client advocacy groups

2. Supervisors must be informed of
   a. illegal activity discovered by social workers
   b. client complaints
   c. treatment outcomes
   d. colleague tardiness

3. Dual relationships between supervisors and supervisees
   a. are inadvisable
   b. are illegal
   c. are encouraged
   d. are not covered in the NASW Code of Ethics

4. A supervisor's ultimate ethical responsibility is to
   a. those he/she supervises
   b. society
   c. funding sources
   d. clients

Ethical Practice

5. Supervisors' responsibility for the actions of a supervisee is referred to as:
   a. tort law
   b. vicarious liability
   c. professional liability
   d. negligence

6. The main function of evaluating employee performance is
   a. to meet state laws regarding outcomes
   b. to satisfy funding sources
   c. to ensure quality of services provided to clients
   d. to promote professional development of supervisees

Engage Assess Intervene Evaluate

7. Which of the following functions of a supervisor is most useful in measuring effectiveness of services?
   a. supportive function of supervision
   b. educational function of supervision
   c. administrative function of supervision
   d. ethical function of supervision

6

Personal Safety

LEARNING GOALS FOR THIS CHAPTER

▶ To identify the sources and types of danger most often encountered in social work practice

▶ To become familiar with potential dangers and risks in practicum

▶ To become familiar with agency policies and procedures that can reduce risk and protect staff and clients

▶ To become familiar with precautions and preventive actions that can reduce the risk of being harmed

▶ To become familiar with steps and actions that can de-escalate an already dangerous situation and protect a social worker in such a situation

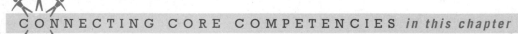

CONNECTING CORE COMPETENCIES *in this chapter*

| Professional Identity | Ethical Practice | **Critical Thinking** | **Diversity in Practice** | Human Rights & Justice | Research Based Practice | **Human Behavior** | Policy Practice | **Practice Contexts** | Engage Assess Intervene Evaluate |

Although social workers see themselves as helpers and expect most clients to be cooperative, at times they find themselves in situations in which they must deal with clients who are angry, volatile, and threatening. Accounts of violence toward social workers are increasing, due to client frustration with human service systems; cutbacks in services; increased levels of crime, drug use, and violence in society; and antiauthority or antigovernment attitudes on the part of clients.

In addition to the physical dangers associated with certain circumstances and types of practice, exposure to job-related danger can lead to worker anxiety, low morale, burnout, family stress, and high staff turnover. As a social work practicum student, you must be cognizant of the dangers you face. You will need to exercise certain precautions so as to reduce risks to your safety. Moreover, you must know what steps to take when you encounter a dangerous situation.

BACKGROUND AND CONTEXT

Broadly speaking, the potential sources of danger to social workers include the following:

- Clients who are angry and feel mistreated by the agency and its staff.
- Clients who present a special threat because of high-risk factors such as alcohol or drug use, a pattern of violent behavior, antiauthority attitudes, or unstable mental condition.
- Persons who are not clients, but who are acquainted with or related to clients and are aware that the clients feel mistreated by the agency and its staff.
- Persons with criminal intent and inclination who are found in neighborhoods near the agency or in areas where the social worker travels and works. These individuals are not clients, nor do they have a relationship with the workers' clients.
- Biohazardous and toxic materials that may be encountered in hospitals and other health-care facilities and during visits to clients in their homes.

In addition, certain practice settings present more risk to social workers than others do. Such settings include child protective agencies, programs in correctional settings, forensic units of psychiatric hospitals, shelters for the homeless, and residential facilities for youth who may be aggressive and impulsive. These settings are inherently dangerous because some of those served have tendencies toward the use of violence. However, any practice setting can be threatening, because client–worker interactions often involve emotionally charged situations and concerns. Even clients with no previous history of violence or high-risk behaviors can, under certain circumstances, pose a threat to social workers.

Individuals with mental illnesses are not inherently more dangerous than persons who do not suffer from such impairments. However, a small percentage of those with certain symptoms are a potential threat. Included in this group are persons who experience visual or auditory hallucinations that may lead them to harm others. It may also include those who hold bizarre, fanatical, or paranoid beliefs or delusions, and who as a result may feel especially threatened by social workers. Clients with extreme antigovernment or antiauthority beliefs may see social workers as threats and may feel justified in resorting to violence.

Practice Contexts

What characteristics of organizations and communities might serve to make clients distrustful of social workers?

Critical Thinking

Without overreacting, how can you make sure you accurately assess the risk you may face in your agency?

Certain social work practices and interventions have a greater likelihood of placing the worker at risk. Such activities include the initial investigation of child abuse allegations, the involuntary removal of a child from a parent's home, providing protection to a victim of domestic violence, outreach to youth involved in gangs, treatment of aggressive youth, intervention with drug- and alcohol-involved clients, the transporting of clients who do not wish to be moved, the behavioral management of persons with certain forms of brain injury or mental retardation, and the monitoring of clients in correctional settings. In these situations, social work actions can be perceived as threatening or coercive. This may result in heightened emotion or defensiveness on the part of clients, and an inclination to use violence.

Social workers who work with potentially dangerous clients face the difficult challenge of remaining humane, open, and accepting of clients while also being alert to the possibility of danger or attack. It is important not to expect that every client will be a threat, but to recognize a client who might be.

Social workers in some settings experience frequent verbal abuse, and because most of these threats do not result in actual violence, these social workers may become complacent. They may come to view verbal threats as part of their job, mistakenly assuming that the clients are always bluffing and consequently fail to take reasonable precautions. Some social workers mistakenly believe that because they have been trained in basic helping skills, they will always be able to talk their way out of a dangerous situation. These overly confident workers may minimize risk, erroneously conclude that they do not need special training in how to respond in truly dangerous situations, and put themselves at risk.

If you are doing your practicum in a hospital or other health-care setting, you should be alert to the existence of biological or chemical hazards and receive instruction on how to protect yourself against infectious diseases and how to avoid or properly handle biohazardous materials such as used tissues, clothing, bed sheets, or pillows that have been stained with body fluids. In

---

Food for Thought

Many of us choose social work as our profession because we want to help other people and make the world a better place. We do not anticipate that we may become targets of violence by the very individuals we want to help, but today risk is a reality of work life for many practicing social workers (Newhill, 2003, 237).

• • •

Agencies which ignore worker safety issues, or accept them as a normal part of the job, imperil both their staff and the families they serve. Staff who ignore their own gut feeling about personal risk and fail to take defensive precautions are not dealing realistically with danger (Farestad, 1997, 2).

• • •

One major potential obstacle in assessing danger is the strong commitment toward helping others. This desire may lead to overlooking or dismissing the danger signs and failing to recognize that some

people do not want to be helped. . . . With no weapon, no power of arrest, no bulletproof vest, and generally no backup . . . [social workers] go into battle armed with only a genuine concern for their fellow human beings and a mission (Harman and Davis, 1997, 15).

• • •

Due to the increased safety risks faced by social workers in many settings, it is critical that you be able to assess potential risk accurately. Although you will not always be able to determine risk accurately in advance of an actual threat to your safety, you should be aware that certain factors may increase the risk of harm (Birkenmaier and Berg-Weger, 2007, 8).

• • •

Looking for the best in people and wanting to help can sometimes override normal protective caution (Newhill, 2003, 200).

some instances, you may need to wear a mask and gloves when interviewing a patient. In some cases this will be done to protect yourself from disease and in other cases to protect a vulnerable patient. Practicum students may also be exposed to client threats over the telephone or via e-mail. You will need to be trained in agency responses to such threats in order to protect yourself, your coworkers, and your clients.

GUIDANCE AND DIRECTION

Diversity in Practice

Is it possible that anger and threats of violence on the part of clients could be influenced by factors related to diversity?

It is important to remember that much violence toward social workers could be prevented if they understand the process of escalation and how to intervene or reach at each phase. Most dangerous interpersonal situations are the result of tensions that have grown and intensified over time. It is vital to understand the phases of escalation, the client's needs and feelings during each phase, and what actions or interventions by the social worker might reduce the tension and level of risk. It is preferable to intervene as early as possible in order to prevent escalation and eventual loss of control by the angry client. Irwin (1997, 8–10) describes four stages of crisis management and suggests approaches to use at each stage to reduce the likelihood of violence. Consider these principles and employ these approaches if you feel threatened by the behavior of a client or another person. Discuss them with your field instructor in order to anticipate potentially dangerous situations and how he or she recommends dealing with clients at each of the following stages:

Stage 1: Initial Tension and Frustration

At this stage, individuals who may become violent are anxious and experiencing high levels of emotion, but are still rational and in control of their behavior. They are not acting on their feelings, so will respond to an approach that helps them vent emotions, reflect on the situation, and devise a solution on their own. Active listening will help them express and examine their feelings and usually reduce the level of tension. Basic listening skills also help build rapport and assess the severity of the crisis and the danger it presents.

Stage 2: Verbal Attack

During this second stage, individuals feel threatened, vulnerable, and defensive. They go on the offensive with verbal attacks. Irrational thoughts and strong feelings begin to override their self-control. They may direct anger toward the worker, using verbal abuse and intimidation. Verbal communication becomes more difficult and further escalation is likely. Effective threat-reducing approaches include calm body language, a nonthreatening tone of voice, reflecting clients' feelings and behaviors, and setting limits on what behavior is allowable. The social worker should calmly validate the feelings being expressed and provide clear guidelines, choices, and alternatives if possible.

Stage 3: Loss of Control

Individuals at this stage have lost control over their behavior. They have physically struck, or are very close to, striking others. They pose a real danger. Workers need to immediately assess the level of danger and their ability to provide control. They should prepare to escape, if necessary. Because most clients will fear their own loss of control, workers are more likely to

Human
Behavior

Considering these
stages, what might you
conclude about how
human behavior is influ-
enced by organizational
responses?

gain control of the situation by empathizing with clients' fear of doing something they will regret. Workers must remain calm and continue to build rapport, while shifting focus to the threatening behavior. The out-of-control
person must be controlled, either by the worker or by legal authorities.

Stage 4: Recovery after the Outburst

At this stage, the crisis has peaked and imminent danger has passed.
Individuals struggle to regain their composure and need help putting
themselves back together. Workers should allow them to further vent
their anger, explain their feelings, and come to some closure regarding
the incident. Allowing people to stabilize themselves decreases the risk
of re-escalation. At this stage, people may gain insight, allow mutual
problem solving with the worker, and plan ways to prevent another such
incident in the future.

Dealing with the Potentially Violent Client

Following is a list of guidelines for anticipating potential danger, identifying
situations that might put you at risk, preventing or dealing with risky situations, and resolving violent situations should they arise.

- Understand that past behavior is the best single predictor of future
  behavior. Before meeting with a client that you do not know who may
  be dangerous, consult agency records or the local police in search of
  information that may help you assess the risk.
- Remove all potential weapons from your office when dealing with a
  potentially dangerous client, including scissors, staplers, paperweights,
  and other small but heavy objects.
- Leave your office door partly open during an interview with a potentially dangerous client.
- Notify others if you are planning to meet a potentially dangerous client
  in your office and arrange for a way to signal for help. Arrange your
  office so that you are closest to the door. Place a desk or other barrier
  between you and the dangerous client.
- Avoid meeting with clients when you are alone in the office. If you
  must have the meeting, turn lights on in other offices and lead clients
  to believe that others will be coming into the office.
- When meeting with an angry client, provide him or her with as much
  privacy as possible without compromising your safety.
- Make use of all safety procedures and devices available such as call
  devices or code systems to alert coworkers that you need help.
- Be very cautious when dealing with a person who is under the influence of alcohol or drugs, even when you know the person fairly well. A
  person under the influence of chemicals should be viewed as inherently unpredictable.
- Be cautious when around persons who may be involved in illegal
  activities such as manufacturing or selling drugs and may feel threatened by your presence or by what you have seen. They may be willing to harm you in order to protect themselves from discovery by
  authorities.
- Remember that worker attitudes play a role in either controlling or pro-
  voking threatening behavior. Maintain a positive, nonjudgmental attitude toward clients.

◗ Remember that clients use threats and violence when other forms of communication fail them, so utilize skills that facilitate communication and help clients express themselves in words.

◗ Recognize that both increased structure and decreased stimuli may help clients remain calm and gain self-control.

◗ Remember that an attack by a client is almost always the reaction of someone who is afraid and feeling threatened. Thus, strive to speak and act in ways that lessen the client's need to be afraid of you. Demonstrate empathy and that you understand the reason behind their anger and fear.

◗ Address the person by name. Do not argue with or criticize an angry person. Avoid doing anything that might be perceived as ridiculing or embarrassing the person.

◗ Trust your instincts. Assume that you have a built-in unconscious mechanism that can recognize danger more quickly than your rational thought processes. If you feel afraid, assume that you are in danger, even if you cannot clearly identify why you feel this way.

◗ Avoid standing above others. If possible and safe, take a sitting position. Standing is more authoritarian and threatening than sitting.

◗ Attacks are most likely when clients feel trapped or controlled, either psychologically or physically. To the extent possible, give clients options and choices. Your location in a room should be one that allows the client to escape without having to come close to you.

◗ Be alert to signs of an imminent attack such as rapid breathing, teeth grinding, dilated pupils, flaring nostrils, choppy speech, clenched fists, and threatening movements of the body.

◗ Allow angry persons to vent their feelings. Most angry persons will begin to calm down after two or three minutes of venting or name calling. While this is going on, it is usually best to listen respectfully and allow them to express their feelings. Some people are stimulated by their own words and grow even angrier because of what they are saying. If that occurs, the level of risk is increasing.

◗ Do not touch an angry person, especially if they may be under the influence of a substance, and do not move into their personal space. Remain at least four feet away from the person.

◗ Remember that an angry or dangerous person is more likely to attack someone who appears weak, insecure, and unsure. Therefore, present yourself as calm, composed, and self-confident, but not haughty.

◗ If an individual threatens you with a gun or other weapon, assure him or her that you intend no harm and slowly back away. Do not attempt to disarm the person. Leave that to the police or security staff with special training.

Handling the Potential Dangers of a Home Visit

◗ Do not enter a situation that could be dangerous without first consulting with others and formulating a plan to reduce risk. Do not hesitate to seek the assistance of other social workers or the police.

◗ When visiting clients in their homes, keep your agency informed of your plans and itinerary and check in by phone on a prearranged schedule. When away from the office, carry a means of calling for help (e.g., cellular phone, push-button emergency signals, or radio).

◗ Assign two staff members for potentially dangerous home visits whenever possible.

Which of these suggestions might apply to the work you will be doing?

▶ Do not enter a home or apartment building until you have taken a few minutes to determine its level of danger. Listen for sounds of violence or out-of-control behavior. Consider whether other people are nearby and if they would respond to a call for help. Identify possible escape routes.

▶ Be aware that guns are most often kept in bedrooms and that kitchens contain knives and other potential weapons. Leave immediately if a threatening person appears to be moving toward a weapon.

▶ Be aware that clients who leave a room could return with a weapon.

▶ Do not sit in an overstuffed chair or couch from which you cannot quickly get to your feet. Select a hard and movable chair. If necessary, it can be used as a shield or barrier between you and a threatening person.

▶ Park your car in a way that allows for a quick escape if necessary.

▶ Keep your vehicle in good running order and full of gasoline so that you will not find yourself stranded in a dangerous or isolated area.

▶ Educate yourself about drugs and illegal drug labs so that you can recognize the dangers inherent in entering such a place.

▶ Know as much as you can about the people living in the home you are visiting in order to anticipate negative attitudes toward authorities, previous history of violence, or previous experiences with social service agencies.

▶ If you are being followed, go immediately to a police or fire station or to a public place. Do not go to your home if you believe someone is following you or watching your movements.

▶ If you are likely to encounter dangerous situations while at work (or while walking to work), wear shoes and clothing that permit running. Avoid wearing long earrings or jewelry that could easily be grabbed and twisted to inflict pain and prevent your escape.

▶ Consider carrying a defensive device such as pepper spray, and learn to use it before making home visits.

Handling an Intense Argument between Two or More People

▶ When two or more individuals are in a heated argument and you need to intervene, begin by gaining their attention. Anything short of physical force may be used. A shrill whistle, a loud clap, a loud voice, a silly request (e.g., "I need a glass of water"), or other attention-getting devices may be used for this purpose.

▶ Ask those in conflict to sit down. If they will not sit, remain standing also.

▶ Separate the disputants as necessary without compromising your own safety. Bring them back together only after they have quieted down and gained self-control.

▶ If possible, always intervene in a crisis situation with a partner.

▶ Do not physically intervene if those in conflict are threatening each other with weapons or if they are engaged in a high level of physical violence.

Agency Procedure and the Dangerous Client

▶ The agency should develop policy and protocols on how staff members are to respond to dangerous situations, such as bomb threats or hostage taking. These procedures should be rehearsed regularly.

- The agency should provide training on personal safety and related agency procedures to staff and students and repeat or update this training on a regular basis.
- The agency should develop a protocol about when and how to use police assistance, including a written agreement with local law enforcement officials.
- The agency should keep waiting rooms and offices clean and create a pleasant and inviting physical environment. Dirty, unpleasant, or unkempt locations convey disrespect to clients and tend to generate hostility.
- The agency should post in waiting rooms and in other prominent places a statement explaining that alcohol, drugs, and weapons are not allowed in the building and that threats and violence or the possession of a weapon will prompt an immediate call to the police.
- The agency should make sure that the exterior of the agency's building and parking lot are well lighted.
- The agency should designate a specific office or room for meetings with potentially violent clients. This room should be one that is easily observed by others nearby.
- The agency's record-keeping system should use color codes or other markings that identify individuals or households with a history of violence.
- The agency should institute security measures within the building. This might include the installation of a call-for-help button in each office space and establishing telephone code words that are requests for police assistance.
- The agency should maintain a log of all threats of violence so staff can identify those individuals and situations that present a special risk.
- The agency should file criminal charges against those who harm or threaten physical injury to either the worker or the worker's family.
- When a worker is harmed, the agency should respond with appropriate counseling and emotional support to lessen the effects on the worker and the worker's family.

Reducing the Risk of Harm: A Workbook Activity

1. What training is provided in your agency to help social workers prevent and deal with threatening or violent clients or situations?

   _____

   _____

   _____

2. What kinds of high-risk clients or situations are you likely to encounter in your practicum? How will you prepare yourself to deal with them?

   _____

   _____

   _____

3. What agency policies and procedures are in place to ensure personal safety and reduce risk to agency employees and clients?

   _____

   _____

   _____

4. Have any employees in your practicum agency been threatened or harmed by clients or consumers? If yes, describe the circumstances that gave rise to the incident.

   _____

   _____

   _____

5. What precautions, if any, might have prevented the above incidents or reduced their seriousness?

   _____

   _____

   _____

6. Do agency workers carry defensive devices such as mace or pepper spray? What are the pros and cons of doing so?

   _____

   _____

7. Given the area served by your agency, what specific locations or neighborhoods are known to be especially dangerous?

   _____

   _____

8. Does your agency have a formal, written agreement with the police detailing when they are to be called for assistance?

_____

_____

9. Are there any clients or situations that frighten you? If so, how can you deal with your concerns and fears?

_____

_____

10. If your practicum is in a hospital or health-care setting, what precautions are you to take in order to protect yourself and your vulnerable clients from infectious diseases or biohazards?

_____

_____

11. Does your agency have an incident reporting system for documenting threats and violence toward workers?

_____

_____

12. What services does your agency provide to workers who are threatened, injured, or traumatized by threats or violence (e.g., counseling, critical incident stress debriefing, or support groups)?

_____

_____

SUGGESTED LEARNING ACTIVITIES

- Invite a local police officer to offer guidance on how to reduce risk in and around your agency.

- Interview experienced social workers and get their advice on how to reduce personal risk.

- Role-play situations that illustrate each of the four stages of crisis management described in this chapter.

- Educate yourself on the specific safety issues faced by your agency (e.g., methamphetamine abuse, use of restraining orders).
  - Attend training offered by your agency on safety.
  - Determine what services (i.e., counseling or legal services) would be offered to you or others in your agency should you experience a threat or actual incident of violence.

- In Sheafor and Horejsi (2008), read the section entitled "The Dangerous Client" (224-227).

Log onto **www.mysocialworklab.com** and select the **Interactive Skill Module** videos from the left-hand menu. Answer the questions below. (*If you did not receive an access code to* **MySocialWorkLab** *with this text and wish to purchase access online, please visit* www.mysocialworklab.com.)

1. **Watch page 7 (Confrontation) in the child welfare module.** When confronting a client who believes that custody of her children is at stake, what is the risk of danger to a social worker?

2. **Watch page 19 (Exploring Feelings) in the domestic violence module.** What safety issues for clients and social workers need to be addressed in domestic violence situations?

PRACTICE TEST

The following questions are similar in phrasing and content to those asked in social work licensing examinations. They should help you prepare to take the licensing examination in your state.

Practice Contexts

1. The main purpose of clear agency protocol in regard to social worker safety is
   a. to protect clients
   b. to protect social workers
   c. to avoid lawsuits
   d. to measure effectiveness of services

2. Social workers who do not follow agency protocol about safety
   a. may not be protected legally if they are injured
   b. will be sanctioned by their agency
   c. have violated the NASW Code of Ethics
   d. are covered if they have their own liability insurance

3. The use of weapons by professionals in their work
   a. is governed primarily by state law and agency
   b. is governed primarily by local law enforcement agencies
   c. is governed by federal law
   d. is governed by the NASW Code of Ethics

4. Which is true in regard to agency agreements with law enforcement agencies?
   a. agreements should be developed on an ad hoc basis
   b. agreements should be formalized in advance of a threat to workers
   c. agreements should be informal
   d. agreements should be made between individual officers and workers

5. Premature use of physical containment of threatening clients may
   a. deescalate the situation
   b. escalate the situation
   c. violate trust between social worker and client
   d. undermine the effectiveness of interventions

Human Behavior

6. The best predictor of client violence toward social workers is
   a. mental health diagnosis
   b. threats of violence
   c. social worker skill and ability
   d. previous history of violent behavior

7. Agencies who provide personal safety training to their workers
   a. will be immune from prosecution if injuries occur
   b. will be able to demonstrate reasonable efforts to protect workers
   c. are required to provide training to each worker once
   d. do not need to carry professional malpractice insurance

7

Communication

LEARNING GOALS FOR THIS CHAPTER

▶ To identify the communication systems used by your agency

▶ To learn skills and guidelines for effective verbal and written communication

▶ To identify common sources and occasions of miscommunication and misunderstanding

▶ To identify barriers to effective communication

CONNECTING CORE COMPETENCIES *in this chapter*

| Professional Identity | Ethical Practice | Critical Thinking | **Diversity in Practice** | Human Rights & Justice | Research Based Practice | **Human Behavior** | Policy Practice | **Practice Contexts** | Engage Assess Intervene Evaluate |

Communication is at the heart of social work practice. A social worker must be able to communicate with clients or consumers, other social workers, members of other professions (such as physicians, teachers, lawyers, and judges), agency supervisors and administrators, leaders and decision makers (such as elected officials), and with a cross section of the people who make up the community. The social worker must be able to communicate in a one-on-one situation, within the context of a small group, and sometimes before a large audience. The worker must also be able to use several modes of communication effectively, including the written word, the spoken word, and nonverbal communication. A social worker must also understand communication within an organization, and how effective organizational communication can enhance the quality of services.

Students are often surprised at how much time social workers must devote to reading and writing. Because of the demands of written documentation, effective writing skills will help to reduce unnecessary time spent documenting your written work. Written communication may take the form of a letter, a memo, a case record, the minutes of a committee meeting, a lengthy formal report, or a grant proposal. The extensive use of written and electronic communication in social work requires that the worker be able to write well and read rapidly.

Effective and skilled communication is central to success in any social work setting. A variety of problems can result from insufficient, inaccurate, or somehow distorted and misunderstood communication. Even during the practicum, many of the problems that frustrate students are actually problems in the communication between the student and the field instructor or between the student and the practicum coordinator. This chapter is designed to assist students in developing essential communication skills for use in the practicum agency.

BACKGROUND AND CONTEXT

Communication can be defined as the process by which a person, group, or organization transmits information back and forth between individuals, groups, or organizations Both the sender and the receiver of information, whether on the personal or organizational level, must be skilled in both sending and receiving in order for communication to be successful.

Interpersonal communication refers to communication that involves talking, listening, and responding in ways that place an emphasis on the personal dimensions of those involved. It usually takes place in a face-to-face exchange but may occur on the telephone, in highly personalized correspondence, or by e-mail. Providing direct services to clients requires frequent and fairly intense interpersonal communication.

The term *organizational communication* refers to the somewhat impersonal exchange of messages and information between the various levels, departments, and divisions of an organization, and also between the organization and various individuals and groups outside the organization. As compared to other types of communication, the communication within an organization tends to be more formal and more often in written form. Moreover, the nature and flow of information within an organization is strongly influenced by lines of authority and the chain of command.

Downward communication consists of messages, directions, and instructions from those higher in the chain of command to those working at lower levels in the organization. The term *upward communication* refers to communication to those higher in the chain of command, such as when a supervisor sends a message to the agency's executive director. As a general rule, upward communication occurs less often than downward communication. This can be a source of problems within an organization because those persons lower on the chain of command often feel that they are not heard and that their communication is not valued. ***Horizontal communication*** refers to the exchange of messages among persons or units at the same level within the organization.

A wide variety of communication networks exists within social service agencies. Mainly, they differ in the degree to which they are centralized. In a highly centralized network, all messages must flow through some central office or person who can then control what information moves up or down. A decentralized network is characterized by an exchange of information between people and organizational levels without first passing through a particular channel or central point. As a general rule, centralized networks are faster and more accurate if the information has to do with relatively simple tasks. Decentralized networks are faster and more accurate if the communication is about complex tasks and unique activities. This type of communication network may also be more informal and feel more personal to those within an organization.

A common problem within organizations is ***information overload.*** This refers to frustration and miscommunication caused by an overwhelming volume of messages, instructions, and reports. Centralized communication networks and highly bureaucratic organizations are especially vulnerable to information overload because so many messages must pass through all levels as they move up and down the organization. This overload can also result in lost or delayed messages and subsequent miscommunication.

Modern communication technology (e-mail, fax machines, cellular phones) has solved some problems caused by slow communication, but it has created others. It has probably added to the problem of information overload because it is now very easy to send a message and copies of it to many more people. E-mail encourages the use of written communication over face-to-face communication, thus eliminating the opportunity to observe nonverbal communication in order to accurately interpret a message.

Professions and organizations develop and communicate by the use of a specialized language, or jargon, as a way to simplify communication. However, this has the effect of making many of their messages unintelligible to outsiders, including students and clients. You will need to learn agency-specific terminology, acronyms, and jargon quickly in order to understand what is said and written on a daily basis.

The goal of communication is for the receiver to accurately understand the message being sent by the sender. That sounds like a simple process, but as everyone knows, communication is complex and many factors can prevent or disrupt the process. Sheafor and Horejsi (2006, 135–136) observe that communication problems develop whenever:

‣ We speak for others rather than let them speak for themselves.
‣ We do not take the time or make the effort to really listen.
‣ We allow prejudices, stereotypes, and presumptions to color how we interpret what others are saying.
‣ We keep things to ourselves because we fear others will disapprove of what we believe and feel.
‣ We make no attempt to communicate because we assume others already know, or should know, how we feel and what we think.
‣ We discourage or suppress communication by ordering, threatening, preaching, patronizing, judging, blaming, or humoring.

Practice Contexts

Is the communication network in your agency centralized or decentralized? Does this meet the needs of the organization?

Human Behavior

How can an understanding of human behavior help you develop positive inter-personal communication skills and avoid barriers to good communication?

Practice Contexts

What did you learn about organizations in previous classes that might help you learn how your agency manages communication?

▶ We allow negative feelings about ourselves to keep us silent, fearing that we have nothing worthwhile to say and that no one will want to hear what we think or feel.

Organizational communication has its own set of unique challenges and requires as much practice and special skill as does communication with clients. Chapter 8 ("The Agency Context of Practice") will help you learn what you need to know about organizations to communicate effectively. Trust between the sender and the receiver is a critical prerequisite to effective communication. It determines how the receiver will respond to the sender's message. There are major barriers to the development of trust, including insincerity, time pressures, and defensiveness. In verbal communication the sender may speak too fast or too slow, or the receiver may not listen. The sender may write or speak without first planning his or her message or use words that the receiver does not understand or words that mean different things to different people.

Defensiveness and fear are also major barriers to communication. When people are in an environment in which they feel safe, accepted, and supported, they concentrate more on the content and meaning of the message, rather than spending time protecting themselves or searching for the sender's hidden agenda. Behaviors that tend to lower defenses include messages that give facts without value judgments, are spontaneous and genuine, offer mutual trust and respect, and display a willingness to consider different points of view. You may observe many of these barriers to communication, and you will need to learn how to deal with them because your clients may be negatively impacted by ineffective organizational communication.

Food for Thought

We use communication to create a new understanding of something, or to express what is unexpressed (Payne, 2007, 62).

• • •

Grasp the subject, the words will follow.
—*Cato the Elder*

• • •

I cannot overemphasize how important clarity is to your writing. Clinicians simply must learn to be extremely careful about their words. You must know and say precisely what you mean. It is not enough to defend with "C'mon, you know what I meant." That may work in everyday discourse, but it is unacceptable in professional work. If the reader does not know exactly what is meant, the responsibility falls on the writer, not the reader (Bair, 2008, 126).

• • •

There are several problems with paper. One is that there is so much of it around that most of us are . . . wasting lots of time dealing with it. . . . Another problem with paper is that from time to time you have to write on it. And whenever you do, you put a little bit of yourself down on the paper to be examined and judged by someone else. Solely on the basis of what you set down

on paper, someone may decide whether you . . . have exercised your professional judgment wisely.

There is something fleeting about a judgment or opinion that is expressed orally; it is less available for scrutiny than is the written word and it will probably be less far reaching in its impact. But ideas can be transformed by writing. Once put down on paper, mere suggestions or daily routines become rules and policies. And one person's (perhaps ill-informed) opinion becomes the last word on the subject.

So . . . you cannot afford to be a poor writer. If the words you put down on paper are not clear to your reader, they can take on a life of their own that is contrary to your intent. Or they can die on the spot, when you want them to come alive and make the reader take action (Kantz and Mercer, 1991, 221).

• • •

As a clinician, you cannot afford to be careless or haphazard about what you say or write. You must be aware of all the subtleties of language and learn to say what you mean. This is especially true of written reports, because once a report is written others may read it without you being present to explain, clarify, or correct mistakes (Baird, 2005, 106).

Social workers often refer to communication styles, which refer to very individualized ways they have learned to communicate with clients and colleagues. These styles build on individual skills such as building rapport, communicating genuineness, and enhancing trust with clients. Although communication styles may differ greatly, the goals of communication are essentially the same—to engage clients in a helping relationship. Over time you will develop your own professional style of communication that will allow you to engage with clients.

Psychosocial factors can become barriers to communication, including the sender's or the receiver's moods, emotional state, level of stress, defensiveness, and lack of trust. Expectations have a great deal to do with communication. We hear what we hope to hear and pay most attention to positions and information with which we agree. We also have a difficult time accepting criticism or negative feedback. Finally, previous ineffective communication between social workers, coworkers, or clients can color subsequent communications.

Communication is also influenced by such factors as one's life experiences, culture and ethnicity, familiarity with the language being used, social class, religious beliefs, and education. The symbols we use in language do not have universal meanings—they are influenced by our background, experiences, and the cultural content of the exchanges between sender and receiver. (See Chapter 12, "Diversity and Cultural Competency," for additional helpful information on cross-cultural communication.)

Diversity in Practice

What can you do to open yourself to feedback about your communication skills with diverse clients and colleagues?

GUIDANCE AND DIRECTION

Good communication skills, verbal and written, are of central importance in social work practice. Do your best to learn communication skills now because you will need them throughout your career. You will continually be challenged to develop these skills and identify methods to monitor the effectiveness of your communication.

Carefully observe the patterns and processes of communication in your agency. For example, when you attend a staff meeting or committee meeting, consider the following questions:

- Who selects topics for discussion and develops the agenda?
- Who initiates communication and who introduces new topics for discussion?
- Who are the active communicators? Who are the quiet ones?
- Who speaks to whom? Who interrupts whom?
- Is there a certain hierarchy that affects the direction of the messages?
- Are the meetings formal or informal? Are the meetings structured by an agenda and the use of *Robert's Rules of Order*?
- What topics are appropriate for discussion?
- Which staff members work hard at listening and understanding others?
- Which ones seem quick to assume they know what others are trying to say without really listening?
- How are decisions made? Is the process guided by a majority vote or is consensus sought?

In nearly every organization you will have the opportunity to observe effective and ineffective, functional and dysfunctional communication. Take note of which styles and methods work and which do not. Consider why communication may be especially difficult and flawed at times. Knowing some of the following pitfalls of communication may keep you from making these same mistakes.

▶ People who are busy and hurried sometimes forget or neglect to communicate with those who are in need of a certain message or information.
▶ People take shortcuts in communication to save time.
▶ People make erroneous assumptions about how much other people know and do not know.
▶ Communication often must go through several levels within an agency, and the meaning or clarity of the message can change at each level.
▶ Personal communication styles vary, and people may not be able to adapt to or appreciate other styles.
▶ People do not see the need to share information, and those who need it may not receive it.
▶ The message itself is confusing or flawed in logic and content.
▶ People do not feel empowered or listened to, so they withdraw and avoid communication with others.
▶ Differences in culture, gender, age, or socioeconomic status can impact effective communication in subtle ways that may increase the chances of misunderstanding between parties.

Sheafor and Horejsi (2008, 140) offer the following suggestions as ways to improve your listening skills:

▶ Stop talking. You cannot listen when you are talking.
▶ Put the message sender at ease. Do what you can to lessen his or her anxiety and remove distractions (e.g., close the door).
▶ Be patient with the message sender. Do not interrupt.
▶ Ask questions if it will help you understand or help the sender clarify his or her message.
▶ Do not show disapproval of what the sender is saying. Do not criticize or enter into an argument, for that will erect a barrier to further communication.

When sending a message, follow these rules:

▶ Use clear, simple language. Speak distinctly and not too fast.
▶ Pay attention to your body language, making sure it is congruent with your message. Maintain appropriate eye contact and utilize gestures.
▶ Do not overwhelm or overload the receiver with information. Break up a lengthy or complex message into several parts so it can be more easily followed and understood.
▶ Ask for comments, questions, or feedback so you will know whether you are being understood. (Sheafor and Horejsi, 2008, 140)

Depending on your practicum assignments, you will probably be surprised at the amount of documentation required in agency practice. You will learn to write memos, letters, case notes, assessments, treatment plans, reports, and perhaps public relations material and grant proposals. At various times your writing will be used to document important events or actions, provide information to the general public, persuade someone to take some action, provide a base for legal action, or report to a funding source. First and foremost, all such written materials must be clear, accurate, and as concise as possible. Follow these guidelines in your written communication:

▶ Be sure you understand who your audience is, what they need to know, and how they want the information presented.

- Organize your material before starting to write, and recognize that you may need to make several revisions.
- Use language that is professional, but do not overuse jargon.
- Avoid slang and language that could be seen as judgmental, derogatory, or that could be interpreted in more than one way.
- Use direct, clear language rather than tentative, insipid words.
- Anticipate the reader's questions and answer them.
- Adhere to the KISS principle (Keep It Short and Simple).
- Use the format required by your agency.
- Make copies of all written communication that is sent out of the office, including correspondence, reports, and grant proposals.
- Incorporate feedback from your supervisor into your revised drafts.
- Seek input from your supervisor about the content and style of your writing.

Agencies differ somewhat in their standards and expectations. Ask your field instructor for specific directions on how to prepare required written materials. Also, ask your field instructor for feedback regarding the quality of your writing. Doing so will demonstrate your openness to learning and willingness to receive constructive criticism. It will also help you to better understand your strengths and limitations and help you avoid patterns of ineffective communication. Be appreciative of constructive feedback on your writing, because improved writing skills improve your chances of securing grants, of developing linkages with other agencies, and or representing the views of clients as shown in treatment plans and case notes that will greatly impact their lives.

You may wonder how much detail is required. A good guideline to follow regarding documentation about clients is to include enough detail to bring the client or issue to life for anyone reading it, but not to overwhelm the reader with unnecessary and extraneous information. When writing about programs or client systems, remember to be clear, convincing, and attuned to the needs, requirements, or motives of those who may be the readers.

Because computer systems are used to record a wide variety of very personal information about clients, be very aware of confidentiality of client records, and learn to anticipate potential breaches in confidentiality that could occur when sharing information between agencies. Learn what can be shared and what cannot. Learn when and how to use release of information documents that demonstrate clients' permission and approval to share information with other professionals or agencies that need this information. Remember that even though clients waive some of their rights to confidentiality in order to be eligible for third-party payments for services, this does not mean that they understand the degree to which their confidentiality may be compromised. Informed consent means that clients understand the impact of what they are signing or agreeing to, and it is often the social worker's responsibility to advocate for clients, making sure they truly do understand and agree.

Be cautious with the use of computerized client database information, faxes, voice mail, and e-mail, so that client confidentiality is always guarded. Remember that each form of communication can be very helpful to social workers and managed-care organizations, but potentially very harmful to clients if confidentiality is compromised.

Developing Communication Skills: A Workbook Activity

Organizational Communication

1. What are the major forms of written communication expected of social workers in your agency (e.g., assessments, treatment plans, reports, case notes, minutes, press releases, memos, letters, grant proposals)?

    _____

    _____

    _____

2. Do social workers in your agency receive special training in the use of written communication (e.g., use of medical terminology, report writing, grant proposal writing, correspondence)? Can you participate?

    _____

    _____

    _____

3. What specific policies does your agency have regarding written communication (e.g., deadlines for completion, suggested or required formats, and supervisory review of documentation) that are relevant to your work?

    _____

    _____

    _____

4. What might be the effects of communication problems on agency operations and clients?

    _____

    _____

    _____

5. What types of communication styles, patterns, and problems have you observed in the following situations? Case conferences including social workers and others involved with clients

    _____

    _____

    Meetings between social workers and clients

    _____

    _____

    Meetings with agency administrators

    _____

    _____

Meetings with board members or funding sources

_____

_____

Meetings between you and your supervisor

_____

_____

6. How do your agency's chain of command and organizational chart affect communication patterns and the flow of information? Is communication between management and staff mostly one way and from the top down, or does it flow easily both ways?

_____

_____

_____

Interpersonal Communication

7. What effective communication styles and skills have you observed between social workers and clients? How can you learn these skills?

_____

_____

_____

8. What ineffective communication styles and skills have you observed between social workers and clients? How can you avoid these pitfalls?

_____

_____

_____

9. How might forms of diversity such as culture, life experience, gender, and special training enhance or limit your ability to communicate with agency clients?

_____

_____

_____

10. Ask your field instructor to tell you about your own communication style, including what to build on to become more effective and what you could change to become a more effective communicator.

_____

_____

_____

SUGGESTED LEARNING ACTIVITIES

▶ Ask your field instructor to show you examples of both well-written and poorly written letters, memos, reports, and case records. Examine these materials and observe how writing style, organization, and choice of words affect their quality. Compare your written work to these examples.

▶ Rewrite a report you have written (three to five pages in length), using only half the space. Pay attention to eliminating unnecessary words. Shorten your sentences. Eliminate all repetition of content.

▶ Seek opportunities to make a speech or presentation before either agency staff members or a community group.

▶ Schedule time with your field instructor to focus exclusively on the quality of your oral and written communication and identify specific steps you can take to improve your skills in communication.

▶ In Sheafor and Horejsi (2008), read the sections entitled "Report Writing" (182–184), "Letter Writing" (184–185), and "Using Information Technology" (187–190).

Log onto **www.mysocialworklab.com** and select the **Interactive Skill Module** videos from the left-hand menu. Answer the questions below. (*If you did not receive an access code to* **MySocialWorkLab** *with this text and wish to purchase access online, please visit* www.mysocialworklab.com.)

1. **Watch page 22 (Seeking Client Feedback, Reaching for Feelings) in the child welfare module.** Why would clients hesitate to reveal their feelings regarding social work interventions?

2. **Watch page 11 (Exploring Underlying Feelings) in the child welfare module.** What techniques can be used to help a client identify and explore his or her underlying feelings?

PRACTICE TEST

The following questions are similar in phrasing and content to those asked in social work licensing examinations. They should help you prepare to take the licensing examination in your state.

1. Social workers who do not document their interventions in writing and need to testify in court about their assessments or client outcomes
   a. may not be able to prove what they actually did
   b. can provide verbal testimony that will be legally acceptable
   c. are in violation of HIPAA requirements
   d. can provide written documentation after the fact

2. If clients request to see written documentation about them and their case, agencies
   a. must comply with their request
   b. must have written requests to see them first
   c. must provide copies of documentation to third parties also
   d. do not have to comply with their request

3. Language barriers between clients and social workers
   a. can be addressed with translators
   b. can negatively impact client outcomes
   c. necessitate cultural competence training
   d. can be addressed with written materials

Diversity in Practice

4. Translators are
   a. legally required when clients do not speak English
   b. indicated when clients do not speak English
   c. indicated when clients speak English but are not citizens
   d. legally required when minor clients do not speak English

5. Clients may have to waive their rights to confidentiality
   a. To third party payers
   b. When they have violated agency policies
   c. When they request to see their own records
   d. When they cannot pay for services

Ethical Practice

6. Public funding sources will
   a. allow agencies to design their own reporting systems
   b. use agency documentation as a way to influence social policy
   c. require agency workers to sign confidentiality agreements
   d. require standardized documentation of services and outcomes

7. Social workers' responsibility to make sure they understand clients' concerns
   a. is a legal responsibility
   b. is a documentation responsibility
   c. is an ethical responsibility
   d. is an agency responsibility

Answers

1) b 2) a 3) a 4) d 5) b 6) b 7) c

The Agency Context of Practice

LEARNING GOALS FOR THIS CHAPTER

- To understand your agency's mission, goals, and objectives

- To understand your agency's organization and administrative structure

- To understand your agency's sources of funding and operating budget

- To identify ways in which your agency relates to and interacts with other agencies within the overall social welfare system

- To identify changes in your agency that could improve services to its clients

CONNECTING CORE COMPETENCIES *in this chapter*

| Professional Identity | Ethical Practice | Critical Thinking | Diversity in Practice | Human Rights & Justice | Research Based Practice | Human Behavior | Policy Practice | Practice Contexts | Engage Assess Intervene Evaluate |

The daily activities and decisions of a social worker are heavily influenced by the nature and purpose of the organization that employs him or her. Throughout its history, social work has been an agency-based profession. A majority of social workers are employed by agencies, and they provide their services within an organizational context. Given this reality, you must examine and understand your practicum agency's mission, goals, structure, funding sources, and level of effectiveness.

BACKGROUND AND CONTEXT

The word *agency* refers to an organization that is authorized or sanctioned to act in the place of or on behalf of others. An agency performs activities that some larger group or organization desires and is willing to fund. This larger entity might be a community, a church, or a governmental body. It is important to understand much about your agency in order to work effectively within it.

Most social workers are employed by human services agencies that fall into two broad categories: private nonprofit agencies and public agencies. *Public agencies* are created by a legislative body made up of elected officials (e.g., a state legislature, the U.S. Congress, or county commissioners) and funded by tax dollars. The goals of public agencies are described in legal codes and government regulations. Elected officials are ultimately responsible for the operation of public agencies and staff members of public agencies are considered government employees.

Private nonprofit agencies (also called *voluntary agencies*) are created by a legal process known as incorporation, which has the effect of creating a legal entity known as a *nonprofit corporation*. These corporations are given nonprofit status under section 501(c)3 of the Internal Revenue Service guidelines for charitable and nonprofit organizations. This type of agency is governed by a board of directors whose basic responsibilities are to establish the agency's mission and direction, set policies for its operation, set and approve budgets, ensure adequate funds for the agency, maintain a communication link with the wider community, and hire and regularly evaluate the executive director. The basic responsibilities of an agency's *executive director* are to implement policy set by the governing board, hire staff and regularly evaluate their performance, make programmatic decisions, and direct and monitor day-to-day operations.

A subcategory of private nonprofit agencies is the *sectarian agency,* which means an agency affiliated with or operated by a religious organization (e.g., Jewish Community Services or Catholic Social Services). The term *membership agency* is used to describe an agency (e.g., YMCA) that derives some of its budget from membership fees and in which members are involved in setting policy.

In contrast to a public agency or a private nonprofit agency, a *for-profit agency* is a business corporation that sells a set of services and is designed and operated to yield a profit for investors and stockholders. Increasingly, not-for-profit hospitals, treatment centers, and nursing homes are being purchased by large corporations and operated as for-profit organizations.

Many social workers are employed in *host settings* in which the organization's primary mission or purpose is something other than the delivery of social services. Examples include schools and hospitals where the primary missions are the provision of educational and medical services. In these host settings, the social worker must work with many other professionals (e.g., doctors, nurses, physical therapists, teachers, or school psychologists) and may be under the supervision of someone who has only a limited understanding of social work and possibly holds professional values somewhat different from those of a social worker.

Private nonprofit agencies are funded by private contributions, by grants and contracts, and sometimes by fees charged for the services they provide. Some conduct their own fund-raising activities and some receive funds from the local United Way organization. Private agencies may receive tax dollars indirectly through contracts with public agencies. Both public and private agencies may establish ***advisory boards*** that provide advice and guidance to the executive director or to the board of directors. As suggested by the name, an advisory board does not have the authority to make final decisions or set policy. It simply serves in an advisory capacity. An advisory board often has members who are agency clients; this is intended to solicit client input and perspective on agency policies and services.

A typical social agency is designed and structured to provide one or more ***social programs.*** A social program is an organized and planned activity designed to accomplish one of the following:

- ▶ ***Remediation of an existing problem*** (i.e., address a problem such as child abuse, unemployment, or delinquency)
- ▶ ***Enhancement of social functioning*** (i.e., improve functioning when no significant problem exists, such as programs of marriage enrichment)
- ▶ ***Prevention of a social problem*** (i.e., prevent a problem from developing, such as reducing teen pregnancy)

Social programs may use one or more broad strategies to achieve their purposes:

- ▶ ***Socialization:*** assisting and encouraging people to understand, learn, and abide by the norms of society
- ▶ ***Social integration:*** encouraging and helping people to interact more effectively with other individuals and with the social systems or resources they need in order to function effectively and cope with special problems
- ▶ ***Social control:*** monitoring and restricting those who exhibit self-destructive or dangerous behavior
- ▶ ***Social change:*** expanding the number and types of life-enhancing opportunities available to people, taking actions that will improve the environment in which people must function, and taking action necessary to reduce or eliminate negative and destructive forces in their social environment

An agency's budget describes anticipated income and expenses for a given period of time, usually one or two years. The common categories of expense include salaries, employee benefits, payroll taxes, consultation fees, staff training, malpractice insurance, supplies and equipment, telephone, printing and copying, rent, property insurance, staff travel, and membership dues. Once a budget has been set or approved, the agency administrator has only limited authority to shift funds from one category to another. Agency budgets are influenced by many factors, including public attitudes, political changes, and shifts in funding priorities.

It is important to understand that the donations, grants, and legislative allocations received by an agency typically have many "strings attached." In other words, the money is given or allocated to the agency for a specified purpose and cannot be spent for other purposes. In addition, the agency's acceptance of

Practice Contexts

How will understanding the mission, structure, and focus of your agency help you in knowing what you are supposed to do and why?

money from a certain source (e.g., United Way or a federal agency) may require that it adhere to certain rules, regulations, accounting, and auditing procedures that add administrative costs. When much of an agency's money is earmarked for very specific purposes, the agency has limited capacity to modify its programs and little flexibility in responding to emergencies or unanticipated expenses. However, many human services agencies are quite bureaucratic, especially public agencies. Bureaucracies are characterized by:

▶ A clear chain of command in communication and assigned authority.
▶ An organizational structure consisting of a vertical hierarchy with numerous units, each of which has a designated leader responsible for that unit's operation and who has authority over those working in the unit.
▶ A set of written rules, policies, and guidelines that outline procedures to be followed in performing work.
▶ A division of labor giving each employee a specific job to perform with an accompanying job description.
▶ Supervision of each employee's work.
▶ An emphasis on formal communication, written documentation, and record keeping.
▶ A higher level of job security than that which exists in a business or in nonprofit organizations.

Research Based Practice

What empirical evidence is there to support the theoretical approach of your agency?

Some agencies have developed less bureaucratic structures in an effort to be more responsive to clients and to their ever-changing environments. They often use feminist, partnership, and empowerment principles; seek to involve their clients in the work of the agency; promote shared power and decision making at all levels; develop flexible guidelines and approaches; and strive to individualize and customize their interventions and services. As a general rule, these agencies are more flexible and provide a less stressful environment for the social workers working for them. Agencies that operate on these principles often are private, smaller organizations that do not need to be bureaucratic in order to be efficient or to provide equal services to all clients.

Organizations develop policies and procedures as ways of dealing with recurring situations, problems, and questions and include them in a ***policy and procedure manual.*** The content of the manual will reflect the mission and goals of the agency and, usually, certain social policies that impact the operation of the organization. The content of an agency's manual is shaped, directly and indirectly, by many external forces. They include:

▶ Federal and state laws, rules, and regulations that could impact agency function
▶ Court decisions and legal opinions relevant to the work of the agency
▶ Accrediting bodies that require adherence to standards and requirements
▶ Formal interagency agreements that specify the ways in which collaborative work will be done
▶ Requirements established by local fund-raising organizations that support the agency
▶ Requirements of managed-care organizations
▶ Contracts with employee unions

Be alert to the fact that all organizations have both a formal and an informal structure. The ***formal*** or ***official structure*** of an agency is described by organizational charts, policy and procedure manuals, and documents that explain the structure and function of various organizational units and the official chain of command. The term ***informal structure*** refers to various networks of employees

Study your agency. Learn about its history, mission, goals, structure, culture, funding sources, budget, and decision-making processes. Strive to understand the special challenges your agency faces and the external economic, political, and community forces that push and pull it in one direction or another. Having such knowledge is a form of power that can be used to address various organizational problems, and it will help you to place your specific work and assignments within a wider context (Sheafor and Horejsi, 2008, 584).

. . .

If there is one overall concept that explains why evaluations are so important, it is accountability. Partially because of past failings of social programs, governmental and most privately funded agencies now require that all agencies be held accountable for how they use their funds and what they achieve for clients (Dudley, 2009, 7).

. . .

. . . [A] mission statement articulates a common vision for the organization in that it provides a point of reference for all major planning decisions. Mission statements are like lighthouses in that they exist to provide directions. A mission statement not only provides clarity of purpose to persons within the agency but also helps them to gain understanding and support from those stakeholders outside the agency who are influential to the agency's success (Unrau, Gabor, and Grinnel, 2007, 54).

. . .

. . . [C]utting-edge thinking in social work now sees the whole agency as needing to become a "learning organization" . . . a term which implies harnessing the practice, wisdom, and skills of the workforce within the overall mission of the agency to give the most effective response to users. It is the culture of the workplace that brings out the best in staff, and even the best of workers and team will become demoralized in poorly managed organizations (Coulshed, Mullender, Jones, and Thompson, 2006, 83).

and unofficial channels of communication. This informal structure is sometimes cynically described by staff as "the way the agency really works." It becomes apparent only after working in the agency for an extended period of time.

Rae and Nicholas-Wolosuk (2003, 13) remind us that there is a difference between **organizational climate** and **organizational culture.** Positive organizational climate attributes include mutual respect, teamwork, and effective communication, all of which contribute to a good working environment and ultimately to high-quality services to clients, whereas negative organizational climate can negatively impact clients. Organizational culture refers to the values and norms that motivate and drive the organization, that are generally internalized by the social workers employed there, and that guide the way services are provided.

GUIDANCE AND DIRECTION

Your practicum agency will be a learning laboratory in which you will develop professional social work skills, observe other social workers providing services, and learn how agencies are organized and structured to address social needs and problems. You will begin to understand how organizations are administered and managed, learn about the common problems of organizations, and see how to work effectively with others within an organizational context.

Learn about your agency's history, why and when it began, and how it has evolved over time. Inquire about how your agency may have modified its original mission, changed its structure, and adapted to a changing community and

What legislation and social policies, if any, shape or dictate the work of your agency? Can they be changed if social conditions change?

What human rights does your agency commit to, and what social justice issues does it address?

What assumptions or evidence about the interaction between human behavior and the social environment does your agency use to design and deliver services?

political context. This will help you understand how agencies survive within an ever-changing environment and continually adjust and adapt their efforts to address the changing social problems and needs on which they focus.

Find out whether your agency was established as a response to state or federal legislation, and how that legislation has guided its development. If it began as a project of a religious organization, try to understand how specific values and religious beliefs may have influenced the agency's formation and operation.

Ask your field instructor about external forces that shape or limit your agency, such as funding priorities and sources, community attitudes, client feedback, regulatory bodies, political pressure, and research findings. Ask how much influence internal forces such as staff suggestions, changes in personnel, and staff morale have on the agency and its programs.

Agencies are always changing. Notice how shifts, increases, or cuts in funding cause changes in the services that can be provided. Observe how public attitudes and political forces shape the ways in which your agency functions. Your agency may go through some significant changes during your practicum. You may even observe the birth of a new agency, or perhaps the dismantling of one that has lost its support or outlived its usefulness. You will learn about the dynamic nature of human services organizations if you closely observe the functioning of your own agency and that of others in the community.

Notice how your agency's type (e.g., public or private, for-profit or nonprofit) affects its work. For instance, public agencies will tend to be quite attentive to the decisions of elected officials, sectarian agencies will reflect the values of the religious organizations that sponsor them, and for-profit organizations may at times focus on making a profit for their owners to the potential detriment of clients.

Your agency will use one or more specific perspectives, theories, models, or approaches in the design and provision of its services and programs. Determine what they are, and why they were chosen. Does your agency use the strengths, ecological, or diversity perspective? Does it operate on social systems theory? Does your agency use a behavioral, psychodynamic, or family systems approach to intervention? Does your agency invest its resources in prevention, early intervention, or rehabilitation? Is the approach therapeutic or correctional? Does your agency hire generalist social workers or those with specializations in certain fields of practice? Does your agency see itself as working toward social change? Review courses you have taken and books you have read to help you understand why a particular approach was chosen by your agency to address the problem or concern identified. Consider what other theoretical approaches might also be used.

Become familiar with your agency's methods of evaluating its programs and services. Find out how your agency assesses its effectiveness, determines whether it is reaching its goals, measures client or community satisfaction, and decides whether it is making a difference. Your agency may use formal or informal methods of evaluation, process or outcome measures, and collect quantitative or qualitative data. Ask your field instructor whether he or she thinks these approaches or evaluation tools are valid and adequate. Ask what methods he or she would ideally recommend using to evaluate services provided enough time, money, and staff were available.

Finally, consider how your agency is perceived by its clients, including their view of your agency's openness, effectiveness, and ability to address their needs. Observe the ways in which your agency works to maintain links to clients, opens itself to client feedback, and works in partnership with client

Diversity in Practice

What types of clients might feel positively about your agency, and which might not? Why?

groups. In the end, clients are best served by agencies that continue to value their input and continually work to improve services.

Agencies regularly reexamine their effectiveness, review their mission and goals, adjust their objectives, and engage in strategic planning for the future. This is done to maintain focus on the mission and vision of the organization, to shift priorities in light of changing political climates or financial resources, and to continuously search for better ways to serve those to whom they are committed. If you have the opportunity to become involved in such efforts, count yourself lucky to participate in an agency's work to redefine itself or improve its services.

Agencies may do this work through staff retreats where they review history and mission, and identify new ways to meet their goals. They engage in strategic planning, identify strengths and weaknesses, as well as clarify challenges and opportunities. Agencies that are most effective are those that stay current, adjust priorities as needed, build on past success, measure their effectiveness, and look to the future. Watch for these qualities in your organization.

Agency Analysis: A Workbook Activity

1. Does your agency have an official mission statement? If yes, what is it?

   _____

   _____

   _____

2. What are your agency's goals and objectives?

   _____

   _____

   _____

3. What types of problems, concerns, or needs bring people to your agency or cause them to be brought to the attention of your agency (e.g., child abuse, delinquency, poverty, health concerns)?

   _____

   _____

   _____

4. List your agency's major programs and services.

   _____

   _____

   _____

5. Is your agency a public agency? A private agency? A nonprofit agency? A for-profit agency?

   _____

6. If your agency is a public agency, is it a federal, state, county, or city agency? What legislation created the agency and assigned responsibilities to it?

   _____

   _____

   _____

7. If your agency is a private, nonprofit agency, why was it formed?

   _____

   _____

8. Describe the members of the board of directors in terms of such variables as their age, sex, ethnicity, race, socioeconomic class, occupation, and personal experiences with the agency's programs and services.

_____

_____

_____

9. What percentage of the board of directors fall into the following categories?

_____% Human services professionals

_____% Business or community representatives

_____% Current or former agency clients or consumers

10. If your practicum is in a private sectarian agency, with what religious organization or denomination is it affiliated?

_____

11. If your practicum agency is a membership organization, how does someone become a member?

_____

_____

_____

12. If your agency is a for-profit organization, who are its owners? For whom is it to make a profit (e.g., stockholders, another corporation, a partnership)?

_____

_____

_____

13. Does your agency have an advisory board? Who serves on this advisory board?

_____

_____

_____

14. What is your agency's overall or total operating budget for the current year?

_____

15. Is the agency's budget or income fairly predictable and stable from year to year, or is it uncertain and unpredictable?

_____

16. About what percentage of the budget is derived from each of the following sources?

_____% Allocations by the U.S. Congress

_____% Allocations by the state legislature

_____% Allocations by the county commissioners

_____% Allocations by the city council

_____% Allocations by the United Way or other combined giving program

_____% Grant from a federal agency, state agency, or private foundation

_____% Fees paid by the clients or consumers of services

_____% Fees paid by a third party (e.g., insurance)

_____% Private donation made directly to the agency

_____% Other

17. Do the clients served by your agency often fall into certain demographic categories such as age, sex, ethnicity, socioeconomic class, level of education, religion, or language?

_____

_____

18. What statistics are recorded on a regular basis by agency personnel (e.g., number of clients served each month, number of cases opened and closed, or characteristics of clients)?

_____

_____

_____

19. How does the agency determine if it is effective (e.g., recidivism rates, client's completion of treatment plans, number of clients served, level of client satisfaction, quality assurance, objectives achieved, social change)?

_____

_____

_____

20 Is your agency required to submit reports to a state or federal agency regarding its programs and services? If yes, what is the nature and the purpose of those reports?

_____

_____

_____

21. Is your agency regularly subjected to on-site inspections, surveys, or reviews by personnel from an oversight or regulatory body? If yes, what is the purpose of these reviews?

_____

_____

_____

22. Is your agency accredited by a national organization or licensed by a state organization? If yes, what is the name of this accrediting body and how often is your agency reviewed by this accrediting body? Can you read reports submitted to this body?

_____

_____

_____

23. Does your agency compete with other agencies for funding? If yes, with what agencies?

_____

_____

24. In what interagency planning and coordinating bodies is your agency an active participant?

_____

_____

_____

25. Do the employees in your agency belong to a union? If so, what is its name?

_____

_____

26. What efforts or programs are in place within the agency to help reduce job-related stress and worker burnout?

_____

_____

_____

27. Is the agency meeting its mission? What evidence can be used to determine that?

_____

_____

_____

SUGGESTED LEARNING ACTIVITIES

- Study your agency's organizational chart. Locate your field instructor and his or her department.
- Attend meetings of the agency's board of directors or advisory board and consider how the topics discussed relate to the agency's mission, goals, programs, and funding.

⬥ Examine your agency's monthly, quarterly, or annual reports to understand its goals and performance.

⬥ Find out how ordinary citizens or the general public view your agency. Speak with friends and acquaintances who know little about social work and ask what they know or have heard about your agency.

⬥ Attend public meetings sponsored by the United Way organization or other social welfare planning groups in order to better understand how your agency fits into the overall social welfare system.

⬥ Accompany a client applying for services at another agency and identify attitudes reflected in how agency staff treat clients and handle client requests.

⬥ Read about the Appreciative Inquiry approach to organizational change at David Cooperider's website (www.ovation.net.com/learning.htm).

⬥ Visit other agencies that provide similar services to those of your agency and compare approaches and programs.

⬥ Ask for instruction and guidance on agency procedures, format and protocol related to record keeping, record storage, and client confidentiality.

⬥ Collect a set of agency pamphlets, brochures, newsletters, and other materials used to inform the public about your agency and its services.

⬥ In Sheafor and Horejsi (2008), read the sections entitled "Preparing a Budget" (429-432), "Coping with Bureaucracy" (583), and "The Process of Agency Planning" (351-354).

Succeed with **PEARSON mysocialworklab**

Log onto **www.mysocialworklab.com** and select the **Interactive Skill Module** videos from the left-hand menu. Answer the questions below. (*If you did not receive an access code to* **MySocialWorkLab** *with this text and wish to purchase access online, please visit* www.mysocialworklab.com.)

1. **Watch page 4 (Introductions and Clarification of Roles) in the child welfare module.** Why will interventions be more effective if you can explain the role of your agency clearly?

2. **Watch page 7 (Giving Information) in the domestic violence module.** Why is it important to provide accurate information about an agency and its programs during the initial meeting with a client?

PRACTICE TEST

The following questions are similar in phrasing and content to those asked in social work licensing examinations. They should help you prepare to take the licensing examination in your state.

Practice Contexts

1. The nonprofit status of agencies known as 501(c)3 is
   a. a designation given by states
   b. a designation given by the federal Internal Revenue Service
   c. a designation given by United Way
   d. a designation given by local city ordinances

Practice Contexts

2. An agency dealing with exploitation of elders is working toward what end?
   a. prevention of a social problem
   b. remediation of a social problem
   c. enhancement of social functioning
   d. social integration

Practice Contexts

3. The primary concern of agencies dealing with dangerous clients is the safety of:
   a. these clients
   b. these clients' families
   c. social workers who work with these clients
   d. judges who work with these clients

Practice Contexts

4. The main advantage of a bureaucratic structure for an agency to clients is that
   a. Services are standardized and equally provided.
   b. There is a clear chain of command.
   c. This structure reduces staff turnover.
   d. Each employee is well supervised by a superior.

Practice Contexts

5. When there is a conflict between agency policy and state law,
   a. agency policy is legally binding
   b. state law is primary legally
   c. agency directors and state employees can negotiate an outcome
   d. the particular situation will dictate which is primary legally

Practice Contexts

6. A public agency is
   a. funded with grant money
   b. mandated or directed by state or federal legislation
   c. either nonprofit or profit-making
   d. accountable to legislators

Practice Contexts

7. Public social agencies are required to account for their work through
   a. client comments at public hearings
   b. statistical record keeping
   c. website postings
   d. evaluation of outcomes against mission, goals, and objectives

9

The Community Context of Practice

LEARNING GOALS FOR THIS CHAPTER

- ▶ To identify and analyze community resources and needs

- ▶ To understand the impact of the community on the social functioning of clients

- ▶ To understand community forces that impede or support social change

- ▶ To develop community analysis and organization skills

CONNECTING CORE COMPETENCIES *in this chapter*

| Professional Identity | Ethical Practice | Critical Thinking | Diversity in Practice | Human Rights & Justice | Research Based Practice | Human Behavior | Policy Practice | Practice Contexts | Engage Assess Intervene Evaluate |

As you become acquainted with both your agency and your community, watch for the ways in which your agency is influenced by community factors and characteristics.

Ask your agency field instructor for suggestions about how to understand the ways in which your agency addresses social problems.

Practicum agencies exist in and are influenced by the communities of which they are a part. Because of this, it is important to study the community in which your practicum agency is located. First, it is obvious that agencies do not exist in a vacuum. In fact, an agency's mission, programs, and operation are often a reflection of the community's characteristics, such as its values, politics, history, and special problems.

Second, most of your clients live and work in this community. It is not possible to understand your clients without understanding their wider social environment and both the positive and negative conditions and forces within that environment. If you work within a direct services agency, the client assessments and intervention plans you develop must consider your client's interactions the community, as well as the resources available in it.

Third, your informal study of the community will allow you to begin identifying unmet human needs as well as the gaps in the service network that should be addressed in order to better serve the people of the community. Finally, by gathering information about the community's values, history, power structure, economic base, demographics, and decision-making processes, you will be able to identify those groups or individuals who have the power and influence to either facilitate or block needed social change within the community.

Learning about a community takes time and effort. However, you will find this to be an invaluable and interesting experience. You will become fascinated as you begin to observe and understand the interplay between the functioning of individuals and families and their neighborhood and community. If your practicum agency is concerned mostly with micro-level practice, you will soon see how your clients' lives are either enriched or harmed by community factors. If your practicum is in an organization heavily involved in macro-level practice, you will come to understand that every community has its own personality and profile, and that in order to deal effectively with social problems and bring about needed social change, you must understand and appreciate that uniqueness.

BACKGROUND AND CONTEXT

The term **community** refers to a group of people brought together by physical proximity or by a common identity based on shared experiences, interests, or culture. There are two major types of communities: communities of interest and identification and communities of place or location.

A **community of interest and identification** can be described as a group of individuals who share a sense of identity and belonging because they share a characteristic, interest, or life experience such as ethnicity, language, religion, sexual orientation, or occupation. The social work community, the business community, the gay community, the African American community, the Islamic community, the Catholic community, and the university community are examples of a community of interest and identification.

The second type of community, a **community of place or location,** is defined mostly by geography and specified boundaries. Such communities include neighborhoods, suburbs, barrios, towns, and cities. The boundaries of a community of place might be a legal definition, a river, or a street. They may have formal or informal names such as Woodlawn, the South Bronx, Orange County, the Blackfeet Indian Reservation, the university area, the west side, and the warehouse district. The people living in these areas or places may share some level of identification, but typically they are more diverse in terms of values, beliefs, and other characteristics than are the people of a community of interest and identification. Also, it is common for the people within this type of community to be in conflict over a variety of issues. Living in proximity to others, in and of itself, does not create a social bond and a sense of belonging. In fact, for many of your clients, the community in which they live does not provide a sense of belonging and may even negatively impact their quality of life. Within a given community of place, there may be many different communities of interest and identification.

It can be useful to examine communities of location in terms of their usual functions. Sheafor and Horejsi (2006, 242) describe these functions as follows:

- **Provision and distribution of goods and services.** Water, electricity, gas, food, housing, garbage disposal, medical care, education, transportation, recreation, social services, information, and the like are provided.
- **Location of business activity and employment.** Commerce and jobs exist from which people earn the money needed to purchase goods and services.
- **Public safety.** Protection from criminal behavior and hazards such as fires, floods, and toxic chemicals is provided.
- **Socialization.** Opportunities are available to communicate and interact with others and to develop a sense of identity and belonging beyond that provided by the family system.
- **Mutual support.** Tangible assistance and social supports beyond those provided by one's family are available.
- **Social control.** Rules and norms necessary to guide and control large numbers of people (e.g., laws, police, courts, traffic control, pollution control, etc.) are established and enforced.
- **Political organization and participation.** Governance and decision making related to local matters and public services are in place (e.g., streets, sewer, education, public welfare, public health, economic development, zoning of housing and businesses, etc.).

Social workers and social agencies must be knowledgeable about how power and influence are used in the community. ***Power*** is the ability to make others do what you want them to do, whereas ***influence*** is the capacity to increase the chances that others will do what you want. Successful efforts to develop a new agency program, pass a law, modify social policy, and bring about social change all depend on the skilled use of power and influence. By themselves, social workers may possess little power or influence. Thus, in order to promote social change, they must have access to and relationships with those individuals and organizations that have power and influence and are willing to use it on behalf of the social agency or its clients.

There are various forms of power and influence within the community context. Different types are more or less important, depending on the issue being addressed and the kind of change desired. Below are examples of various individuals and groups with power and influence:

- Elected officials (e.g., mayor, members of city council, county commissioners, or state legislators)
- Those who control credit, loans, and investments (e.g., banks)
- Those who control information (e.g., newspapers or television stations)
- Executive directors of corporations that employ large numbers of people
- Respected religious and moral leaders
- Recognized experts in their profession or field

- Longtime and respected residents of the community
- Natural leaders (i.e., persons who are charismatic, articulate, and have attracted a loyal following)
- Advocacy organizations that are known for their solidarity, persistence, and devotion to a cause
- Client groups that are skilled in self-advocacy

It is important to remember that the movers and shakers of a community (i.e., those with real power and influence) are not always the visible leaders. Many key decision makers work behind the scenes and hold no formal positions, but are capable of contributing greatly to social change. Those are the individuals with whom you will develop relationships in order to call attention to issues you care about and to help you work toward social change.

Community dynamics differ depending on the size of a community. For example, in a large community, those with power tend to be more specialized and exercise their power only in relation to selected issues. By contrast, in smaller and more rural communities, those with power tend to become involved in a wide range of issues and decisions. These differences will impact the work of social agencies.

Community size also affects how individuals experience the push and pull of social forces and prevailing attitudes. For example, an individual who is a member of a sexual minority may be more likely to experience discrimination and rejection in a small, rural community and feel more isolated than if he or she lived in an urban area. In a larger city, he or she may have access to a more clearly identified gay community to provide positive role models, socialization, and a nurturing environment that can buffer negative societal attitudes toward homosexuals.

GUIDANCE AND DIRECTION

Human Rights & Justice

What is the social work profession's stance on the role of communities in promoting and protecting human rights and social justice?

Coming to understand the community context of practice will help you see that we are all shaped in both positive and negative ways by our life experiences. We are supported or undermined, protected or put at risk, guided or controlled, served or stressed, and encouraged or discouraged by our interactions with the individuals, groups, and organizations that make up the communities in which we live. These interactions have a profound effect on our social functioning and quality of life.

Always be conscious of the fact that the clients or consumers served by a social agency are members of a particular community of place and probably members of several communities of interest and identification. You need to understand the meaning of these groups for clients and the ways in which they impact clients both positively and negatively.

When working directly with clients, identify their social roles (e.g., spouse, parent, or employee) and then consider how specific community characteristics may make it easier or more difficult to fulfill those roles. As you examine the influence of a community on the social functioning of individuals and families, consider the following questions:

- Has my client had the benefits and opportunities provided by schools that are intellectually stimulating and physically safe?
- Does my client have adequate employment opportunities to support himself or herself and a family?
- Does my client live in adequate, safe, and affordable housing?
- Does my client feel safe when at home and on the street, and feel adequately protected by the law enforcement agencies of the community?

Food for Thought

As social workers, we need to understand the multiple communities of our clients as well as our own communities. Communities provide us with a rich social and personal life. They shape the way we think and act. They surround us with values and norms of behavior, explicit laws, and unwritten rules of conduct. They furnish us with meanings and interpretations of reality, with assumptions about the world. They provide resources and opportunities, albeit unevenly—places to work, to learn, to grow, to buy and sell, to worship, to hang out, to find diversion and respite, to be cared for. They confront us with traumas and problems, they intrude on our lives, and they hold out the possibilities for solutions (Hardcastle, Powers, and Wenocur, 2004, 92).

• • •

Environmental capital includes the natural features and resources of the area. *Physical capital* refers to things that have been added to the natural environment by human hands. This includes roads, buildings, and other forms of infrastructure. *Economic capital* comes in the form of financial wealth, as well as mechanisms for producing and exchanging things of monetary value. *Human capital* is the central source of wealth for the community. It involves the storing of and access to the skills, talents, and energy of the members of the community and members' willingness to contribute them. *Political capital* involves access to the system of policy setting and enforcing in the community. It includes the ability to exchange something, for example, votes or public attention, for political forms. *Information capital* is the generation, accumulation, storage, retrieval, and exchange of data, information, and knowledge. Research and educational activities help provide information capital. *Social capital* is the system of community norms and interrelationships that produce trust, collaborative action, and community consciousness (Homan, 2004, 40).

• • •

The goal of community participation is broad involvement of citizens in all phases of the improvement process until residents "own" it and it is sustainable (Hardcastle, Powers, and Wenocur, 2004, 406).

• • •

Several themes and assumptions permeate community practice. First, economic and social injustice results from the failure of the larger society to assist all individuals in meeting their potential. Second, all citizens have the right to participate directly in decisions that affect them. Third, when provided with information, citizens will participate in the decision-making process. Fourth, failure of citizens to participate in the democratic process is attributable either to their lack of knowledge about the process or injustices that disenfranchise them. Outside intervention is sometimes required to promote citizens' participation in order to achieve a socially just society (DiNitto and McNeece, 2008, 65).

▶ Does my client feel encouraged, supported, and empowered by his or her interactions with others in the community?

▶ Is my client subjected to rejection, discrimination, or stereotyping by others in the community?

▶ Is my client's social functioning limited by a lack of public transportation, education and training, or accessible and affordable health care in the community?

▶ What services or programs are needed and wanted by my client but not available in the community?

▶ Is my client aware of groups or organizations in the community that can act as advocates for his or her needs?

▶ What natural helpers and informal resources of the community or neighborhood are used by or available to my client?

▶ Is my client a real or imagined threat to others in the community?

▶ Has my client chosen to live in this neighborhood or community? If so, why? If not, what social and economic circumstances necessitate that he or she live in a particular neighborhood or community?

Diversity in Practice

How might clients answer these questions differently depending on the diverse groups to which they belong?

▶ What significant life experiences have shaped my client's attitudes toward the community and toward my practicum agency, its services, and programs?

Remember that your clients may view the community very differently than you or other members of the community do. If you have not been exposed to the negative aspects of community life as your clients may have been, acknowledge that your privileged position may make it difficult to understand your clients' views of the community.

As social work students gain experience and carefully observe and participate in a given community, they often become aware of factors that are common to many communities. For example, be alert to the following community dynamics:

▶ All communities and neighborhoods have social support networks and informal helpers. However, special effort may be required to identify and access these resources for clients or social workers.

▶ There may be a degree of overlap and duplication in the functions and programs of various agencies in the community. Sometimes this duplication is unnecessary and wasteful, but in many cases the duplication is beneficial to clients and healthy for the total system of services.

▶ There may be "turf" issues and conflicts between agencies, brought on in part by their competition for funding, the differences in how they define and explain problems, and what they consider to be their territory.

▶ The people of a community expect agencies to cooperate and collaborate. However, this can be inherently difficult when the agencies must compete with each other for funding and because cooperation and collaboration are time consuming and labor intensive.

▶ An agency with the support of powerful and influential individuals can secure funding and gain recognition, even when its mission may be less important and worthy than that of other agencies in the community.

▶ Negative community attitudes toward a certain client group or a certain type of agency can be a major obstacle to developing and providing needed services to a particular group.

▶ Certain groups are better organized and better able to act as advocates for themselves than are others.

▶ Community attitudes and values affect social agencies and their ability to carry out their mission.

▶ Communities under economic stress are sometimes ripe for the development of social problems, and may not be able to support their citizens in positive ways.

Practice Contexts

Including this list, what have you learned about communities in your social work courses that will help you in your role as a community organizer?

Work to understand how clients and those in need of the services provided by your agency perceive your organization and its work. Be cautious regarding the conclusions you reach about why the people of the community may not fully utilize the services available in the community, such as the ones offered by your agency. For example, you might assume that they are not fully informed or sufficiently motivated, when in reality they see your agency as culturally insensitive or irrelevant to their needs. Perhaps the agency's hours of operation do not mesh with their hours of employment or their lifestyle. They may also see your agency as representing a set of values and beliefs significantly different from their own. They may not even be aware that your organization exists.

Remember that social workers involved in mezzo- and macro-level practice need to understand the community because the focus of their work may

In what ways is intervention on the community level similar to intervention with individuals and families?

What challenges do you see for the social work profession as it works at both the individual client and community levels of practice?

What research-based information on your community is available that will help inform your practice?

be the community itself rather than individual clients. This level of practice sees the community itself as the client, the target, or the focus of service. When social workers engage in this level of practice, they must use their knowledge of community, their communication skills, their commitment to creating healthy communities, and their ability to partner with others to this important work.

Watch for opportunities to engage in the community level of practice. You may have the chance to participate in such efforts as grant writing, community development, self-advocacy efforts by community groups, and interagency collaborations. Reread the portions of your textbooks that refer to the roots of the social work profession, and you will be reminded of the historical focus on community development as a way to enhance social functioning and the interplay between individual well-being and the health of communities.

Because it is vital to have an accurate and informed assessment of your community in order to practice effectively, make certain that your conclusions are well founded and not a result of first impressions, hasty judgments, faulty assumptions, or poor data gathering. It is as important to do good community assessments as it is to do good client assessments. Community-level social work needs to be based on thorough, careful, and ongoing assessment.

Beginning a Community Analysis: A Workbook Activity

The following questions are designed to help you understand your community and its effects on your agency and its clients. Answer each one to the degree that you can, recognizing that you will obtain additional information over time. You can obtain some of this information from other social workers or administrators in your agency and some from organizations such as the U.S. Census Bureau, local chambers of commerce, and economic development groups.

1. What geographical area is served by your agency?

   _____

   _____

2. What are the names of the communities, neighborhoods, or areas served by your agency?

   _____

   _____

3. How many people live in the area served by your agency? What is the population density of the area?

   _____

   _____

4. Of the people in the community, about what percentage are in various age groups (e.g., preschool, grade school, teen, young adult, middle age, and old age)?

   _____

   _____

   _____

5. What are the major and ethnic backgrounds represented in the community? Which are considered minorities?

   _____

   _____

6. To what extent has the community experienced intergroup conflict based on ethnicity, culture, class, religion, or other factors?

   _____

   _____

7. Are there significant numbers of immigrants, refugees, or undocumented workers in your community? How does this impact the community?

   _____

   _____

8. What major languages are spoken by the people of the community?

   _____

   _____

9. Of the people living in the area served by your agency, what can be said about their income levels? Median per person income

_____

Median household income

_____

Percentage of families receiving some form of public assistance

_____

10. How do these data on income compare with the state and national averages?

_____

_____

11. How does the cost of living in this community compare with communities or cities of similar size in the state or region?

_____

_____

12. What are the rates of unemployment in the community? How do these compare with figures for the state, region, and nation?

_____

_____

13. How many people in the community live below the poverty line?

_____

_____

14. What is considered a living wage in the community?

_____

_____

15. Of the adults living in the community, about what percentage are in each of the following categories of educational achievement? (Consult U.S. Census data.)

_____% 8th grade or less   _____% Some college/Associate degrees

_____% 12th grade or less (no diploma)   _____% Bachelor's degree

_____% High school graduate   _____% Graduate degree

16. What groups wield considerable power and influence in the community? (i.e., ethnic, racial, religious, political groups) What is the source of their power and influence?

_____

_____

17. What problems (e.g., crime, pollution, lack of affordable housing, poverty) does the community have?

_____

_____

18. Of what is the community especially proud (e.g., physical beauty, history, climate, schools, sports teams)?

_____

_____

19. About what is the community especially fearful or embarrassed (e.g., environmental problems, corruption, violence, poor roads, high taxes)?

_____

_____

20. What six social welfare planning councils or interagency coordinating bodies exist in the community? How might you observe or participate in their work?

_____

_____

_____

21. What mutual aid or self-help groups in the community might be especially helpful to the clients you serve in your practicum agency (e.g., Alcoholics Anonymous, adoptive parent support group, Alliance for the Mentally Ill, caregiver support group)? Can you attend and observe their meetings?

_____

_____

22. Does your community have a United Way or another combined fund-raising program that raises money for numerous human service agencies? By what process does this fund-raising organization decide which agencies it will support?

_____

_____

_____

23. What significant gaps exist in the array of human services and programs within the community? Why do they exist?

_____

_____

_____

_____

24. Are there significant, unnecessary, or wasteful duplications among the human service programs of the community?

_____

_____

_____

25. Do "turf" conflicts and unhealthy competitions exist between human services agencies within the community? If so, how do they affect your clients?

_____

_____

26. In the opinion of experienced human services professionals and experts of the community, how adequate are the following community elements?

Housing	Good	Adequate	Inadequate

_____

Schools	Good	Adequate	Inadequate

_____

Police and fire protection	Good	Adequate	Inadequate

_____

Recreational programs	Good	Adequate	Inadequate

_____

Public transportation	Good	Adequate	Inadequate

_____

Health care and hospitals	Good	Adequate	Inadequate

_____

Mental health services	Good	Adequate	Inadequate

_____

Day-care centers for children	Good	Adequate	Inadequate

_____

_____

Family support programs	Good	Adequate	Inadequate

_____

_____

Programs for troubled youth	Good	Adequate	Inadequate

_____

_____

Chemical dependency treatment	Good	Adequate	Inadequate

_____

_____

Programs for persons with disabilities	Good	Adequate	Inadequate

_____

_____

Programs for the elderly	Good	Adequate	Inadequate

_____

_____

SUGGESTED LEARNING ACTIVITIES

▶ Participate in interagency committees or task groups that are made up of representatives of various community organizations.

▶ Read grant proposals and reports written by your agency to see how it claims to meet community needs.

▶ Locate and study community resource directories, census data, and historical materials to help deepen your understanding of a particular social problem addressed by your agency.

▶ Use the Internet to examine census data related to the area served by your agency.

The home page for the U.S. Census Bureau is www.census.gov. Once there, click on Access Tools, then click on American FactFinder.

▶ Attend meetings of support groups whose goals are related to the problems addressed by your agency.

▶ In Sheafor and Horejsi (2008), read the sections entitled "Learning about Your Community" (241–245) and "Community Decision-Making Analysis" (317–321).

Succeed with PEARSON mysocialworklab

Log onto **www.mysocialworklab.com** and select the **Interactive Skill Module** and **Career Exploration** videos from the left-hand menu. Answer the questions below. (*If you did not receive an access code to* **MySocialWorkLab** *with this text and wish to purchase access online, please visit* www.mysocialworklab.com.)

1. **Watch page 18 (Identifying Next Steps) in the domestic violence module.** How might a domestic violence shelter be designed so that it can become a community of support to those fleeing domestic violence?

2. **In the Career Explorations videos, watch question 22 of the interview with Karen Cowan.** In what ways did it help the residents of the group home to be perceived as contributing members of the community they served during Hurricane Katrina relief efforts?

PRACTICE TEST

The following questions are similar in phrasing and content to those asked in social work licensing examinations. They should help you prepare to take the licensing examination in your state.

Practice Contexts

1. Community of place or location refers to
   a. geographic community
   b. the community in which a social agency is located
   c. same as a community of identification
   d. same as neighborhood

2. A community of interest or identification
   a. refers to voluntary groups outside of social work intervention
   b. is the same as a geographic community
   c. is most often a negative association for clients
   d. may be the focus of an intervention

3. If a community is not able to support the social functioning of its members
   a. it would qualify for federal funding
   b. social workers need to utilize family support instead
   c. agencies are likely to be underfunded
   d. the community could be the target of community-based intervention

4. The difference between formal power and social influence
   a. Is minimal
   b. Is important because those who can support social change may not be those who have formal power

   c. Is a legal one
   d. Is irrelevant

5. Community level social work practice is considered
   a. micro social work practice
   b. macro social work practice
   c. mezzo social work practice
   d. all levels of practice simultaneously

6. Social capital refers to
   a. informal social networks
   b. organized social networks
   c. the collaboration and trust within a community that can be built upon
   d. support groups in a community

7. Community asset mapping
   a. refers to the grids of transportation systems in a community
   b. is required by United Way
   c. refers to community focus groups
   d. is often done in conjunction with community needs assessments to identify the strengths of a community

Answers

1) a 2) d 3) d 4) b 5) b 6) c 7) d

10

The Social Problem Context of Practice

LEARNING GOALS FOR THIS CHAPTER

▶ To understand the social conditions, needs, and problems faced by your clients

▶ To understand how social problems are influenced by historical, political, and cultural forces

▶ To understand how theories of the causation of social problems influence social policies and social programs

▶ To understand how political power and influence can determine whether a particular condition comes to be defined as a social problem

CONNECTING CORE COMPETENCIES *in this chapter*

| Professional Identity | Ethical Practice | Critical Thinking | Diversity in Practice | Human Rights & Justice | Research Based Practice | Human Behavior | Policy Practice | Practice Contexts | Engage Assess Intervene Evaluate |

Most of the agencies and organizations that employ social workers were created in response to specific social problems or needs as perceived and understood by elected officials (in the case of public agencies), by powerful and committed community leaders (in the case of private nonprofit agencies), or by investors (in the case of for-profit organizations). In order for you to understand your agency's purpose, policies, and operation, it is important to carefully examine the social problems or conditions on which it focuses its attention and resources.

The definition and conceptualization of a social problem is a complex process that is shaped by historical, political, and cultural forces as well as by existing scientific knowledge. There can be intense disagreement over whether a particular condition is to be defined as a problem. Even when there is agreement that a problem exists, there can be much debate over its cause, its severity, and what can and should be done about it. There can also be great disagreement over whether those experiencing a social problem are to be blamed or held accountable for their situation or are to be supported by others as they attempt to cope with or change their situation.

For example, one segment of society may view the situation of child abuse as the failure of an individual parent to treat a child well and not consider the impact of a history of child abuse, family stress, and financial insecurity as contributors to inadequate parenting. Homelessness may be viewed as the responsibility of the individual by some, whereas others may see this problem as related to low wages, high cost of living, lack of health insurance, and an inadequate safety net during financially stressful times.

How a problem is defined and the predominant beliefs about its causation have a profound effect on the formulation of social policies and the design of social programs that are intended to address the problem. Moreover, as an understanding of the problem changes, agencies must modify their guiding principles and adapt their services and interventions to these new interpretations.

BACKGROUND AND CONTEXT

A *social condition* is a factual reality. Examples include the fact that many marriages in the United States end in divorce, the fact that growing numbers of people in the United States are homeless, the fact that in some high schools a majority of students do not graduate, the fact that a high percentage of homeless people are families, and the fact that a growing number of Americans go without health insurance. These are facts, but are they actually social problems? If yes, why? Who decides that a particular condition is a problem that requires action by the community or government? Whose values, norms, and beliefs are to be used in forming a judgment?

A *social problem* can be defined as a social condition that negatively impacts individuals or communities, and as a situation in which the welfare, values, and well-being of society may be threatened. A social problem is considered as such because many people believe that its existence is wrong, harmful, or immoral. Some people may view a given condition as a problem that violates the values they hold dear and that demands collective action and an investment of resources. Others, however, presume that it is simply an acceptable part of life that requires no special response. A condition becomes a problem when it threatens the values, the sense of morality, the security, or safety of those in a community or a society who have the power and influence to bring forth collective action and, eventually, the new policies, programs, and agencies that will address this problem. For example, teenage pregnancy may

Ethical Practice

What social problems addressed by your agency are at odds with the social work profession's values about individual or community well-being?

Policy Practice

Ask your agency field instructor about the historical ways in which agencies such as yours have dealt with social problems, and what has shaped the evolution of such approaches.

be defined as a social problem because it is associated with increased high school dropout rates and reliance on public assistance.

When powerful and influential individuals and groups come to view a social phenomena or condition as a problem and a threat to what they value, they must decide what social policies and actions are needed to solve this problem or lessen its negative impact. Many different solutions or actions may be proposed. Each will rest on a particular set of assumptions, values, and beliefs about the cause of the problem and what interventions will be feasible and effective. There may be several competing theories of causation, each of which purports to explain why the problem exists and what can and should be done about it.

Those in decision-making positions may sponsor research into the causes of the problem and seek the advice of experts, but in the final analysis, the decisions about the nature and cause of the problem will be heavily political and will reflect the views and preferences of those who have power and influence. That is why social workers must become competent in the political and social policy arena if they are to effect change in the social policies that impact their clients. For example, in recent years powerful political forces have redefined poverty as a problem caused by an unwillingness of people to work and by the existence of welfare programs thought to create dependency. Their approach has been to reduce access to welfare benefits and to place limits on those benefits. Others would say that not addressed in this approach are questions of whether the poor have the education and skills needed to obtain and hold such jobs, and whether the available jobs provide health insurance and a wage high enough to support economic independence.

SOCIAL CONDITION

    An existing situation or phenomenon is observed, measured, and acknowledged by a community or society.

SOCIAL PROBLEM

    The people of a community or society judge the social condition to be unacceptable and are motivated to do something about it. The condition is now perceived as a social problem. For a condition to "become" a social problem, its existence must somehow threaten or disturb those groups that have the power or influence to bring about a collective and political response and move others to address the problem.

SOCIAL POLICIES

    The existence of a social problem calls forth or requires some type of action. A social policy is an agreed upon course of action. Policy makers propose various policy options based on their values, beliefs, and knowledge about the nature and cause of the problem. A political process determines which of the possible options is chosen. These policies are then expressed in laws, in administrative rules and regulations, and in the budgeting process and the allocations of monies.

    Policies change over time in response to new knowledge or a shifting political climate.

SOCIAL PROGRAMS

    Social programs flow from social policy. A program is a planned and organized effort that reflects the social policies. A program is designed to accomplish a certain outcome. A program exists as an organization or as a component of a formal organization. Programs require funds for staff, office space, travel, training, equipment, and client services.

PRACTICES

    Practices are actions performed by those hired to perform the tasks and activities required by the social policies and social programs.

Figure 10.1
The Evolution of Social Policies, Programs, and Practices

The decisions made concerning which actions should be taken to address a social problem eventually give rise to specific **social policies.** Social policies, described in detail in Chapter 11, are the federal, state, and local laws, statutes and ordinances enacted to address social problems. Social policies can mandate services to be provided, enable organizations to provide services, fund programs, set priorities for social programs, or set standards for types and quality of services to be provided. Many of the social agencies that serve as social work practicum settings have the responsibility of carrying out these social policies and designing specific programs and interventions to solve the problem. The specific actions by agency employees can be viewed as their **practices.** The relationship between a social condition, a social policy, a social program, and practices is outlined in Figure 10.1.

GUIDANCE AND DIRECTION

Critical Thinking

Why is it imperative to analyze a social problem in the following ways before designing a strategy to address it?

In any community or society, there is great variety in the perspectives of its members as they try to understand and explain the social problems they observe and experience. These different viewpoints will be based on personal experiences, attitudes, values, information, misinformation, and even stereotypes. You may think that some of these perspectives are biased or uninformed, but it is important to realize that the beliefs make sense and seem valid to those who hold them. Not everyone agrees that a social condition is a social problem, and not everyone agrees on the causes of social problems. Further, there is much disagreement on what social policies should be put in place to address social policies.

Although this can be confusing and may make it hard for you to know how to begin addressing social problems, it may be helpful to ask yourself the following questions in order gain a broad perspective on a social problem that concerns you.

- What is the actual social condition that you are concerned about?
- How is it described by those who observe it? What definitions are used by those individuals or groups?
- Who considers it to be a social problem and who does not?
- How do groups with different viewpoints frame their perspectives?
- What is the scope and scale of the condition? Is it worsening? How does it compare to the same condition in other geographic areas?
- What societal values about human existence are potentially threatened by the social condition?
- What are some of the proposed theories of causation of this social condition?
- How do these theories of causation impact the development of social policies to address this condition?

The different viewpoints and the political debate that arises from them will sometimes result in social policy that you support and, at other times, in policy that you see as ineffective or harmful. Remember that the democratic political process is influenced by public attitudes, values, information, and power. In order to influence the process, you will need to venture into the process of politics and use your skills to advocate for social policies that benefit those you serve. This will rarely be easy because of the strongly held beliefs of everyone involved in the issue and because those negatively impacted by existing social problems or policies may not have access to power.

The action we take to remedy social problems . . . depends largely on whether we find the causes of those problems within individuals or in the contexts in which the individuals live (Becker, 2005, 138).

• • •

One of the most critical skills a social worker can possess is the ability to shape public opinion (Lieberman, 1998, 19).

• • •

A clinician ordinarily sees but one aspect of individuals who are surrounded and sustained by a community of immense complexity. It is as if the professional stands before the open top half of a Dutch door, conversing without seeing the operations of the household or even a single whole person. The same is doubly true of our view of a social problem, many dimensions of which are veiled (Hardcastle, Powers, and Wenocur, 2004, 62).

• • •

Modern history reveals that Americans do not like to stand by and do nothing about social problems. . . . Solutions require social action—in the form of social policy, advocacy, and innovation—to address problems at their structural or individual levels (Guerrero, 2009, 19).

• • •

Generally, the more visible the social problem, the more likely it is that individuals will take action (Unrau, Gabor, and Grinnell, 2007, 123),

• • •

It is relatively simple to measure the magnitude of welfare dependency among single women with children because public authorities issue data about the number of persons who receive welfare checks. Other problems, such as homelessness and substance abuse, are more difficult to measure because people who have these problems often do not seek public services. Policy advocates often have to demonstrate that specific problems are sufficiently important to merit the attention of agency staff, funders, government officials, and legislators (Jansson, 2008, 245).

• • •

Definitions of social problems are expressed in terms that describe the condition, reflect attitudes toward the condition, and give numerous other hints as to how that condition is considered offensive or problematic. Groups vie for control of the definition of a problem. When one group wins, its vocabulary may be adopted and institutionalized while the concepts of the opposing group fall into obscurity. When terminology changes, when new terms are invented, or existing terms are given new meaning, these actions signal that something important has happened to the career or history of a social problem (Spector and Kitsuse, 2001, 8).

Diversity in Practice

What might get in the way of truly listening to and learning from others whose opinions about social problems differ from yours?

As our society becomes more diverse and pluralistic, there will be even more diversity in how people think about social conditions and social problems. Strive to understand perspectives that are different from your own and think about how these perspectives lead to definitions and potentially different solutions. Expect increasing numbers of lively discussions, heated debates, and conflicts between groups with very different views about what constitutes social problems and what ought to be done about them. If you wish to address social problems at the community or societal level, you will need to contribute reason, reliable data, and political influence to this debate.

To a large extent, your understanding of social conditions and social problems will be rooted in your liberal arts background, including course work in sociology, psychology, economics, political science, anthropology, and history. You may also have had personal experiences that deepen your understanding of certain problems, or perhaps these experiences serve to bias your viewpoint, particularly if the associated pain and conflict have not been satisfactorily resolved at an emotional level. Work to understand what you truly believe and why.

It is important to remember that clients who are experiencing problems firsthand may view them very differently from the way you do. A situation that you or other professionals define as a problem may not seem like a problem to your client or vice versa. If you have never been poor or homeless, were not raised in an unsafe home or neighborhood, or have not been affected by racism, you may not fully appreciate the profound effects these experiences can have on people. Listen sensitively to client accounts of their life experiences so that you can better understand their importance and the impact on their lives.

Continually deepen your knowledge about how social problems such as poverty, crime, or racism develop not only so you can help clients improve their social functioning, but also so you can work toward the prevention of these social problems. As you have learned, most social problems are a result of interplay between individual, family, community, and societal forces. Because of this interaction, attempts to address large-scale social problems such as poverty or racism need to be multifaceted and geared toward societal changes as well as support for individuals experiencing poverty or racism directly. If you are familiar with the multitude of interrelated individual, family, community, and economic factors associated with various social problems, you will be better equipped to devise effective strategies of intervention and prevention.

Draw on your understanding of the ecological perspective and social systems theory to examine how social problems develop and change over time. Identify the many factors, conditions, and circumstances that interact to create a social problem. As you gain experience, you will see more clearly how one social problem can lead to or exacerbate others, or how several problems clustered together can overwhelm clients or communities and have devastating consequences. You will also see that social change at the macro level must take place in order to enhance the social functioning of individual clients and families.

Think hard about the concept of prevention and the ways in which you could become involved in preventing the social problems you are attempting to address. What changes at the community and societal level are needed in order to prevent adverse conditions and social problems from developing in the first place? Do existing prevention programs appear to be effective? Do we have the knowledge, the resources, and the political will to launch effective programs of prevention? What would various solutions cost and from where would this money come? As you ponder various strategies, consider the advantages, disadvantages, feasibility, and probable effectiveness of various prevention efforts at the micro, mezzo, and macro levels. What groups might oppose prevention programs and why? Can something that did not happen be measured?

During your practicum, you will most likely meet clients who are truly remarkable, positive human beings despite the fact that they grew up in very challenging or destructive environments. For reasons that we are just beginning to understand, some individuals are resilient and able to resist the negative influences of a corrosive environment. There may have been social supports available at a variety of levels to these individuals that enhanced individual strengths and coping skills, allowing them to function well in spite of their experiences. Seek to understand why one environment can affect people differently. Learn from your clients about the strengths and resiliency factors that have made it possible for them to overcome adversity. However, refrain from believing that your work is only to empower individuals, although that is crucial. Remember that it is also crucial to be involved in macro-level practice that prevents negative environments from developing in the first place.

Finally, begin to identify ways in which you as a social worker might be able to impact the identification of a social problem by a community in order for it to be addressed. Find ways to empower your clients to articulate their experiences effectively so their needs are not ignored or their views discounted.

Human Behavior

What is the nature of the interplay between your clients and the social environments of which they are a part that have led to the social problems they are experiencing?

Research Based Practice

In order to engage in research-informed practice to address social problems, where can you find the answers to these questions?

Human Behavior

What classroom knowledge about the ways in which individuals and families are shaped by their environments will help you understand your clients' situations?

The Problems and Needs Addressed by Your Agency: A Workbook Activity

1. What specific social conditions, needs, or problems does your practicum agency address?

   _____

   _____

   _____

2. Within the geographical area served by your agency, how many people are estimated to have the specific conditions, problems, or needs addressed by your agency?

   _____

3. How do these numbers and data compare with state and national statistics regarding the prevalence of this social problem or condition? If the numbers are higher for your area, to what do you attribute the severity of this problem?

   _____

   _____

   _____

4. What particular subpopulations are most likely to experience these problems, needs, or conditions? Is there a particular age group, gender, ethnic group, socioeconomic class, or occupational group that is most likely to experience the problems or conditions addressed by your agency?

   _____

   _____

   _____

5. How will the community be harmed if these conditions or problems grow larger and more serious?

   _____

   _____

   _____

6. What groups and organizations in your community have argued that the concerns or conditions addressed by your agency should indeed be defined as problems that require action in the form of programs, services, and interventions? In other words, who believes in and supports what your agency is trying to do?

   _____

   _____

   _____

7. Have any groups and organizations in your community argued that the concerns or conditions addressed by your agency should not be viewed as real or significant problems and that the programs and services provided by your agency are unnecessary, misdirected, or of low priority? In other words, does anyone not believe in and support what your agency is trying to do?

_____

_____

_____

8. What groups, individuals, or organizations, if any, stand to benefit economically or politically (e.g., by access to a low-income employee pool or lower taxes) from the continued existence of these social conditions, problems, and needs?

_____

_____

_____

9. What groups or organizations, if any, might be penalized or in some way harmed (e.g., by higher taxes and loss of power or status) by an extensive effort to eliminate or reduce these social conditions, problems, and needs?

_____

_____

_____

10. Has the problem or concern addressed by your agency become more or less serious in the past ten years? How does this change compare with changes in state and national statistics on the prevalence of this problem?

_____

_____

_____

11. What criteria or measures are used to document the seriousness of the problem or condition?

_____

_____

_____

_____

12. In what ways, if any, are new research findings in the social and behavioral sciences changing the way your agency conceptualizes and explains the problems, conditions, and needs that it attempts to address?

_____

_____

_____

_____

13. Are there different opinions and perspectives about the seriousness of the problem? If so, are these differences based on different definitions of the problem, different statistics, or differences in attitudes toward the problem?

_____

_____

_____

_____

14. How are the problems and concerns addressed by your agency related to other broad social problems such as poverty, crime, racism, violence, high rates of divorce, substance abuse, lack of affordable health care, lack of jobs, or changes in societal values and attitudes?

_____

_____

_____

_____

15. What specific steps and actions would be needed to prevent these problems or conditions? What would it take to eliminate these problems altogether?

_____

_____

_____

_____

16. What research or demonstration projects would you recommend be done in order to build knowledge about the social problems your agency addresses (e.g., impact of welfare reform on poverty rates, genetic influences on chemical dependency, principles of violence prevention, long-term costs associated with lack of health care)?

_____

_____

_____

SUGGESTED LEARNING ACTIVITIES

▸ Conduct interviews with experienced professionals in your agency to better understand the theories of causation that shape the agency's programs and interactions with the agency's clients and consumers.

▸ Attend public meetings (e.g., city council meetings) and read the letters to the editor of the local newspaper in order to better understand the various ways in which people explain the existence of social problems and the variety of solutions that may make sense and seem logical to them.

▸ Attend the meetings of a group or organization that defines the problem addressed by your agency much differently than does your agency. Try to understand the basis for their views.

▸ Identify a self-help group that addresses the social problem your agency addresses. Attend a meeting to determine if it explains the social problem and its solution differently from your agency.

▸ Examine the *Encyclopedia of Social Work* for chapters that offer summaries of basic information related to the various problems addressed by social workers and social agencies.

▸ Examine the most recent edition of the *Social Work Almanac* or a similar reference book that presents national statistics on the social problem addressed by your agency and compare them with those of your area.

▸ Read print and electronic media descriptions of social problems. Pay attention to whether the media takes a strengths or deficit perspective on these social problems.

Succeed with **mysocialworklab**

Log onto **www.mysocialworklab.com** and select the **Interactive Skill Module** and **Career Exploration** videos from the left-hand menu. Answer the following questions. (*If you did not receive an access code to* **MySocialWorkLab** *with this text and wish to purchase access online, please visit* www.mysocialworklab.com.)

1. **In the Career Exploration videos, watch the interview with Sue Dowling.** What human behavior theories attempt to explain the existence of child abuse?

2. **In the Interactive Skill Modules, watch the domestic violence module.** What human behavior theories attempt to explain the phenomenon of domestic violence?

PRACTICE TEST

The following questions are similar in phrasing and content to those asked in social work licensing examinations. They should help you prepare to take the licensing examination in your state.

1. Disagreement on whether a social condition is a social problem
   a. is because of a lack of information
   b. is because of differing values and views of what social conditions should exist
   c. is because there is no clear definition of a social problem
   d. is because social workers have not succeeded in public relations

Ethical Practice

2. Social problems
   a. fit federal criteria for disaster relief
   b. cannot be adequately addressed through social policies
   c. often get in the way of agency work
   d. are social conditions that violate human rights and social work ethics

3. Public social programs
   a. Are mandated or required to address identified social problems
   b. Do not have to address social problems
   c. Receive funding based on how well they address social problems
   d. Are focused primarily on prevention of social problems

Practice Contexts

4. Looking at social problems as the result of a number of interrelated causes is
   a. critical social work theory
   b. strengths perspective
   c. structural family theory
   d. ecosystems perspective

5. The prevention of social problems is best achieved through
   a. recognition of the multi-faceted etiology of social problems
   b. school-based primary prevention programs
   c. reliance on evidence-based practice
   d. increased state funding

Engage Assess Intervene Evaluate

6. The social worker who addresses social problems with multi-level interventions
   a. is a specialist
   b. is a broker
   c. is a generalist or integrated practitioner
   d. is a networker

7. Social programs need to be based on a good assessment of social problems
   a. because money is limited
   b. because funding sources require this
   c. because interventions are more effective if based on a good assessment
   d. outcomes must be measured against assessment data

11

The Social Policy Context of Practice

LEARNING GOALS FOR THIS CHAPTER

▶ To identify, become familiar with, and analyze the social policies that most directly affect the clients served by your agency

▶ To identify, become familiar with, and analyze the social policies that most directly influence the activities of your practicum agency

▶ To understand how and why social policies are formulated and change over time

▶ To understand the concept of social policy practice

CONNECTING CORE COMPETENCIES *in this chapter*

| Professional Identity | Ethical Practice | Critical Thinking | Diversity in Practice | Human Rights & Justice | Research Based Practice | Human Behavior | Policy Practice | Practice Contexts | Engage Assess Intervene Evaluate |

Previous chapters focused on the agency context, the community context, and the social problem context of social work practice. This chapter examines a fourth context, the social policy context. The clients or consumers served by your practicum agency, the other social workers and staff within this agency, and even your practicum experiences are affected by social policy.

The study of social policy can be an exciting activity because it involves the examination of what we as a society believe about people, the problems experienced by people, and what can and should be done about these problems. It forces us to carefully examine our own assumptions, beliefs, and values and in the process we are sometimes surprised by what we discover about ourselves and our views. Although stimulating, the study of social policy is also a complex undertaking. For example, the analysis of a particular social policy requires students to be able to locate relevant governmental documents and legal codes, understand the legislative process, and acquire a basic understanding of the many historic, political, cultural, and economic forces that shaped the development of a particular policy.

This chapter attempts to clarify the nature of social policy by defining and distinguishing between various terms and by explaining the impact of social policy on a social agency and on those that it serves. Specific suggestions are offered on how you can identify and locate information concerning the social policies most relevant to your practicum setting.

BACKGROUND AND CONTEXT

For purposes of this chapter, **social policy** is defined as a decision made by public or governmental authorities regarding the assignment and allocation of resources, rights, and responsibilities and expressed in laws and governmental regulations. In this definition, **resources** refer to various social and economic benefits and opportunities, both tangible and intangible. The terms **assignment** and **allocation** imply that a policy may either offer or curtail these resources for all people or for certain individuals. **Responsibilities** refer to the expectations of those providing services and those receiving services. **Rights** refer to the protection of guaranteed freedoms or entitlements.

Needless to say, lawmakers and government officials formulate policies on a wide variety of topics. Thus, there are public policies on international relations, economics and the monetary system, the tax structure, interstate and international commerce, military and defense, highways, use of public lands, environmental safety, education, and the like. For the most part, social policies address matters or issues related to the social well-being of people and the relationships between various groups within society. Thus, social policies focus on such concerns as marriage, divorce, adoption, domestic abuse, the special needs of the elderly, juvenile delinquency, mental health, discrimination against minority groups, training and job opportunities for the disadvantaged, economic assistance to the poor, availability of affordable housing, immigration, and other similar concerns. The term **social welfare policy** is often applied to those social policies that focus primarily on the distribution of economic benefits to those in need (e.g., public assistance, subsidized housing, Medicaid, or subsidized child care). These approaches account for the ways in which many federal and state laws and social policies have been enacted, some of which results in effective social policy, and some of which do not.

Social policies are directly related to social problems, and are intended to address them. Thus, once a social problem is identified, various groups, all

Policy Practice

How can you learn about the social policies that impact or direct your agency's work and impact the lives of your clients?

with different values, belief systems, and political affiliations, begin the process of addressing these social problems in the form of a law that may actually change the social structures that contribute to or add to the social problems. Social policies are in a constant state of evaluation and are impacted by the following:

▶ Whoever holds political power at any given time
▶ Whether a social problem is a crisis or can be tolerated
▶ Evidence about how former and current social policies have impacted the social problem
▶ Pressure by constituency and advocacy groups.

Social policies often direct agencies to do what is required, perform to a certain standard, and within a given budget. Further, they provide the tools that are to be used to measure effectiveness and show accountability in the use of public money.

Lowy (1991, 377–379) explains that public social policies are derived from four dichotomous approaches to the legislative process and those who attempt to influence them:

1. ***Generic versus categorical approach.*** A generic approach to social policy development seeks a particular outcome for an entire population, such as health care or housing for all people in society. By contrast, a categorical approach focuses on only one segment of the population, such as housing for the elderly or health care for children.

2. ***Holistic versus segmented approach.*** A holistic approach to policy development attempts to address the needs or concerns of the total person or the whole family, while a segmented approach focuses on only a single factor, such as an individual's income or nutrition. A segmented approach gives rise to a fragmented and confusing service system in which clients must approach several different agencies in order to secure the services or results they need.

3. ***Rational versus crisis approach.*** The rational approach places a heavy emphasis on deriving social policy from a careful and thorough study of the problem and issues. By contrast, the crisis approach creates policy as a hurried and usually highly political reaction to a crisis or serious problem. Very few of our country's social policies have grown out of the rational planning process.

4. ***Future planning versus political context approach.*** The future planning approach gives careful consideration to social trends and probable future developments and tries to anticipate how the various policy options would fit with what can be expected in the future. By contrast, the political context approach is mostly concerned with solving an immediate problem and allows the policy to be determined mostly by popular opinion, political interests, and pragmatic assumptions about what will be supported and tolerated by dominant forces in society.

Social policy planning and implementation would be most effective if the generic, holistic, rational, and future planning approaches were all used because the resulting policies would be more carefully conceived and based on current or future needs. The reality, however, is that most social policies are a result of the categorical, segmented, crisis, and political context approaches. This is because of limited vision and information, monetary constraints, political motivation and power, and a tendency to only enact social policy when social needs reach the crisis stage.

Engage Assess Intervene Evaluate

How is policy practice similar to and different from planned change at the micro level?

Critical Thinking

Which of the above approaches to social policy development best describe the history of the major social policies impacting your agency and its clients?

A social policy is created when a legislative body enacts a law, usually at the federal or state level but in some cases, at the county or city level. Once the law is enacted, high-level governmental officials and various governmental legal departments will usually prepare a set of rules and regulations that clarify the provisions of the law and describe in detail how the law is to be implemented. These directives are often called ***administrative rules and regulations.*** Subsequently, key provisions of the law and many of the rules and regulations are written into a public agency's manual of policy and procedure that guides its day-by-day operation and the decisions and actions of agency staff. Statements of social policy are found in legal codes, in executive orders issued by the president and state governors, in administrative rules and regulations issued by governmental officials, and sometimes in statements and speeches made by high-ranking public officials. In some instances, legal decisions handed down by courts have the effect of creating social policy.

Although an agency policy is not a social policy, social policies do filter down to the level of a local or community agency and find their way into the agency's policy manual. At the local level, social policies have a significant impact on an agency's services and programs and on what a social worker actually does or does not do in his or her work with clients. The impact of social policy on agency policy is most evident in the operation of a public agency in which one will find that many of the statements found in the manual are direct responses to specific legal codes and various governmental rules and regulations.

Ethical Practice

What values underlie the major social policies that impact your agency and your clients?

Social policies are a reflection of values and what is believed to be right and wrong, desirable and undesirable. They are shaped mostly by those who have power and influence. The formulation of social policy is basically a political process and politics are primarily about power. It is the art

---

Food for Thought

One way to institute social justice in society and to lessen the extent of social exclusion and exploitation is through the shaping of governmental policy to those ends. Policy creates the world in which practice is accomplished (van Wormer, 2004, 13–14).

• • •

Suffice it to say that solving the welfare problem is not the answer to solving the poverty problem, as policy-makers often imply. Rather, solving—or at least dealing with—the poverty problem is the answer to solving the welfare problem (Popple and Leighninger, 2004, 181).

• • •

Social policy addresses fundamental values of social inclusion, equity, human rights and widening of human capabilities: It is important that these intrinsic values are always at the forefront of thinking about social policy (Mkandawire, 2004, 31).

• • •

The problem is that U.S. society no longer exhibits . . . commitment, and its political leadership has moved with alarming speed to disassemble the meager vestiges of

past concern for the poor. Rather than "working" the system harder on behalf of their clients' immediate needs, social workers must now seek to work *against* a system that is intent upon denial of moral responsibility for responding to those same needs (Perez-Koenig and Rock, 2001, 10).

• • •

Policy analysis, at every step of the way, is a political activity. Power and oppression go hand in hand. Anti-oppressive policy then means recognizing power imbalances built in the social system and actively working toward the promotion of change to redress the balance of power (van Wormer, 2004, 117).

• • •

Policy advocates need perspective to avoid pessimism and self-recrimination in the wake of defeats or partial successes. No single person or group is likely to prevail on the complex playing field of policy deliberations. Advocates must realize that defeats are more likely when people champion the needs of stigmatized and relatively powerless groups, which lack the clout of more powerful interests (Jansson, 1999, 23).

Research Based Practice

Have the positive and negative impacts of social policies affecting your clients been measured by your agency either formally or informally?

of gaining, exercising, and retaining power in order to influence and enact social policies that are believed to be right and effective. Hopefully the effectiveness of social policies is monitored, measured, and evaluated, and results are shared with policy makers so that social policies can be continually improved in order to address social problems more effectively.

If social policies are ill conceived because the decision makers either do not understand the problem or have erroneous beliefs about its causes, the resulting social programs will also be flawed. Those who understand the concerns being addressed and understand the inadequacies of existing policies and programs, have both an obligation and an opportunity to provide accurate information to the decision makers so they can develop appropriate and effective social policies. In the absence of such information, policy makers will assume that social policies are addressing the needs they were intended to address. Social workers can thus be extremely influential in not only providing needed information, but also lobbying for just, equitable, and effective social policy changes.

GUIDANCE AND DIRECTION

You may be surprised at the degree to which your work is impacted by social policy. You need to learn about social policy so that you can take part in its formulation. Hopefully you are excited at the prospect of working at the macro level to design social policies and social programs that could improve the lives of many people. Social change and social policy development are the most efficient and exciting ways to help large numbers of people and promote social justice. This level of practice is referred to as ***social policy practice.***

Perhaps you see yourself primarily as a direct services provider and you may prefer to help clients and families one by one and in a very personal way. The idea of becoming involved in political action and social change efforts may not be the focus of your emerging practice. However, it is still imperative for you to understand social policy and how it affects your clients, positively or negatively. In order to be an informed advocate for your clients and a skilled provider of direct services, you must understand specific social policies, their strengths and limitations, and why they exist in their current forms.

Depending on your practicum setting, you will need to become familiar with a cluster of social policy issues and concerns. You must acquire a basic or working understanding of the social policies that most directly influence the operation of your agency, its own agency policies, your role and its clients or consumers. Below is a list of social policy domains that are of interest to many social workers and many social agencies.

Abortion	Discrimination and racism
Adolescent pregnancy	Economic development
Adult protection	Education at the preschool, elementary, and secondary levels
Caregiving	
Child care	Employment
Child protection	End of life
Child support	Family planning
Community development	Foster care and adoption
Custody	Health care and rehabilitation

Homelessness	Marriage and divorce
Housing	Mental health and mental illness
Immigration and refugee issues	Parenting
Intimate partner violence	Physical and mental disabilities
Job creation and unemployment	Public assistance/welfare
Juvenile delinquency and adult crime	Public health and safety
Long-term care	Substance abuse

Social policy is constantly evolving as a result of changing societal needs, shifting social values, increases or decreases in financial resources available to implement policy, and, of course, political forces. You will need to keep abreast of proposed legislative changes and find ways to have input into the political process. During your practicum, make a special effort to involve yourself in activities that prepare you for social work practice. Look for the opportunity to participate in task forces or committees working to pass a law or assist grassroots or advocacy groups seeking to change social policy. You may be able to observe and give testimony at public meetings or legislative hearings that solicit public input before social policy decisions are made.

Be aware that when social workers do not engage in the politics of forming social welfare policy and allocating funding for social welfare programs, many client needs and concerns are overlooked by the decision makers, and the insights and values of the social work profession are omitted from the development of social policy. Your knowledge and skills are needed in the ongoing work of social policy development.

You will need to develop and utilize a social policy analysis model or conceptual framework to guide your examination and analysis of the social policies that impact the operation of your agency and either support or undermine the social functioning of your clients. The questions listed in the workbook activity in this chapter are ones often addressed in the various models and conceptual frameworks used in policy analysis. Learn to view such models as tools to help you understand and assess the effectiveness of social policies with which you work. Recognize that these frameworks will not only guide your evaluation of social policy, but can also provide you with the insights needed to improve social policy.

Sources of information regarding a social policy include the original code or statute, administrative rules and regulations, and other governmental documents that describe and explain the policy. Various professional and advocacy organizations (e.g., Child Welfare League of America, National Association of Social Workers, American Association of Retired Persons, Children's Defense Fund, American Public Welfare Association, American Hospital Association, Urban League, Southern Poverty Law Center) distribute reports of their analysis of social policies relevant to their particular concerns. In addition, the observations of social workers and of clients will give you insight into how a given policy affects the lives of individuals and families. The social workers in your agency will have opinions about how social policy could be improved, how it benefits or harms clients, and how it complements or conflicts with other social policies. Clients may also have insights based on their experiences with effective or ineffective social policies, so seek opportunities to learn from them.

As a way of learning about social policy, identify a social problem (e.g., homelessness) that your agency addresses. Next, identify a specific social

Policy Practice

What is the role of social work in the development of social policies that promote social functioning and the well-being of individuals, families, groups, and communities?

Critical Thinking

Building on what you have learned about social policy, what social policy analysis model can you use to understand and assess the effectiveness of social policies in your agency?

policy related to that problem (e.g., public assistance laws, unemployment compensation laws, health care policies, minimum-wage laws). Using the questions found in the workbook activity, analyze this social policy and determine if it is adequate, effective, and positive in its effects.

During your analysis, consider the following categories of social policies, each of which reflects a philosophy, a set of values, and a belief system about how society should deal with social problems:

> ▶ *Policies of social and financial support* are those intended to help or encourage people to carry out their roles and responsibilities and meet their basic needs for food, shelter, and so on. Examples include policies related to financial assistance, medical care for the poor, and subsidized housing for low-income elders.
>
> ▶ *Policies of protection* are those that seek to protect people from harm and exploitation, especially those who are most vulnerable. Examples are policies related to child abuse and neglect, domestic violence, the frail elderly, and to groups often subjected to discrimination and oppression.
>
> ▶ *Policies of rehabilitation and remediation* are those intended to correct or minimize the impact of certain disabling conditions such as serious mental illness, developmental disabilities, and chronic illness.
>
> ▶ *Policies of prevention* are those that attempt to prevent certain social and health problems from developing or increasing. Examples are those that encourage economic development, immunizations, parent education, family planning, proper nutrition, and curfews for youth.
>
> ▶ *Policies of punishment and correction* are those that seek to punish and control persons who violate laws and societal norms. Examples are policies related to crime and delinquency, probation and parole, and the monitoring of convicted sex offenders.

The social policy you are analyzing will probably be one of these types, and thinking about it this way will help you understand the overall intent of the policy, the values that drive it, and how it may reflect public attitudes and political ideology. You will soon be able to understand, describe, and analyze it in terms of the following:

> ▶ Its authority and auspices (federal, state, or local law)
> ▶ Its history and the reasons for its development
> ▶ Its stated purpose and goals
> ▶ The assumptions, values, and beliefs upon which it is based
> ▶ Its key principles and main provisions
> ▶ Its impact on your agency's operation
> ▶ Its impact on your clients
> ▶ Its advantages and positive effects
> ▶ Its disadvantages and negative effects
> ▶ Its relationship to other social policies
> ▶ Its gaps and need for revision

After you have become familiar with a specific social policy and its effects, consider how it could be improved and what steps or actions would be necessary to achieve those improvements, such as changes in existing legislation, changes in administrative rules, or the creation of incentives to adhere to the policy.

Social Policy Analysis: A Workbook Activity

Identify one public social policy that has a significant impact on the operation of your agency and/or on the clients or consumers served by your agency. Then, in relation to that specific policy, answer the questions presented below.

1. What is the official name of the social policy being studied?

   _____

2. What is the legal citation of the policy (e.g., public law number or state statute code number)?

   _____

3. When was the social policy enacted or established and when, if ever, was it significantly modified?

   _____

   _____

   _____

4. Which of the four approaches to social policy development described in this chapter best explains how this social policy was formed?

   _____

   _____

5. What programs are commonly associated with or mandated by this policy?

   _____

   _____

   _____

   _____

6. What conditions, problems, or needs does this social policy address (e.g., violence, poverty, homelessness, addictions, unemployment)?

   _____

   _____

7. What are the overall goals of this social policy (e.g., protection of a vulnerable population, provision of public assistance, or social control)?

   _____

   _____

   _____

8. Which of the types of social policies listed on page 116 best describes the social policy you are studying?

_____

_____

9. If this policy creates certain benefits or services, what are the criteria for eligibility? Why do some people receive benefits, services, or protection while others do not?

_____

_____

_____

10. What underlying values, beliefs, or assumptions about people and their needs or problems are reflected in this policy? How do these values fit or not fit with the values of the social work profession?

_____

_____

_____

_____

11. Who benefits from this social policy? Who loses or is placed at a disadvantage from this policy?

_____

_____

_____

12. Does the funding required to implement this social policy need to be reauthorized regularly (e.g., each year or every two years)?

_____

13. Based on your work in your practicum site, is this social policy doing what it is supposed to do? If not, why?

_____

_____

_____

14. How could this social policy better address the needs of those it is designed to assist (e.g., fill gaps in services, coordinate with related programs, increase funding, and change eligibility criteria)?

_____

_____

_____

_____

15. What would it take to actually change this policy (e.g., legislation, amendments, coalition building, or lobbying)?

_____

_____

_____

16. Does one political party support this policy more than another does? If yes, why?

_____

_____

_____

17. What interest groups, advocacy groups, or grassroots organizations support this social policy? Why?

_____

_____

_____

18. What interest groups, advocacy groups, or grassroots organizations oppose this social policy? Why?

_____

_____

_____

19. How are the roles and duties of social workers in your agency shaped, constrained, or expanded by this social policy?

_____

_____

_____

20. What other social policies are interrelated with this particular policy? Do they fit together well or are they in conflict with one another?

_____

_____

_____

_____

_____

SUGGESTED LEARNING ACTIVITIES

- Interview a social worker in your agency about a social policy that most directly affects his or her clients and obtain his or her recommendations for improving the social policy.

- Review the NASW *Code of Ethics* (1999) guidelines regarding the social worker's responsibility in the area of social policy (www.socialworkers.org).

- Read *Social Work Speaks,* which describes NASW's position on a wide variety of social issues.

- Attend legislative or public hearings that gather public input before a social policy is enacted or modified.

- Identify your personal position regarding a controversial area of social policy, such as abortion. Attend meetings of an organization that takes an opposing position to try to understand that perspective, including the values, beliefs, knowledge, and assumptions on which it is based.

- Invite a state legislator to discuss his or her experiences with proposing, formulating, and passing legislation.

- Use the Internet to monitor the progress of a bill before the U.S. Congress or your state legislature. For information on federal legislation relevant to social work, explore the legislative page at the web site of the National Association of Social Workers.

- Explore the web sites of organizations that monitor social policy, such as the Electronic Policy Network, Center for Law and Social Policy, U.S. Department of Health and Human Services, and World Wide Web Resources for Social Workers.

Succeed with PEARSON mysocialworklab

Log onto **www.mysocialworklab.com** and select the **Interactive Skill Module** and **Career Exploration** videos from the left-hand menu. Answer the questions below. (*If you did not receive an access code to* **MySocialWorkLab** *with this text and wish to purchase access online, please visit* www.mysocialworklab.com.)

1. **In the Career Exploration videos, watch question 9 of the interview with Sue Dowling.** She said that her greatest challenge was keeping up with new social policies, changes in administration, and political issues. How can you prepare yourself for policy practice?

2. **In the Interactive Skill Modules, watch the domestic violence module.** How important is it for a social worker to understand social policies when working in domestic violence programs?

PRACTICE TEST

The following questions are similar in phrasing and content to those asked in social work licensing examinations. They should help you prepare to take the licensing examination in your state.

Policy Practice

1. The term agency policy
   a. is the same as social policy
   b. refers to laws that an agency must abide by
   c. refers to agency guidelines and procedures
   d. refers to human resources rules

Policy Practice

2. The term which refers to the assignment of federal economic resources in a social policy is:
   a. allocation
   b. guidelines for oversight
   c. rights and responsibilities
   d. entitlements

Policy Practice

3. The Social Security Act of 1935 is an example of what approach to social policy?
   a. future planning approach
   b. holistic approach
   c. crisis approach
   d. political context approach

Policy Practice

4. Federal administration rules and responsibilities
   a. are the standards of a social policy
   b. clarify the provisions of the social policy and implementation guidelines
   c. set job descriptions for agency employees
   d. specific budget amounts and categories

Policy Practice

5. The level of social work practice that focuses on social change and policy formation
   a. is advocacy
   b. is mezzo level practice
   c. is evidence based practice
   d. is policy practice

Policy Practice

6. Social work roles involved in policy practice include
   a. advocate
   b. researcher
   c. organizer
   d. all of the above

7. Social policies which support mental health services are which type of social policy?
   a. policies of financial support
   b. policies of rehabilitation or remediation
   c. policies of punishment or correction
   d. policies of protection

Answers

1) c 2) a 3) c 4) b 5) d 6) d 7) b

12

Diversity and Cultural Competency

LEARNING GOALS FOR THIS CHAPTER

▶ To become familiar with the NASW Standards for Cultural Competency

▶ To learn how social services agencies address the concerns and needs of diverse clients

▶ To understand how client experiences with minority status might influence their use of human services

▶ To become aware of the legal and ethical prohibitions against discrimination

▶ To understand how your own values and beliefs might affect relationships with persons different from you

▶ To understand how human rights apply to social work practice

CONNECTING CORE COMPETENCIES *in this chapter*

Professional Identity	Ethical Practice	Critical Thinking	Diversity in Practice	Human Rights & Justice	Research Based Practice	Human Behavior	Policy Practice	Practice Contexts	Engage Assess Intervene Evaluate

We live in an increasingly diverse and pluralistic society made up of many distinct ethnic, religious, and cultural groups. Consequently, people have different values, beliefs, traditions, and languages. Social workers and social services agencies are being challenged to find ways of recognizing, respecting, and accommodating differences while treating all clients with fairness and equality under the law.

Members of the social work profession believe that all people have worth, simply because they are human beings. All persons are entitled to fundamental human rights, and all have basic responsibilities, including the responsibility to treat others with respect, dignity, and fairness. These beliefs are prerequisites to peaceful relations among people, to social justice, and to the effective and proper operation of human services organizations.

Public and private human services agencies must be thoughtful and fair in decisions about who is eligible for the services they offer and how best to allocate limited resources. Agencies must avoid discrimination based on race, color, sex, national origin, age, religion, creed, and physical and mental disability.

Human Rights & Justice

Upon which specific human rights is the work of your agency most committed?

BACKGROUND AND CONTEXT

Culture refers to the learned patterns of thought and behavior that are passed from generation to generation. One's culture consists of the unspoken and unquestioned assumptions and ideas about the nature of reality, the human condition, and how life should be lived. Everything we do is influenced by ways of thinking, values, beliefs, expectations, and customs that make up our culture. Our professional knowledge and practice, all social policies, and all agency policies and procedures are shaped by culture. Broadly defined, culture includes not only references to ethnicity or background, but also such variables as age, disability, and sexual orientation. Each form of diversity shapes clients' thoughts, behavior, and world views.

Whittaker and Tracy (1989) astutely observe that every contact between a social worker and client is, at some level, a cross-cultural encounter.

> On the one hand, the worker brings a particular knowledge base, set of value components, and methods of helping—all of which have been shaped in part by his or her own cultural background, by that of the dominant culture, and by the values and ethics of the professional helping community. These influences shape the manner in which a social worker will define social problems, what aspects will be considered relevant to assess, and what specific interventions will be employed to ameliorate the problem. On the other hand, the client also brings cultural elements to the social work relationship, including culturally determined patterns of help seeking and service utilization. (147)

As you work toward cultural competency, you must recognize that we are all limited by *ethnocentrism,* which is the tendency to assume that one's own culture is normal and even superior and that it is an appropriate standard for judging the beliefs and behaviors of others. We cannot avoid being ethnocentric to some degree because our own beliefs, values, and patterns feel natural and normal and seem rooted in common sense and our daily lives. These are so integral to us that it is difficult to realize there are other ways of thinking and living. We must strive to become aware of how our culture influences our thoughts, decisions, and actions in order to avoid misunderstanding our clients and failing to recognize and respect their unique culture. Sheafor and Horejsi (2006) explain that ethnocentrism exists when:

▶ Stereotyped explanations are given for the behavior of persons of a specific ethnic or minority group.
▶ The same helping strategies are used for all clients who are members of a particular ethnic or minority group.
▶ The importance of culture and ethnicity in a person's life are minimized, or at the other extreme, used to explain nearly all behavior. (175)

Prejudice can breed ***discrimination,*** which refers to decisions, behaviors, or actions that deprive an individual or a whole group of certain rights and opportunities. Discrimination can be either intentional or unintentional, depending on whether it was motivated by prejudice and the intent to harm and depending on the person's understanding of or denial of the potential to be discriminatory. However, either can be harmful to clients. Discrimination can also be personal or institutional. In ***personal discrimination,*** an individual behaves in ways that cause harm to the members of a group. In ***institutional discrimination,*** beliefs and practices that are embedded in law, in social and economic systems, and in governmental or organizational policy cause harm to members of certain groups. Examples often given of institutional racism include policies requiring English as a primary language, those restricting refugees' or illegal immigrants' access to basic services, and those that disallow insurance and governmental benefits to same-sex partners. It is possible for social workers to engage in unintentional discrimination, which is usually understood as behavior rooted in denial of one's own racism or stereotypical thinking. In this case, denial of one's own biases gets in the way of an honest self-assessment and may keep us from seeing our own limitations.

Clients' membership in a minority group may have a more significant influence on their interaction with a social worker or agency than does their membership in a specific cultural group. Typically, the members of a minority group experience some level of discrimination and, according to Schaefer (2006, 6), "a narrowing of life's opportunities—for success, education, wealth, the pursuit of happiness—that goes beyond any personal shortcoming he or she may have."

Minority status is not simply a function of numbers. In a given society, a particular group may be in the majority in terms of percentage of the overall population, but still have minority status because they are discriminated against. For example, even though females are slightly more numerous than males, women are often considered a minority group because they have less power and control over their lives than do men, and because they experience prejudice and discrimination based on gender. Minority status may also be tied to age, sexual orientation, physical or mental disability, socioeconomic status, educational background, or religion. If people perceive themselves as different from others or as less powerful and more vulnerable, these perceptions have an impact on help-seeking behavior, on how they expect to be treated, on their level of trust in a social worker or agency, and on what they consider to be a useful and relevant service or program.

Social agencies vary in their capacity to respond effectively to culturally diverse clients. Cross (1988, 1–4) suggests that the various levels of cultural competency and cultural sensitivity among human services agencies exist along a continuum. Six levels are identified on this continuum. Consider, based on your observations or formal evaluations of your agency, where your organization might fall on this continuum.

Practice Contexts

In light of ethnocentrism, is it possible for an agency to assess its own level of cultural competency?

Food for Thought

In spite of their training, behavioral science stu dents, researchers, and practitioners are no more immune to racism than is the average person (Lum, 1992, 133).

. . .

In an absolute sense, competence is an unachievable ideal: we cannot be fully and completely competent in *any* culture, including the one we identify as our own. We are always limited by our experiences and perceptions—we receive cultural information, and process it, as unique individuals, individuals who may share certain levels of commonality of experience, but who also retain a relationship to our own cultural experiences that cannot be understood by another person in its fullest sense. If we are thus limited in our ability to become fully "competent" in our own culture(s), how much more so are we limited in our ability to be fully "competent" in another culture? (Rothman, 2008, 1).

. . .

The story of human rights is about the struggle of the human race to ascend to the heights rather than cave in to circumstances (Wronka, 2007, 49).

. . .

Developing critical consciousness is a two-step process that involves learning to perceive social, political, and economic contradictions and taking action against oppressive elements. It is a process through which people come to an understanding of power, empowerment, and oppression. One develops greater critical consciousness through approaching, equalizing, and finding out about situations. It is developed through praxis (the exercise or practice of a skills) or a combination of action and reflection (Lum, 2006, 47).

. . .

It is important to constantly be on the lookout for use of flowery or technical language that masks oppression (Wronka, 2007, 29).

. . .

Membership in an oppressed and vulnerable group or "minority" status does not make a worker an instant "expert" in cultural competence, though it may make her/him especially knowledgeable about that particular culture, and about the ways in which oppression can affect people of any diverse group. It also doesn't necessarily "protect" the worker from biases, prejudices, and oppressive beliefs about other groups (Rothman, 2007, 16).

. . .

Once systems of oppression are in place, they are self-perpetuating (Adams et al., 1997, 17).

. . .

The world view of the culturally different client who comes to counseling boils down to one important question: "What makes you, a counselor/therapist, any different from all the others out there who have oppressed and discriminated against me?" (Sue and Sue, 1990, 6).

1. *Destructiveness*—Agency policies, programs, practices, and attitudes are destructive to certain cultures and to the individuals of the culture. The agency is aware of its negative effect on the peoples' culture and believes its actions are desirable or justified.

2. *Incapacity*—Agency policies, programs, and practices are destructive, but negative effects are unintended and unrecognized.

3. *Blindness*—The agency does not recognize important differences. It assumes that all people are the same and that all clients can and should be treated the same without consideration of different customs and belief systems.

4. *Pre-competence*—The agency recognizes its inability to properly serve minorities or those who are culturally different and is working to improve service to a specific population. Efforts may include recruiting minority personnel, seeking cultural knowledge, and building linkages with the minority community.

Human Rights & Justice

In what direct or indirect ways is the working of your agency based on broad human rights as described below?

5. *Basic Competence*—The agency recognizes and respects cultural differences and conducts ongoing self-assessments of its policies and practices and continually works to expand its cultural knowledge and the special resources needed to adequately serve minority groups.

6. *Advanced Competence*—The agency strives to develop new knowledge of culturally competent practice and is an advocate for changes within the wider human services system and throughout society.

Many of the issues related to diversity that the social work profession deals with are at their core human rights issues with national and international contexts. The work you will be doing in practicum may be very personal and individual for one client or family, but may also be tied to much larger human rights organizations and their declarations. Some of these include:

- United Nations Universal Declaration of Human Rights
- International Covenant on Economic, Social, and Cultural Relations
- International Federation of Social Workers
- Declaration of Human Responsibilities of the InterAction Council
- United Nations Convention on the Elimination of All Forms of Discrimination Against Women
- United National Convention on the Rights of the Child
- Geneva Convention

GUIDANCE AND DIRECTION

Diversity in Practice

How can a diversity perspective and a strengths perspective be used together?

In an effort to see your agency from the perspective of diverse clients, examine its physical environment, its written materials, its internal policies, and its staffing patterns. Assess whether your agency is accessible to persons with disabilities. Look to see if reading material, posters, and artwork would appeal to diverse groups of people, including language adaptations and visual representations of people from a variety of backgrounds. Read agency written materials to determine if they are free of bias and whether they use inclusive language. Finally, learn if the agency staff is diverse and represents people of various ages, cultures, sexual orientations, and other backgrounds.

No doubt you will work hard to be culturally sensitive and respectful of differences among people. However, you, like other people, may not always recognize your own biases, prejudices, or ignorance regarding diverse groups. The practicum offers an important opportunity for self-examination and self-correction in terms of such personal limitations.

You may believe that people are more alike than different, and also that treating all clients alike is fair and reasonable. However, these beliefs do not recognize the importance of diversity, and may cause you to overlook unique aspects of a client's background and the powerful impact of minority status. Although it is true that people have much in common, it is also true that there are differences and these can greatly affect social work practice. Sue and Sue (1990, 165) remind us, "In counseling, equal treatment may be discriminatory."

Recognize the positive experiences resulting from minority group status, such as ethnic pride, bilingual abilities, community solidarity, extended family cohesion, and a strong sense of history. These experiences are strengths on which a professional relationship and a possible intervention can be built. Do not assume that membership in a minority group has only negative implications.

Work to understand any negative experiences your clients may have had because of their minority status, such as discrimination in school, housing, or employment, inappropriate placement in foster homes, or threats and violence in the form of hate crimes. Remember that many personal problems such as depression, poverty, dropping out of school, substance abuse, suicide, and even physical illness may have some roots in the stress and inner turmoil a person feels when subjected to discrimination or oppression.

If you are a member of a minority group, you may be better able to understand the effects of prejudice and discrimination, as well as the unique benefits that are a result of such membership. It is also important for you to have satisfactorily resolved any related personal issues, anger, and resentment in order to be objective and to perceive the uniqueness of every situation and individual. However, such negative experiences of personal discrimination or marginalization can provide motivation and passion for the work you may do with others who are experiencing oppression. If you have experienced discrimination because of your minority status, do not assume your minority clients will have the same experiences or conclusions about them as you do.

Social work with diverse clients is complex and demanding. Stereotypical adaptations of usual approaches or slight changes in the agency's standard operating procedures are not likely to be effective. Rather, you will need to develop distinct methods that are acceptable, relevant to, and appropriate for the specific group with which you are working, and this necessitates involving them in any such steps.

Be alert to the fact that misunderstandings and misinterpretations in cross-cultural interactions can occur in many areas and situations including:

What evidence exists to support the effectiveness of culturally sensitive interventions with diverse clients and groups?

- Spoken language (e.g., misunderstanding words, accent, and nuances)
- Nonverbal communication (e.g., misunderstanding gestures, facial expressions, touch, and tone of voice)
- Interpersonal differences such as appropriate level of directness, assertiveness, and self-disclosure
- Male–female relations and beliefs about appropriate touching and expressions of attraction for another person
- Judgments concerning appropriate dress, body decorations, and level of modesty
- Importance assigned to punctuality, use of time, and planning ahead
- Use of physical space and judgment as to what is appropriate distance between people
- Ways of learning and teaching and giving and taking direction
- Ways of negotiating, handling conflict, and expressing emotion
- Ways of seeking and utilizing professional or culturally valued helpers
- Differences in definition of family and the involvement of family in social work interventions

Seek to understand your clients' beliefs about the appropriateness of asking for help and receiving help from professionals and agencies. Some ethnic groups may believe that personal and family problems should not be discussed with anyone outside the family. Some may feel great shame if they must seek help from a stranger. Others may prefer to seek help from religious leaders, and some may view social workers with mistrust for historical reasons.

Recognize that different groups may hold very different beliefs about the nature and cause of personal problems. For example, some ethnic groups may view depression or physical illness as primarily a problem of spirituality (e.g., a consequence of eating a taboo food, having broken one's relationship with God, or of a lack of balance between one's spirit and body).

Different groups have different ideas about what is an appropriate method of helping and about who has the capacity and authority to help with or treat certain types of problems. Some people may choose to use informal helpers and spiritual leaders, prayer, purification ceremonies, and religious rituals rather than the services of a professional helper. You will need to learn how to work cooperatively with spiritual leaders, healers, and clergy. Expect to learn from them about approaches to helping that are valued by your clients.

Remember that clients from a minority group may have had or may expect negative experiences when they must have contact with social workers or social agencies, based on their group's history with the dominant culture. Clients may also be fearful of interacting with social workers because they fear legal recrimination for themselves (e.g., illegal immigrants, or homosexual clients living in states that have laws prohibiting homosexual sexual activity). Their fears may be a barrier to their development of trust and their willingness to invest themselves in a professional helping relationship. Be careful not to interpret such mistrust, fear, or anger as client resistance. Do not automatically interpret client quietness, reticence, or anxiety as pathology or dysfunction. When appropriate, acknowledge to your client that you recognize the differences that separate you, and show your appreciation for their struggles by validating their experiences.

Developing competence in working with diverse people and acquiring the knowledge about diverse client groups required for culturally competent practice will be a long-term, perhaps lifelong process. Relish the possibilities available to you as you venture into work with clients and communities who are very different from you, and remain aware of the limitations of your ability to understand others' experiences and interpretations of them. Even skilled and experienced social workers cannot know the intricacies of every culture or minority group, so try to learn about the world of others in an authentic way.

The NASW Standards for Cultural Competency clearly define what social workers need to know, believe, and be able to do to be considered culturally competent. Monitor yourself regularly for progress in meeting the standards of NASW, summarized below, recognizing that cultural competence is never truly achieved, but remains a lifelong professional goal (NASW Press, 2007, 4).

- **Ethics and Values.** Use the values and ethics of the profession and recognize potential congruence or conflict between professional values and those of clients.
- **Self-Awareness.** Work to understand your own culture, including values and beliefs.
- **Cross-Cultural Knowledge.** Commit to continuous development of cultural knowledge.
- **Cross-Cultural Values.** Use interventions that take culture into account.
- **Service Delivery.** Be aware of available services and make referrals appropriate for diverse clients.
- **Empowerment and Advocacy.** Understand how social policies and programs impact diverse clients and advocate when needed.
- **Diverse Workplace.** Promote diversity in the profession through creation and support of a diverse workplace.
- **Professional Education.** Promote education and training in cultural competence.
- **Language Diversity.** Advocate for the use of interpreters and services in appropriate languages.

Develop what is called a ***dual perspective***, which is the ability to focus simultaneously on the attitudes, values, and customs of the larger, society and

Ethical Practice

Upon which NASW ethical principles is cultural competence based?

the attitudes, values, and customs of the individual client or family. Doing this while being aware of the impact of your own values, attitudes, and customs will help you effectively relate to diverse clients, understand how they are impacted by the larger society, and at least partially view your clients' experiences from their point of view and not just your own.

Agencies sometimes intentionally or unintentionally adopt attitudes, engage in behavior, and enact agency policies that reinforce stereotypes, widen the gap between social workers and clients, and eventually result in clients choosing to separate themselves from these agencies. Watch for agency attitudes, behaviors, and policies that might be uninformed, stereotypical, or inappropriate culturally.

Work to broaden what Anderson and Carter (2003, 154–155) call ***cultural borderlands,*** which refer to the area of overlap between the social worker's cultural identity and the client's cultural identity. This can be done by expanding your knowledge of diverse people, increasing your awareness of the impact of your own cultural identity on your work, and recognizing that communication with your clients and their communication with you are both seen through personal and cultural filters. This will reduce the chances of misinterpretation and inappropriate interventions, while increasing the chances that an effective professional relationship will set the stage for a culturally appropriate and effective intervention. Remember that your own positionality in relation to your clients may be one of privilege. If so, continue working to understand how clients might view you, look for commonalities while respecting difference, challenge oppression, learn from your clients, work to identify any biases, and equalize power when you can.

Identity and Self-Awareness: A Workbook Activity

1. How would you describe yourself in terms of gender? Race? Ethnicity? Socioeconomic class? Religion? Age group? Minority group? Sexual orientation?

   _____

   _____

   _____

2. What are the positive aspects of each of these group identities or memberships for you?

   _____

   _____

   _____

3. What are the negative aspects of each of these group identities or memberships for you?

   _____

   _____

   _____

4. How might your identity, characteristics, and membership in particular groups affect your work with clients who are different from you?

   _____

   _____

   _____

5. What are your most common thoughts and feelings when you encounter people who are different from yourself?

   _____

   _____

   _____

6. What biases and stereotypes, if any, have you identified within yourself as you have encountered clients who are different from you? What can you do to ensure that these do not color your work?

   _____

   _____

   _____

7. What steps can you take to improve your skills in working with diverse clients?

   _____

   _____

   _____

8. How many of the NASW Standards for Cultural Competency do you have? How can you develop the ones you do not yet have?

_____

_____

_____

Cultural Awareness in Your Agency: A Workbook Activity

1. What specific actions has your agency taken to make sure it is in compliance with federal law that prohibits discrimination on the basis of race, color, sex, national origin, age, religion, creed, physical or mental disability, and familial status?

_____

_____

_____

_____

2. In what ways does your agency make accommodations for clients or consumers who have a physical or mental disability or limitation or who are not fluent in or comfortable with the English language?

_____

_____

_____

3. About what percentage of your agency's clients could be described as members of a cultural, ethnic, religious, or racial minority? What groups are they?

_____

_____

_____

_____

4. What special efforts, if any, has your practicum agency made to reach out to and provide relevant services or programs to members of minority groups?

_____

_____

_____

5. What culturally sensitive assessment instruments or practice techniques, if any, does your agency use with clients who are members of minority groups?

_____

_____

_____

6. Is there anything about your agency that might discourage minorities from using its services (e.g., the racial, ethnic, or gender makeup of staff; location; office hours and days of operation; reputation in community; costs; perceived attitude toward minorities)?

_____

_____

_____

7. What grievance procedures are available to clients or consumers if they believe they have experienced discrimination by the agency or its staff?

_____

_____

_____

8. Does your agency or organization have an affirmative action program that is applied when hiring new staff? If yes, does the program achieve its purpose?

_____

_____

_____

9. Where on the cross-cultural continuum described by Cross (see Background and Context section) would you place your agency? Why?

_____

_____

_____

Diversity in Client Behavior: Situations to Discuss

Many factors influence the behavior and decisions of clients. One important set of factors, but certainly not the only one, is the client's cultural and ethnic background. Below is a list of situations that a social worker might encounter. Read each one carefully and answer each of the following questions about each situation.

A. What diverse beliefs, values, minority status, or customs are operating in this situation that might explain or clarify the client's behavior or choices?

B. How might these situations be misunderstood if you are not familiar with the beliefs and customs of the client?

C. What else would you need to know in order to be competent in this situation?

D. What individual family or cultural strengths might be identified in these situations?

1. A low-income couple with six children lives in a small and crowded house and have great difficulty financially. They choose to have additional children, which will strain the family even more financially.

    A. _____

    B. _____

    C. _____

    D. _____

2. A man who needs his job and wants to keep it did not report to work today. Instead, he drove 200 miles to be with a relative who had phoned him last night and requested his assistance.

    A. _____

    B. _____

    C. _____

    D. _____

3. Parents of two children refuse to allow them to participate in their school's sex education programs.

    A. _____

    B. _____

    C. _____

    D. _____

4. The family of a hospital patient moves into the hospital room and begins using cultural healing practices unknown to the medical staff.

    A. _____

    B. _____

    C. _____

    D. _____

5. A family with a child who is deaf refuses to let him learn sign language.

    A. _____

    B. _____

    C. _____

    D. _____

6. A family with conservative. religious views will only accept services from faith-based organizations.

    A. _____

    B. _____

C. _____

D. _____

7. A family chooses to home school their children and refuses to cooperate with governmental guide-lines regarding the education of their children.

   A. _____

   B. _____

   C. _____

   D. _____

8. During the first meeting with a social worker, a client asks the worker many personal questions about the worker's parents, children, marriage, religion, and family history.

   A. _____

   B. _____

   C. _____

   D. _____

9. A client who lives in near-poverty, and expresses a strong desire to obtain a job that pays a living wage, refuses to take a well-paying job in another city 100 miles away.

   A. _____

   B. _____

   C. _____

   D. _____

10. A woman whose husband restricts her movement, and verbally and physically abuses her, returns to live with her husband after seeking shelter for herself and her children in a domestic violence shelter.

   A. _____

   B. _____

   C. _____

   D. _____

11. An immigrant family who was robbed of several valuable possessions refuses to report the crime to the police.

   A. _____

   B. _____

   C. _____

   D. _____

12. An enrolled member of an American Indian tribe is in need of social services, but is reluctant to accept them from an agency that provides these services to individuals and families from many different backgrounds.

   A. _____

   B. _____

   C. _____

   D. _____

13. A family eligible for needed social services available on proof of citizenship chooses not to use these services.

   A. _____

   B. _____

C. _____

D. _____

14. An elderly woman who could benefit from mental health services declines them.

A. _____

B. _____

C. _____

D. _____

15. A person involved in a same-sex relationship is experiencing intimate violence at the hands of his or her partner, but declines to seek legal protection.

A. _____

B. _____

C. _____

D. _____

16. A student with a severe learning disability refuses university-provided accommodations, and is in danger of being placed on academic probation because her grade-point average is below the university requirement for good academic standing.

A. _____

B. _____

C. _____

D. _____

SUGGESTED LEARNING ACTIVITIES

- Attend cultural and religious celebrations and activities that are meaningful to many of the clients or consumers served by your agency (e.g., powwows, religious ceremonies, and gay pride events).

- Invite respected members of various ethnic and religious groups to explain how cultural and religious factors might influence clients' perceptions of the agency's programs and services and whether they would be inclined to use those services.

- Listen to music and read books and poetry by members of cultural or minority groups served by your agency.

- Visit agencies that specifically serve members of minority groups (e.g., refugee programs, women's centers, gay and lesbian community centers, and advocacy groups for persons with disabilities). Ask how their programs differ from yours.

- Seek special training designed to help human services personnel respond more effectively to diverse clients.

- Examine assessment tools used in your agency to determine if they are culture-bound or culturally inappropriate.

- In Sheafor and Horejsi (2008), read the section entitled "Applying Cultural Competence to Helping" (174–180).

- Seek opportunities for cultural immersion experiences.

- Read the novel *Every Good Boy Does Fine* (see bibliography), about a client's perspective on head injuries.

Log onto **www.mysocialworklab.com** and select the **Interactive Skill Module** videos from the left-hand menu. Answer the questions below. (*If you did not receive an access code to MySocialWorkLab with this text and wish to purchase access online, please visit* www.mysocialworklab.com.)

1. **Watch page 16 (Demonstrating Sensitivity to Cultural Context) in the school social work module.** What

NASW cultural competence standards are demonstrated by the social worker?

2. **Watch page 13 (Exploring Cultural Differences) in the group work module.** How can a social worker help a client deal with the challenges faced in intergenerational family cultural situations?

PRACTICE TEST

The following questions are similar in phrasing and content to those asked in social work licensing examinations. They should help you prepare to take the licensing examination in your state.

Diversity in Practice

1. The learned patterns of thought and behavior which are passed form generation to generation and which include values, beliefs, and customs is referred to as
   a. family of origin issues
   b. diversity
   c. ethnicity
   d. culture

Diversity in Practice

2. Evaluating a person negatively based on the group or category to which they belong
   a. is ethnocentrism
   b. is prejudice
   c. is Affirmative Action
   d. is privilege

Diversity in Practice

3. The NASW Code of Ethics tells social workers to avoid discrimination
   a. in practice
   b. by condoning it
   c. by facilitating it
   d. all of the above

Diversity in Practice

4. The belief that one's culture is superior to others, which may be unconscious, is

   a. ethnocentrism
   b. stereotyping
   c. discrimination
   d. equality

Diversity in Practice

5. The NASW cultural competency standards for social workers
   a. set a firm standard in each potential situation
   b. provide specific guidelines for individual interventions
   c. require lifelong commitment to increasing competency
   d. are in conflict with the NASW Code of Ethics

Diversity in Practice

6. The NASW cultural competency standards for organizations
   a. include evaluations that are standardized
   b. include mandatory cultural sensitivity training
   c. focus on service delivery and a diverse workplace
   d. are left to the individual organization

Diversity in Practice

7. The concept of human rights
   a. is separate from the NASW Code of Ethics in concept and values
   b. is in line with the NASW Code of Ethics in concept and values
   c. is restricted to global issues
   d. is the basis of U.S. laws

Professional Social Work

LEARNING GOALS FOR THIS CHAPTER

▸ To understand the purpose, mission, and nature of the social work profession

▸ To clarify how social work is similar to and different from other helping professions

▸ To understand the need to move from the role of student to the role of a professional

▸ To understand the expectations of the generalist social worker

CONNECTING CORE COMPETENCIES *in this chapter*

| Professional Identity | Ethical Practice | Critical Thinking | Diversity in Practice | Human Rights & Justice | Research Based Practice | Human Behavior | Policy Practice | Practice Contexts | Engage Assess Intervene Evaluate |

Social workers see themselves as professionals and they describe their occupation as a profession. As a social work student you are expected to behave in a professional manner during your practicum, but what exactly is a profession and what does professional behavior look like? How does one decide whether clients are being treated in a truly professional manner and receiving truly professional services? Does the presence of professionally trained social workers in an agency have an observable and positive effect on the nature and quality of the services received by clients?

Social work is one of many helping professions. Social workers often work closely with other helpers such as physicians, nurses, speech therapists, psychologists, substance abuse counselors, school counselors, and others. What do social workers do that is not done by the members of other helping professions? Is there anything unique or special about what social workers know or do? How is social work different?

BACKGROUND AND CONTEXT

All professions and all professionals ***profess*** to have special and unique knowledge and skills. They profess to understand certain phenomena better than those who do not have this special training. Because they profess to adhere to a code of ethical conduct, they expect to be trusted by their clients and by the public at large. They profess to be accountable for their decisions and actions. Professionals lay claim to a certain domain of activities. This is the basis for professional licensing and certification. It is important to know that the requirements for licensing and certification vary from state to state. From a legal perspective, professionals are responsible for providing their clients with a certain standard of care, and if they fail to do so, they may be sued for malpractice or professional negligence. Broadly speaking, a ***profession*** is an occupation that possesses certain characteristics:

Professional Identity

Based on the above characteristics, would social work be considered a profession?

- A unique body of knowledge and theories from which special skills and techniques are derived
- Methods of teaching this body of knowledge and skills to persons entering the profession
- Recognition by society that the members of the profession possess a special expertise
- Sanction by the community or state to perform certain activities
- Practitioners who share a distinct culture, specialized language or terminology, sense of purpose, identity, history, and set of values
- A set of professional values and a written code of ethics that guides practice activities
- A professional organization whose members are bound together by a common purpose
- Capacity and authority, usually by law, to regulate practice, including admitting new members
- A sense of "calling" to the profession by those entering it by virtue of their values, interests, or natural abilities

The social work profession uniquely assumes responsibility for promoting the social functioning of individuals, families, and communities at the micro, mezzo, and macro levels. This means that social workers not only provide services to individuals, families, and communities, but just as importantly work to implement social policies and promote societal conditions that will also support social functioning. The term ***social functioning*** refers, in general, to the social well-being of people and especially their capacity and opportunity to meet their basic needs such as food, shelter, safety, self-worth, and to satisfactorily perform their social roles such as spouse, parent, student, employee, and citizen.

Social work professionals focus primarily on the interactions or transactions between the individual and his or her social environment. That environment is composed of a multitude of units and systems such as family; support networks; neighborhood and community groups and organizations; workplace; and various legal, educational, health, and human services systems. This is often referred to as the ***person-in-environment focus*** of the social work profession. Social workers often focus on how well the social environment supports individuals and families, and what clients can do to enhance the social systems of which they are a part. A social worker will perform tasks and activities aimed at achieving these broad goals

- Enhancing the problem-solving and coping capacities of people
- Restoring and maintaining the social functioning of people
- Preventing the occurrence of serious personal and social problems
- Linking people with those systems and resources that can provide needed support, services, and opportunities
- Protecting the community from persons who consistently behave in ways that harm others
- Promoting humane and effective social policy and social services programs
- Planning, developing, and administering social agencies and social programs
- Promoting the effective and humane operation and administration of organizations and human services delivery systems that provide people with resources, services, and opportunities
- Protecting the most vulnerable members of society from destructive social influences
- Conducting research and developing and disseminating knowledge relevant to the practice of social work

Ethical Practice

Which core values of social work do you believe are most central to the work of your agency?

A profession can be viewed as an organized effort to actualize its core values. Social work is often described as a value-driven profession because so much of what a social worker does is guided by a particular set of core values. However, all professions are rooted in a particular set of values. For example, the medical profession values health and physical wellness and the education profession values learning and academic success. The physician strives to develop knowledge and methods that can be used to maintain and restore health, and the educator strives to develop knowledge and methods that facilitate learning.

Professional Identity

How can you learn to conduct yourself in accord with the standards of the social work profession?

The social work profession holds high standards for its members, including the demonstration of professional behavior. This is vital for you as a new social worker to understand, because adhering to these standards will help to ensure that clients receive the highest quality of services. Engaging in nonprofessional behavior puts its clients at risk, reduces the quality of services, undermines the public image of the profession, and may violate the profession's ethical principles. Although social work is a profession, social workers may or may not behave in a professional manner. Nonprofessional behavior leads to diminished quality of services and may also violate the NASW *Code of Ethics.* Sheafor and Horejsi (2006, 166) offer a comparison of professional and nonprofessional behavior in Table 13.1.

Most social workers are employed by some type of social agency or social welfare organization and often experience a push and pull between loyalty to

Table 13.1   Professional and Nonprofessional Behavior

Professional Behavior	Nonprofessional Behavior
1. Views social work as a calling and a lifetime commitment to certain values actions.	1. Views social work simply as a job that can be easily abandoned if something better comes along.
2. Bases practice on a body of knowledge and research findings that have been learned through formal education and training.	2. Bases practice on personal opinions or on agency rules and regulations.
3. Makes decisions primarily on the basis of facts, analysis, and critical thinking.	3. Makes decisions primarily on the basis of personal feelings and traditions.
4. Develops relationships with clients that are purposeful and goal directed; does not expect to meet own emotional needs within these relationships.	4. Develops relationships with clients that are perfunctory or resemble friendships; expects to meet own emotional needs within these relationships.
5. Considers client's well-being and needs to be of primary concern.	5. Considers own well-being and needs to be of primary concern.
6. Adheres to the principles of good practice, regardless of other pressures.	6. Allows political and fiscal pressures to dictate decisions and actions.
7. Uses the professions' *Code of Ethics.*	7. Uses only personal moral judgments and opinions to address ethical concerns.
8. Upgrades knowledge and skills continually so that services to clients can be improved.	8. Learns only what is required to keep the job.
9. Takes responsibility for creating new knowledge and sharing it with peers.	9. Does not see self as responsible for the development of new knowledge.
10. Assumes personal responsibility for examining the quality of services provided and for working to make agency, program, or policy changes that will improve services to the client.	10. Is concerned only about doing the job as assigned or described by others; does not see self as responsible for agency, policy, or program changes.
11. Exercises self-discipline; keeps own emotions under control.	11. Lacks self-discipline; expresses emotions in a thoughtless and hurtful manner.
12. Expects and invites review of own performance by peers.	12. Avoids peer review of own performance.
13. Keeps accurate and complete records of practice decisions and actions.	13. Avoids record-keeping.

Source: Sheafor, Bradford, and Charles Horejsi. *Techniques and Guidelines for Social Work Practice.* 8ed. Boston: Allyn and Bacon, 2008. Copyright © 2000 by Pearson Education. Reprinted by permission of the publisher.

Critical Thinking

What learning experiences can you design for yourself that will help you make the transition from student to professional?

their organization and its managers and loyalty to the social work profession and its values and principles. They believe in the core values and mission of the organization, but find the core values of the social work profession to be more important to them if they are ever in conflict. Much of what a social worker does is shaped—and sometimes driven—by agency policy. For this reason, social workers must be attentive to the nature and purpose of their agency's policies and how these impact clients. From the perspective of professional social work, an agency policy should have the following characteristics:

- ▶ It promotes the well-being of clients and of the community as a whole.
- ▶ It is respectful and fair to those most directly affected by the policy.
- ▶ It serves to empower clients and it recognizes and builds on their strengths.
- ▶ It promotes social and economic justice, directly or indirectly.
- ▶ It is consistent with the core values and principles found in the NASW *Code of Ethics.*
- ▶ It reflects the principle of effective social work based on current knowledge and research findings.
- ▶ It holds social workers and other agency employees accountable for the work they perform and the services they provide.
- ▶ It is clearly written, realistic, and consistent with relevant legal codes and regulations.

GUIDANCE AND DIRECTION

A big challenge you will face in your practicum, but hopefully one you will take on enthusiastically, is making the transition from the status of student to the role and expectations of a professional social worker. As a student in the classroom, you were allowed to listen without responding, or to learn about theory without having to apply it. In the practicum, all that changes. Consider how the roles of student and social worker differ, as shown in Table 13.2.

Table 13.2   Student versus Social Worker Role

Student Role	Social Worker Role
Learns passively	Learns actively and applies learning
Engages in theoretical discussions and hypothetical decisions	Applies theory to real clients
Has occasional absences from class to practicum without consequence to self or client	Needs to be fully present to ensure quality
Defers to others in decision-making and intervention	Takes initiative in developing and implementing interventions
Assumes partial responsibility	Assumes full responsibility
Bases work on theory and academic preparation	Bases work on academic preparation as well as accumulated experience and practice wisdom
May take client feedback personally and react emotionally	Sees client feedback as crucial to professional growth

Engage Assess Intervene Evaluate

In what circumstances might a social worker be expected to simultaneously intervene at the micro and macro levels?

As you move from the role of student to professional, evaluate yourself honestly in terms of where you are on the continuum between them. Push yourself to leave a passive and partial student role behind, choosing to do whatever it takes to assume the roles and responsibilities of a professional. Do not wait until your first social work position to make this transition. Your future clients deserve the highest level of professionalism you can offer now when you are a student as much as they will when you have finished your education and training.

A primary purpose of the practicum experience is to help you develop a professional identity as a social worker. To possess this identity means that you have a clear understanding of the purpose of the profession, your roles and responsibilities as a social worker, the profession's core values and ethical guidelines, and the skills and knowledge needed to perform social work tasks and activities. Most students begin developing a professional identity by observing other social workers and reflecting on their behavior, decisions, and attitudes.

Read the job description for social workers in your agency, and determine if it is consistent with the profession's stated purposes, values, and practice roles. Watch for variation between how social workers define their own roles and responsibilities and how their roles may be defined by administrators or funding sources. Ask your field instructor or other social workers how they attempt to meet the expectations of high-level administrators and fiscal managers while

Food for Thought

Social justice work challenges us to examine the social construction of reality, that is, the ways we use our cultural capacities to give **meaning** to social experience. It guides us to look at the **context** of social problems and question relations of **power**, domination and inequality that shape the way knowledge of the world is produced and whose view counts. It forces us to recognize the importance of **history** and a historical perspective to provide a window into how definitions of social problems and the structuring and shaping of institutions and individuals are time specific and contextually imbedded. Finally, social justice work opens up the **possibility** for new ways of looking at and thinking about programs, policies, and practices, and to envision the people with whom we work and ourselves as active participants in social transformation toward a more just world (Finn and Jacobson, 2003, 32).

• • •

. . . [T]oday's social workers are the heirs of a powerful tradition of social action (Haynes and Mickelson, 2000, 2).

• • •

. . . [T]he "space" occupied by social work is defined, to a considerable degree, by *its position in*

the interface between the mainstream and marginal in society. It can be no surprise, therefore, that social work involves those who are poorest, most disadvantaged and marginalised. It is the nature of social work that this should be so (Sheppard, 2006, 19).

• • •

. . . [S]ocial work is a *political* activity; that is, it operates within the context of sets of power relations—the power of law and the state, the power inherent in social divisions such as class, race and gender, and the micro-level power of personal interactions. Indeed, power can be seen to operate at all three levels, personal, cultural and structural. . . . Also, many of the problems social workers tackle have their roots in the abuse of power (Thompson, 2001, 162).

• • •

Is social work *art?* To what extent does it rely on *reflection?* Is social work, alternatively, a *science?* If so, how adequate is the notion of *evidence-based practice?* On the other hand, is it largely a tool of management—social work being a simple technical activity, which involves a series of relatively straightforward *competencies?* (Sheppard, 2006, 13).

still adhering to the mission and purpose of the profession and fulfilling their obligations to their clients.

You will begin to notice how the values, knowledge base, and approach of the social work professional are different from those of other helping professionals such as clinical psychologists, nurses, school counselors, physicians, occupational therapists, and vocational counselors. The uniqueness of the social work profession will become apparent if you truly understand the profession's core values and ethical principles, as well as the concept of social functioning. The uniqueness of social work lies in its commitment to the overall social functioning of people as well as its commitment to working for social change and social justice. However, contrary to the beliefs of many social work students, social work is not unique because it pays attention to the "whole person," the client's environment, and the ecological perspective. These are ideas also commonly discussed in textbooks for nursing, education, counseling, and occupational therapy. The distinctive identity of social work comes from its commitment to both enhancing the social functioning of clients and to creating social environments, conditions, and social policies that promote positive social functioning.

You are likely to encounter stereotypes and misconceptions about social workers and the social work profession, just as you would for other professions, and this will be frustrating. You may need to inform others about the profession's real purposes and values, as well as about the level of education required for professional social work. You might also ask yourself where these perceptions of social work originated, and consider whether some social workers may speak or behave in ways that perpetuate the stereotypes.

Negative images of the profession are often based on limited information about social work and sometimes on experiences with ineffective or unethical social workers. They could also be based on negative experiences with persons who are assumed to be social workers, but who do not have a degree in social work. Give careful thought to whether social workers are recognized and respected as true professionals. Consider why social workers in certain agencies are viewed as professionals, whereas in other agencies they are not treated as professionals. Do what you can to enhance the image of the profession by purposefully using the title social worker to describe your work, by committing to practicing in the most competent and ethical manner possible, and by taking opportunities to inform the public about the profession.

Finally, you will probably find it helpful to remember that for all the emphasis on social work knowledge, theory, and research, you will not be effective if you do not pay close attention to what many consider the "art" of social work. As Sheafor and Horejsi (2008, 33–41) note, the "social worker as artist" has several components:

What is the importance of both the art and science of practice? What are the limitations of each alone?

What responsibility do you have to address misconceptions about the social work profession?

- **Compassion and courage.** You will daily confront the pain of others, and must join with them in a compassionate manner. You must also develop the inner strength to repeatedly face human suffering and frustration without being consumed by it.
- **Professional relationship.** Your most fundamental tool in practice is the capacity to build meaningful and productive professional relationships, which is rooted in your capacity for demonstrating empathy, genuineness, and nonpossessive warmth.
- **Creativity.** You must be innovative, imaginative, flexible, and persistent as you work to overcome barriers to change.

- **Hopefulness and energy.** You will need to believe in the basic goodness and ability of people, to continue working without becoming discouraged, and to bounce back from failures and mistakes.
- **Judgment.** You will need to develop sound judgment, critical thinking skills, thoughtful decision-making abilities, and the ability to reflect on and learn from successes and failures.
- **Personal values.** Your personal values must be compatible with the core values of social work, including respect for basic rights, a sense of social responsibility, commitment to individual freedom, and support for self-determination.
- **Professional style.** Because you are the instrument of change in practice, you will need to develop your own professional style, which is a combination of professional knowledge and your own personality and personal gifts.

The social worker's professional identity is formed as he or she blends these artistic elements with the science of the profession. Sheafor and Horejsi (2008) explain:

[T]he social worker must combine his or her personal qualities, creative abilities, and social concern with the profession's knowledge in order to help clients enhance their social functioning or prevent social problems from developing. Each person has unique personal qualities that represent the artistic component of social work practice. Professional education cannot teach these artistic features, although it can help the learner identify such strengths and develop the ability to focus on and apply them in work with clients. Professional education can also assist the learner in developing a beginning understanding of the knowledge (or science) that is necessary for effective practice. This merging and blending of one's art and the profession's science is initiated in social work education programs, but it is a lifelong activity, as social work knowledge is constantly expanding and the worker is being continually changed by life experiences. (34)

The Image and Impact of Social Work: A Workbook Activity

It is important to examine the impact of the profession's values, ethical code, practice principles, and knowledge base on the behavior and performance of the social workers in your practicum agency. In light of this, respond to the following questions.

1. Is the NASW *Code of Ethics* discussed by the social workers in your practicum agency?

   _____

2. Does the NASW *Code of Ethics* appear to have a significant impact on decision making and practices within your practicum agency? If yes, in what ways? If no, why not?

   _____

   _____

   _____

3. To what extent and in what ways, if any, do conflicts between personal and professional values, political pressures, or a push to hold down operating costs keep agency staff from following principles of good social work practice and adhering to basic principles of the NASW *Code of Ethics?*

   _____

   _____

   _____

4. Which of the core values of social work are most apparent in your agency? Which are most lacking?

   _____

   _____

   _____

5. Which of the core social work values are most consistent with your own personal values?

   _____

   _____

   _____

6. Which of the following social work roles are most often assumed by the social workers in your agency?

   _____ Broker of services

   _____ Case manager   _____ Educator/trainer

   _____ Advocate   _____ Community organizer

   _____ Social activist   _____ Social policy analyst

   _____ Counselor/therapist   _____ Research/program evaluator

   _____ Collaborator/networker   _____ Administrator/manager/supervisor

_____ Group leader/facilitator   _____ Other (specify)
_____ Program planner

_____

_____

7. About what percentage of the social workers in your agency are members of NASW?

_____

_____

8. What are the requirements for obtaining and retaining a social work license in your state at the BSW and MSW levels (e.g., degree required, examination, years of experience, and hours of supervised practice)?

_____

_____

_____

9. About what percentage of the social workers in your agency have a social work license?

_____

10. What governmental body issues social work licenses and receives complaints about the practice of social workers?

_____

_____

11. Does your agency require a social work degree (BSW or MSW) as preparation for certain positions or jobs? If yes, for what jobs?

_____

_____

12. What professional journals do the social workers in your agency read on a regular basis?

_____

_____

13. What is the public image of social workers in your community? What forces and experiences have shaped this image?

_____

_____

14. What agency policies, procedures, and expectations reinforce and encourage social work professionalism within your agency (e.g., continuing education is expected and rewarded, workers are expected to take personal responsibility for decisions and actions, constant attention is given to professional ethics)?

_____

_____

_____

15. What, if any, agency policies, procedures, and behavioral norms tend to undermine and discourage social work professionalism within your agency (e.g., lack of sanctions for sloppy work, political concerns driving decision making, or bureaucratic regulations taking precedence over individual client needs)?

_____

_____

_____

16. What other professionals do you work with in your agency? How do you perceive your role and code of ethics to be similar to or different from theirs?

_____

_____

_____

SUGGESTED LEARNING ACTIVITIES

- Attend local chapter meetings of NASW or the meetings of other social work–related professional organizations and decide what issues are of greatest concern to the social workers in your community.

- Review announcements of social work conferences and workshops to determine what topics are of interest to social workers.

- Watch for media portrayals of social workers in newspapers, magazines, on television, or on the Internet to determine how social work is described and whether it is usually presented in a positive or negative light.

- Join the National Association of Social Workers as a student member, which will allow you to keep abreast of professional social work issues and programs and support its work

- In Sheafor and Horejsi (2008), read and discuss the section entitled "Improving the Social Work Image" (616–618).

- Investigate a variety of social work membership organizations, such as Association for Community Organization and Administration, the National Association of Black Social Workers, the Association of Oncology Social Workers, the National Association of Puerto Rican/Hispanic Social Workers, the Clinical Social Work Federation, the National Indian Child Welfare Association, the Rural Social Work Caucus, the Society for Spirituality in Social Work Practice, the North American Association of Christians in Social Work, International Federation of Social Workers, and the Social Welfare Action Alliance.

Succeed with PEARSON mysocialworklab

Log onto **www.mysocialworklab.com** and select the **Career Exploration** videos from the left-hand menu. Answer the questions below. (*If you did not receive an access code to* **MySocialWorkLab** *with this text and wish to purchase access online, please visit* www.mysocialworklab.com.)

1. **Watch question 15 in the interview with Beth Harmon.** What rewards do you expect to have as a social worker? How will you balance the rewards with the potential disappointments?

2. **Watch the interview with Christine Mitchell.** Were the reasons you chose social work as a profession similar to those that motivated Christine to choose social work?

PRACTICE TEST

The following questions are similar in phrasing and content to those asked in social work licensing examinations. They should help you prepare to take the licensing examination in your state.

Professional Identity

1. A body of knowledge, theory base, public sanction, code of ethics, and professional regulation are the main characteristics of
   a. a profession
   b. a minority group
   c. a social work school
   d. a licensing body

2. The NASW definition of social work includes an emphasis on
   e. clinical practice
   f. both micro and macro level practice
   g. political action
   h. continuing education

3. The unique focus of social work is on
   a. psychological aspects of life
   b. spiritual aspects of life
   c. social functioning of individuals, families, and groups
   d. ethical standards for practice

4. Service, social justice, dignity and worth of the person, importance of human relationships, integrity, and competence are
   a. continuing education standards
   b. the core principles of the profession
   c. to be measured in each intervention
   d. are the human rights values on which the profession is based

5. The social worker's duty to clients as the highest value is an example of
   a. a professional orientation to practice
   b. a social worker's individual moral code
   c. licensing requirements
   d. state law

6. The practice of minimizing control over clients' lives and selecting appropriate placements is:
   a. the concept of self-determination
   b. the concept of safety
   c. the concept of professionalism
   d. the concept of using the least restrictive environment

7. Professional social workers are held accountable ethically and clinically through
   a. the use of standardized assessment tools
   b. the use of evidence-based practice
   c. the use of standardized evaluation tools
   d. the use of the use of individualized treatment plans

Answers

1) a 2) b 3) c 4) d 5) a 6) d 7) b

Social Work Ethics

LEARNING GOALS FOR THIS CHAPTER

▶ To apply the NASW *Code of Ethics* to practicum

▶ To learn how the NASW *Code of Ethics* guides practice in your agency

▶ To identify the ethical questions and dilemmas that arise most frequently in your practicum setting

▶ To identify and resolve ethical dilemmas

▶ To become aware of how your own moral standards may differ from those of the NASW *Code of Ethics*

CONNECTING CORE COMPETENCIES *in this chapter*

| Professional Identity | Ethical Practice | Critical Thinking | Diversity in Practice | Human Rights & Justice | Research Based Practice | Human Behavior | Policy Practice | Practice Contexts | Engage Assess Intervene Evaluate |

Ethical Practice

How can you recognize and deal professionally with the ethical questions and dilemmas in your practicum?

Every day, social workers make decisions and take actions based on ethical principles. These principles have a profound and far-reaching impact on practice. They also have a significant impact on a student's social work practicum. Prior to beginning your social work practicum, you have studied the NASW *Code of Ethics* and devoted classroom time to the discussion of ethical questions and issues. Up to this point, the topic of professional ethics may have seemed rather abstract, but in your practicum you will meet these questions and dilemmas face to face.

This chapter briefly reviews the nature of professional values and ethics, discusses the content of the NASW *Code of Ethics,* and offers guidance on identifying ethical issues and resolving ethical dilemmas. The workbook activity will heighten your awareness of ethical concerns within your practicum setting.

BACKGROUND AND CONTEXT

Engage Assess Intervene Evaluate

In what ways might a social worker's responsibilities to clients conflict with his or her responsibilities to organizations or to society at large?

Each profession has a code of ethics that provides an ethical base for practice. These codes usually focus on professionals' responsibilities to those they serve, to the organizations for which they work, and to society at large. This is true for the NASW *Code of Ethics,* which you will be asked to apply daily in your practicum. In regard to an understanding of ethics, Ruggiero (1992) explains:

> Ethics is the study of right and wrong conduct. . . . The focus of ethics is moral situations—that is, those situations in which there is a choice of behavior involving human values. [Values] are those qualities that are regarded as good and desirable. (4–5)

Food for Thought

Social workers cannot be non-judgmental and they should not attempt to be. They are merchants of morality and should acknowledge this fact openly (Pilseker, 1978, 55).

• • •

In some ways, it may be helpful to think of ethics as a continuum, where the potential choices and actions are arranged on a spectrum ranging from highly unethical to highly ethical or from ethically unwise to ethically sound. Where your choice falls on that continuum may depend on the factors surrounding the case, or the context, and may depend on your own level of comfort with your options. As such there may be several right answers, but finding them requires a systematic method for addressing the "it depends," and this is where ethical decision-making models come into play (Strom-Gottfried, 2007, 26).

• • •

A moral dilemma exists whenever the conflicting obligations, ideals, and consequences are so very nearly equal in their importance that we feel we cannot

choose among them, even though we must. . . . We can never be completely comfortable in dealing with such dilemmas, but it is a consolation and source of confidence to remind ourselves from time to time that the frustration we experience with them is not a sign of incapacity on our part but rather is a reflection of the complex nature of moral discourse (Ruggiero, 2008, 125).

• • •

In the classroom, topics of values, ethics, and the law are often esoteric, philosophical, pedantic, distant, attenuated, and daunting. . . . In your internship, however, values, ethics, and the law are quite different. The dusty and distant topics actually come to life and play an active role. In your internship you will find that issues of values, ethics, and the law are exciting and something you will encounter fairly regularly (Thomlison and Corcoran, 2008, 59).

• • •

A code of ethics is a map of the minefield of practice (Payne 2007, 12).

The NASW *Code of Ethics* clarifies the profession's values, classifies professional responsibilities to a variety of stakeholders, sets standards for professional behavior, and offers to guidelines to measure ethical and unethical behavior. The term **ethical dilemma** describes a situation in which the social worker has two or more ethical obligations (e.g., to take action to protect the client from imminent harm and also to protect the client's right to privacy) but cannot adhere to one principle without violating another because of their mutually exclusive nature. Rather than providing clear-cut guidance on each dilemma, the *Code of Ethics* provides general principles that the social worker uses to make ethical decisions.

GUIDANCE AND DIRECTION

Engage Assess
Intervene Evaluate

In what ways do these ethical competencies apply to the interventions in which you are involved with your clients?

The standards for ethical conduct by social workers may be described as **ethical competencies** (The University of Montana School of Social Work, 2008, 10–11).

- The ethical social worker understands definitions of ethics and values, both personal and professional.
- The ethical social worker becomes familiar with the National Association of Social Workers *Code of Ethics,* including its purposes, uses, and limitations.
- The ethical social worker develops the ability to identify ethical issues and situations.
- The ethical social worker develops and uses a model of ethical decision making.
- The ethical social worker develops the ability to examine, explore, and resolve ethical dilemmas.
- The ethical social worker understands connections between ethical and legal issues in practice.
- The ethical social worker applies National Association of Social Workers *Code of Ethics* to all levels of practice.
- The ethical social worker understands potential ethical violations and their consequences.
- The ethical social worker applies critical thinking skills to ethics in practice.
- The ethical social worker understands the importance of supervision and continuing education.

Inquire about the agency's process or procedures for resolving ethical issues and dilemmas. These procedures may be written or informal. Your agency may use ethics committees, staff discussions, and outside legal and ethics consultations to help staff members make difficult decisions. Observe and participate in such meetings as often as possible, because this will help you develop awareness of and skill in identifying and resolving ethical dilemmas.

It is very likely that you will observe disagreements over situations involving ethics. Each situation is unique to some degree, and there is seldom only one right way to deal with it. Over time, you will become more comfortable with this uncertainty and be better able to sort out the competing values and potential consequences of each decision.

When you encounter an ethical dilemma, consider the guidelines offered by Sheafor and Horejsi (2008, 168–169) and begin by seeking answers to questions such as the following:

- Who is your primary client (i.e., usually the person, group, or organization that requested the social worker's services and expects to benefit from them)?

⬧ What aspects of the agency's activity or worker's roles and duties give rise to the dilemma (e.g., legal mandates, job requirements, agency policy, questions of efficient use of resources, possible harm caused by an intervention)?

⬧ Who can or should resolve this dilemma? Is it rightfully a decision to be made by the client? Other family members? The worker? The agency administrator?

⬧ For each decision possible, what are the short-term and long-term consequences for the client, family, worker, agency, community, and so on?

⬧ Who stands to gain and who stands to lose from each possible choice or action? Are those who stand to gain or lose of equal or of unequal power (e.g., child vs. adult)? Do those who are most vulnerable or those with little power require special consideration?

⬧ When harm to someone cannot be avoided, what decision will cause the least harm or a type of harm with fewest long-term consequences? Who of those that might be harmed is least able to recover from the harm?

⬧ Will a particular resolution to this dilemma set an undesirable precedent for future decision making concerning other clients?

⬧ What ethical principles and obligations apply in this situation?

⬧ Which, if any, ethical principles are in conflict in this situation and therefore create an ethical dilemma?

⬧ In this situation, are certain ethical obligations more important than others are?

It is likely that you will encounter some very troublesome situations in which all available choices or options are to some degree harmful and destructive to your client and other people. In such cases you must decide which option is the least harmful. Essentially, you are forced to choose the lesser of two or more evils. Although this is hard for even the seasoned social worker, it is a reality you will learn how to address.

In order to function effectively as a social worker, you must be able to distinguish between your values and morals and those of the client. As a general principle, you should not impose your values and beliefs on the client. However, this is a challenging principle of practice because the social work profession and social agencies are built on and represent a set of values and beliefs about what is good for people and desirable in human relationships. Moreover, some clients engage in behaviors that are clearly wrong and a danger to themselves and others (e.g., assault, rape, robbery, child neglect). In such situations, attempting to be value-free or value-neutral can be extremely dangerous, irresponsible, and possibly unethical.

You may find that your personal moral code conflicts with the values of your clients, your field instructor, your agency, or even the NASW *Code of Ethics.* When you encounter such conflicts, do not ignore them. They are important questions and dilemmas that must be faced honestly and squarely. You will need to decide when you can and cannot suspend your personal moral code.

There may be times when you conclude that your agency violates certain ethical principles or violates the rights of certain clients. If this occurs, discuss your concerns with your field instructor or faculty supervisor in order to sort out the issues and determine whether an ethical principle is being violated.

In general, the ethical mistakes made by students tend to be in the following areas of ethical conduct:

⬧ ***Violating client autonomy and self-determination.*** All clients should be given autonomy in life choices unless they are harmful to others. Be prepared to accept your clients' choices, even when you disagree with them.

Critical Thinking

Who can you ask to help you sort through ethical decisions and ethical dilemmas?

Human Rights & Justice

How will you balance the social work values of client self-determination and the protection of vulnerable populations?

Policy Practice

What laws and social policies regulate the ethical decisions of social workers in your agency?

- *Violating client confidentiality and privacy.* Do not release information regarding your clients without their consent, or reveal their identity by carelessness in casual conversation or careless documentation.
- *Violating client right to information and informed consent.* Do not withhold information that clients are entitled to have. Keep fully informed of decisions that will have a significant impact on their situation.
- *Violating client right to competent services.* Do not practice beyond your ability level. When a situation calls for skills that you do not possess, consult your supervisor and refer to someone who can provide the service.
- *Entering into dual relationships.* Maintain a professional relationship with your clients. Never become romantically involved with a client or enter into a buying, selling, lending, or renting agreement with a client.

An ethical area that may be confusing for you is the limits to client confidentiality. Clients have a right to privacy. However, this right is not absolute; there are limits and exceptions to a client's right to confidentiality. You may need to release client information, without your client's permission, when your client is abusing another person, is planning or has committed a serious and dangerous illegal act that places others in danger, or is threatening harm to himself or herself or to another person. Confidentiality also may not apply when you receive a court order requiring you to release client information, or when a contract requires you to share information with a third party, or when your client is a minor.

Be certain that you understand the federal and state laws that apply to confidentiality as well as related agency policy on this matter. Make sure that you understand the concept of *privileged communication,* which refers to the principle that clients can expect that their social worker cannot or will not share information without their consent.

Values, Ethics, and Your Practicum: A Workbook Activity

1. What two or three ethical concerns or dilemmas are most frequently encountered in your practicum setting, according to your field instructor?

    _____

    _____

    _____

2. How do the social workers in your agency deal with ethical questions and resolve ethical dilemmas (e.g., discussions at a staff meeting, presentations to an ethics committee, consultations with experts)?

    _____

    _____

    _____

3. To what degree and in what way does the NASW *Code of Ethics* influence the decisions and behavior of the social workers employed by your agency (e.g., is the *Code of Ethics* referred to during case conferences and staff meetings and do the social workers have a copy of the *Code of Ethics* in their office)?

    _____

    _____

    _____

4. Does your agency have its own code of ethics or a code of conduct for its employees? If yes, how is it similar to and different from the NASW *Code of Ethics*?

    _____

    _____

    _____

5. Are there specific items or sections in the NASW *Code of Ethics* that are particularly difficult to follow in your agency? If yes, what are they and why are they difficult to follow?

    _____

    _____

    _____

6. Does your agency have policies that, in your opinion, are in violation of the NASW *Code of Ethics*? If yes, describe how these policies are in conflict with specific provisions of the NASW *Code of Ethics*.

    _____

    _____

    _____

7. How does your agency handle reports of ethics violations on the part of its staff (e.g., written incident reports, temporary suspensions of staff, formal investigations, grievance policies, reports to state licensing bodies)?

_____

_____

_____

8. Within the past five years, have any agency social workers or other agency personnel been dismissed or reprimanded for ethics violations? If so, what was the nature and type of misconduct?

_____

_____

_____

9. What ethical principles in the NASW *Code of Ethics* do you feel most strongly about? Why?

_____

_____

_____

10. Does your agency have policies that are in conflict with your personal moral code? If yes, how will you handle or resolve these conflicts?

_____

_____

_____

11. Are there statements or sections in the NASW *Code of Ethics* that are in conflict with your personal moral and ethical standards? If yes, how you will attempt to resolve this conflict?

_____

_____

_____

12. What is the name of the agency in your state that is responsible for handling formal complaints about ethics violations by licensed social workers? What process is used to investigate possible ethics violations?

_____

_____

_____

13. What are the possible sanctions in your state for social workers who commit ethics violations (e.g., loss of license, civil action for monetary damages, criminal prosecution, sanctions by the NASW)?

_____

_____

_____

SUGGESTED LEARNING ACTIVITIES

▶ Read and study the NASW *Code of Ethics.* It can be downloaded from the NASW's web site (http://www.naswdc.org).

▶ If members of other professions (e.g., psychologists, nurses, or teachers) work in your practicum setting, secure a copy of their profession's code of ethics and compare it to the NASW *Code of Ethics.*

▶ Interview experienced social workers and ask them to describe the ethical issues they most often encounter and the issues that are especially difficult for them to resolve.

▶ Review your agency's policy manual and identify policy principles that are very similar to the NASW *Code of Ethics.* Identify policies that appear to be in opposition to the *Code of Ethics.*

▶ In Sheafor and Horejsi (2008), read the section entitled "Making Ethical Decisions" (168–173).

Succeed with **mysocialworklab**

Log onto **www.mysocialworklab.com** and select the **Interactive Skill Module** videos from the left-hand menu. Answer the questions below. (*If you did not receive an access code to* **MySocialWorkLab** *with this text and wish to purchase access online, please visit* www.mysocialworklab.com.)

1. **Watch page 12 (Exploring Confidentiality) in the school social work module.** What is the basis for the great emphasis placed on confidentiality in social work?

2. **Watch page 19 (Clarifying the Role of the Agency) in the child welfare module.** Upon what values about the well-being of children and families is the work of child protective services based?

PRACTICE TEST

The following questions are similar in phrasing and content to those asked in social work licensing examinations. They should help you prepare to take the licensing examination in your state.

Ethical Practice

1. A practice situation in which two ethical standards are in conflict is
   a. a values conflict
   b. an ethical dilemma
   c. an ethical violation
   d. malpractice

2. Social workers who find their moral code in conflict with legal codes should
   a. consult a supervisor for help in reconciling the conflict
   b. consult with an attorney for help in reconciling the conflict
   c. consult with a spiritual advisor for help in reconciling the conflict
   d. all of the above

3. The NASW Code of Ethics provides:
   a. a clear guide for every potential ethical situation or conflict
   b. a general guideline of ethical principles that professionals use to make decisions
   c. a standard for client behavior
   d. a description of legal standards for social work

4. The clarification of who the primary client is in a potential intervention is helpful
   a. in resolving ethical dilemmas
   b. in setting ethical standards for practice
   c. in abiding by state laws regulating practice
   d. in understanding clients' points of view

5. Weighing potential consequences and harm to parties involved in an intervention
   a. is required by state law
   b. is required by agency policy
   c. is helpful in resolving ethical dilemmas
   d. is required by client bills of rights

6. An ethical dilemma is a situation in which
   a. choosing one value means that another value will be violated
   b. clients are empowered to make the choices about their lives
   c. legal codes take precedence over ethical codes
   d. social workers are empowered to make choices about clients' lives

7. Violations of professional ethics can lead to
   a. legal sanctions
   b. licensing sanctions
   c. agency sanctions
   d. all of the above

Legal Concerns

LEARNING GOALS FOR THIS CHAPTER

▶ To become familiar with the specific state and federal statutes and codes relevant to your practicum setting and its programs and services

▶ To become familiar with the legal terminology frequently used within your practicum setting

▶ To become familiar with the laws affecting and regulating your agency and its services

▶ To become aware of the types of practice situations that could give rise to an allegation of wrongdoing or professional negligence

▶ To become aware of precautionary steps that may reduce the chances of being named in a malpractice suit

CONNECTING CORE COMPETENCIES *in this chapter*

Professional Identity	Ethical Practice	Critical Thinking	Diversity in Practice	Human Rights & Justice	Research Based Practice	Human Behavior	Policy Practice	Practice Contexts	Engage Assess Intervene Evaluate

Policy
Practice

Watch for opportunities
to learn about the laws
and social policies that
regulate social work
practice in your agency
and your state.

Social work, like all professions, is guided and impacted greatly by the law. Every social services agency and program is shaped and guided by specific codes or legal considerations. Some agencies were formed in response to a law requiring states or the federal government to provide specific programs and services. In some agencies, a client's eligibility for services is defined by law. In many instances, a social worker's actions are dictated by law, as in the case of mandated reporting of child abuse. Many social workers are licensed by state law and must conform their practice to the provisions of that law and its provisions.

As a social work practicum student, you must understand the legal context of your professional practice. You must be alert to the actions that may violate the law and to the types of situations that might give rise to a lawsuit against an agency, a professional social worker, and even a social work student.

BACKGROUND AND CONTEXT

There are three broad categories of laws that guide, direct, and sometimes mandate the actions of social workers and agencies:

1. ***Laws regulating services or actions related to a specific client.*** Such laws may determine whether a client is eligible to receive a certain service or benefit, whether a specific client can be forced to accept intervention (e.g., involuntary hospitalization), or whether a particular family situation can be defined as suspected child or elder abuse or neglect that must be reported to the authorities.

2. ***Laws regulating a field of practice or type of social services program.*** Specific social work arenas may have laws that affect the clients served by agencies providing services in this arena. For example, if an agency provides service to youth, many of its policies and procedures for dealing with young clients will be shaped by laws related to the notification of parents regarding services to be provided to their children. In hospitals, laws related to informed consent, release of patient records, and durable power of attorney for health care are daily concerns to a medical social worker. Social workers who provide services to refugees and immigrants must understand laws relating to refugee and immigration status.

3. ***Laws regulating the professional practice of social work.*** Laws guiding professional social work practice dictate how social workers must conduct themselves in order to practice competently. These laws may deal with matters such as confidentiality, privileged communication, informed consent, duties to clients, duty to warn, and requirements for obtaining a social work license. They set standards for professional conduct, provide procedures for dealing with allegations of social work misconduct, and specify disciplinary actions against social workers who violate laws or the ethics of the profession.

Because laws directly impact social workers and clients, social workers must acquire a basic understanding of the laws and legal procedures that most directly impact their practice setting and clients served. In addition, they must become familiar with specific laws related to their practice roles, duties, and job description. For example, if a social worker functions as a case manager, he or she must be conversant in the laws relating to sharing of confidential information with other agencies and the eligibility requirements for services needed by clients.

Social workers must be familiar with the court system and know proper conduct when testifying in court. Practitioners in the fields of child welfare and in probation and parole may testify in court on at least a weekly basis. However, all social workers, regardless of field of practice or agency setting, can expect to be occasional witnesses in court proceedings.

Practitioners and social work students must operate on the assumption that any of their professional records, case notes, reports, and correspondence may eventually become the target of a subpoena, gathered and reviewed by attorneys, and read in court. They need to be thoughtful and cautious about what they put into a written record and how they write it, for at some point they may be asked to explain and defend their statements.

A growing number of social workers are being sued for malpractice. This possibility must be considered daily, even as a practicum student. Malpractice and professional negligence fall under a category of law known as tort law. A **tort** is a private or civil wrong or injury that results from actions other than the breach of a formal legal contract and the commission of a crime.

The person who alleges the negligence and brings a malpractice lawsuit against a social worker or agency is termed the **plaintiff.** In this instance, the social worker or agency would be termed the **defendant.**

In order for the plaintiff (e.g., the social worker's client or former client) to be successful in this type of lawsuit, the plaintiff's attorney must prove four points:

1. The social worker had a professional obligation or duty to provide the plaintiff with a certain level of service, a certain standard of care, or a certain manner of professional conduct.

2. The social worker was negligent or derelict in his or her professional role because he or she did not live up to this recognized obligation or duty, standard of care, or expected professional conduct.

3. The plaintiff suffered injury or harm (e.g., physical, mental, emotional, or financial) as a result of what the social worker did (act) or did not do (omission) and this act or omission had a foreseeable harmful consequence for the plaintiff.

4. The social worker's act or omission was a direct or proximate cause of the harm experienced by the plaintiff.

Sheafor and Horejsi (2008) explain how the actions of social workers are judged:

Whether a breach of duty has occurred is determined by measuring the allegedly harmful act or omission against published standards of practice, agency policy, and the performance of social workers in similar settings. The client's injury must be one that would not have occurred had it not been for the social worker's negligence. Despite this traditional *proximate cause* requirement, juries are increasingly finding liability without fault (i.e., finding providers of services negligent even when they are not the proximate cause of the injury). (588)

A wide variety of acts or omissions can place social workers or the agencies for which they work at risk of being sued and held liable for causing harm to their clients or to individuals harmed by their clients. Such acts or omissions on the part of the social work might include:

⬧ Failure to clearly outline duties of social worker and client
⬧ Sexual or romantic involvement with a current or former client so that both parties understand and agree

Engage Assess
Intervene Evaluate

Select an intervention in which you are involved. Identify the precautions you need to take to prevent allegations of negligence and malpractice.

Critical
Thinking

How can you learn about potential pitfalls to avoid the following acts or omissions?

- ▶ Failure to warn others when a client discloses clear intent to inflict serious physical harm on someone
- ▶ Failure to alert others when a client discloses intent to harm self
- ▶ Failure to attempt to prevent a client's suicide
- ▶ Failure to properly diagnose and treat a client
- ▶ Failure to provide appropriate treatment and services to a client
- ▶ Failure to ensure continuity of service to a client under the care of a worker or agency
- ▶ Failure to maintain and protect confidentiality
- ▶ Failure to maintain accurate professional records and a proper accounting of client fees, payments, and reimbursements
- ▶ Misrepresentation of professional training, experience, and credentials
- ▶ Breach of client civil rights
- ▶ Failure to refer clients to other services or professionals when indicated
- ▶ Use of harmful or ineffective interventions
- ▶ Failure to protect a client from harm caused by other clients in a group, program, or facility
- ▶ Failure to report suspected child or elder abuse, neglect, or exploitation

Human Rights & Justice

How does this list of acts and omissions relate to social justice principles of working with clients?

Certain clients and certain situations place social workers and agencies at a higher risk of being sued. These clients and situations may include:

- ▶ Clients who are a real physical danger to others
- ▶ Clients who have been separated from their children because of actions taken by the social worker or agency (e.g., foster care placement and custody evaluations)
- ▶ Clients with complex and intense needs requiring social workers to provide highly technical and competent services

---

Food for Thought

Even if one's practice is perfectly within standards, there is no guarantee that a lawsuit will not be filed or that one would emerge unscathed from such a suit. A practitioner who is successfully sued could be required to pay damages as high or higher than hundreds of thousands of dollars. Furthermore, regardless of income, the process of defending against the suit can be financially and emotionally expensive (Baird, 2008, 67).

• • •

Even a social worker employed in settings that provide group liability coverage should seriously consider obtaining their own individual coverage. When both a social worker and the worker's employer are named in a liability claim, the employer could argue that the social worker, and not the employing agency, was negligent. Individual coverage would thus protect workers who find themselves at odds with their employers in relation to a liability claim (Reamer, 1994, 24).

• • •

Although you are a student, you are acting in the same capacity as a professional social worker in your responsibilities with clients and, as such, are accountable for upholding the same legal, professional, and ethical standards as other social workers (Birkenmaier and Berg-Weger, 2007, 239).

• • •

The typical professional liability insurance policy provides benefits including the cost of defense, settlements, and judgments within the stated policy limits. Most policies provide a benefit for representation and defense before licensing boards. That is the good news. The bad news is that these same policies contain between 15 and 20 stated policy exclusions. . . . Complaints regarding certain ethical violations are not covered by the policy leaving the offending mental health professional exposed to damage awards that must be paid from personal assets or future earnings (Bernstein and Hartsell, 2005, 168).

▶ Clients who may commit suicide
▶ Clients who are very suspicious of others and quick to blame and accuse others of some wrongdoing
▶ Clients who have a history of alleging malpractice and negligence and bringing suits against various professionals
▶ Clients who are very manipulative and deceptive
▶ Clients who have a history of using sex as a way of manipulating others

GUIDANCE AND DIRECTION

Make a special effort to become familiar with the laws relevant to your practicum setting, including the laws that regulate the services your agency provides and the laws that regulate professional social work practice. Depending on the nature and purpose of your agency, you will need to become familiar with federal and state codes, and sometimes local ordinances, that apply to your clients and the services your agency provides. Your clients' lives are affected directly and indirectly by such laws. For example, you may need to understand laws pertaining to the following:

▶ Marriage, parenthood, divorce and child custody
▶ Partner violence and abuse
▶ Voluntary and involuntary termination of parental rights, foster care, and adoption
▶ Guardianship, conservatorship, power of attorney, durable power of attorney for health care
▶ Child or elder abuse and neglect
▶ Involuntary hospitalization of persons with mental illness
▶ Detention or involuntary hospitalization of persons who are suicidal or a threat to others
▶ Parental notification regarding treatment for minors
▶ Adult and juvenile adjudication, probation and parole
▶ Crime victim assistance
▶ Immigration and refugee status
▶ Buying and selling of illegal drugs
▶ Family planning, reproductive rights, and abortion
▶ Education of children with disabilities
▶ Discrimination in employment and housing
▶ Confidentiality in health and mental health care settings
▶ Reporting of contagious diseases and public health hazards
▶ Personal debt and bankruptcy
▶ Disability accommodation

Social work supervisors and administrators will need a basic understanding of laws related to employee matters, financial management, and the like. Although as a practicum student, you will not be engaged in administration, laws that impact your agency are an important part of the context of providing quality services and of maintaining good employees and employee relations. Watch for opportunities to learn about laws pertaining to:

▶ Contracts
▶ Leases and rental agreements
▶ Property and liability insurance
▶ Employee compensation and benefits

How might Affirmative
Action be interpreted by
both clients and agency
staff as alternately
positive and negative?

What ethical dilemmas
could arise in such
situations in your
agency?

▶ Workers compensation and unemployment insurance
▶ Hiring and dismissal of employees
▶ Employee unions
▶ Financial record keeping
▶ Receipt of charitable contributions
▶ Accessibility for persons with disabilities
▶ Job classification related to public employees
▶ Restrictions on political action and lobbying by public employees
▶ Nonprofit corporations
▶ Sexual harassment
▶ Drug-free workplaces
▶ Affirmative action

If social workers in your agency commonly appear in court, request the opportunity to observe their testimony. Determine their role and function in court, how they prepare for a court appearance, what types of questions they are asked by attorneys, what written documents they provide the court, and if their recommendations tend to be followed by judges. Give special thought to legal and ethical issues that may arise when social workers advocate for their clients, when they are asked to participate in involuntary treatment of clients, or when they must testify on behalf of one client and against another. Identify the social work interventions that follow those documents and orders. Learn about social workers who testify as expert witnesses and what is required of them.

If possible, read the case records of clients whose cases are heard in court. Read the petitions and other legal documents filed on behalf of or against your agency's clients. Read the court orders found in client records. If you have questions about what these records mean, ask your field instructor to explain their significance and what is expected of social workers in these situations.

As mentioned earlier, some situations put social workers at greater legal risk than others. Learn about the types of situations and clients that present the highest legal risk to social workers in your agency. Ask how often lawsuits are threatened or actually filed against social workers or the agency. Ask about your agency's policy regarding legal defense expenses for employees who are sued. Find out if practicum students who may be sued are covered in your agency's liability or malpractice insurance policy. If not, obtain liability insurance for yourself that will cover you for a possible malpractice suit.

An agency's policy and procedures manual generally describes a standard of care and service owed to, and expected by, the client. Thus, in a malpractice lawsuit, a social worker's failure to follow agency policy may be used as evidence of professional negligence. An agency places itself at higher legal risk when it has an official policy that is not or cannot be regularly followed by its employees. Agency policies will not protect social workers who do not abide by them. The best way to avoid becoming involved in a malpractice lawsuit is to be proactive in learning about and acting on the following guidelines:

▶ Read the NASW *Code of Ethics* regularly and abide by its guidelines.
▶ Adhere to agency policy, procedure, and protocol.
▶ Make every effort to practice competently and avoid situations beyond your level of competence.
▶ Utilize supervision regularly to ensure that your techniques are legal, ethical, and therapeutically sound.
▶ Recognize situations of high legal risk.
▶ Consult with your agency's legal counsel whenever confronted with troublesome legal issues or questions.

Ethical Practice

Make a plan for learning about your agency's policies with these ethical guidelines and watch for situations in which you will be expected to abide by these policies.

- Obtain malpractice insurance if your agency does not provide it for you.
- Avoid dual relationships with clients.
- Protect client confidentiality.
- Inform clients about the limits of confidentiality.
- Maintain up-to-date, accurate, and complete client records.
- Maintain client records that are free of judgmental language and hearsay.
- Obtain written permission from clients to release information about them to others.
- Document any client complaints or grievances, and the steps you took to resolve them.
- Understand laws pertaining to privileged communication for social workers in your state.
- Abide by all mandatory reporting laws requiring you to report suspected abuse or neglect.
- Refer clients to other professionals and programs when you are unable to provide the services they require and document your efforts to make a referral.

You are not likely to become entangled in a malpractice lawsuit if you follow the guidelines described above, so do not let concerns over legal risk and malpractice keep you from learning or acting in the best interests of your clients. However, it is important to be careful to avoid legal consequences. Adhere to what would be considered by an average citizen, a jury, or a judge to be reasonable, customary, and prudent practices. The actions you take on behalf of clients must be fair, in good faith, and in keeping with how other professionals would tend to act. If you need clarification in any particular area, seek guidance and consultation from your social work supervisor and/or agency legal counsel.

Legal Issues and Concerns: A Workbook Activity

The following questions are designed to heighten your awareness of the legal context of social work practice and the legal considerations that are relevant to your practicum agency. Discuss these questions and issues with your field instructor and with experienced social workers in your agency. Your agency may have a legal department and staff attorneys who can respond to your questions and explain legal principles.

1. Is eligibility for your agency's services in any way defined by law? If so, what statutes, legal rules, and regulations are used to determine who is and is not eligible?

   _____

   _____

2. Are certain individuals legally required or mandated to obtain services from your agency (e.g., those on probation and subject to court-ordered treatment or those whose children are in foster care)? If so, what specific statutes apply to these individuals and situations?

   _____

   _____

3. Do those individuals who are pressured to make use of your agency have a right to refuse to participate? If so, do they face any consequences for that action?

   _____

   _____

4. Is your agency licensed by the state (e.g., a licensed child placing agency, licensed hospital, and licensed residential center for youth)? If yes, identify the specific license(s) and the laws and regulations that apply to these licensures.

   _____

   _____

5. What outside agencies or organizations (e.g., governmental agencies, accrediting bodies, and citizen review boards) are authorized to interview staff about their practices and review the records kept by your agency (e.g., client records, client services, and financial records)?

   _____

   _____

6. What percentage of the social workers in your agency have a social work license?

   _____

7. Does your agency have liability insurance that provides employees with legal defense against allegations of wrongdoing and/or pay the assessed damages if found guilty? If so, what limitations and restrictions apply (e.g., must the employee be following agency policy and behave in an ethical manner before he or she be covered the insurance policy)?

   _____

_____

_____

8. Does the agency's liability insurance cover the actions of social work practicum students? If yes, what limitations and restrictions apply?

_____

_____

_____

9. What are the possible legal consequences for a social worker who takes action that conflicts with or violates the agency's written policy?

_____

_____

10. Has the agency or any staff member been sued for negligence or malpractice? If yes, what was the nature of the allegation(s) and the outcome of the lawsuit(s)?

_____

_____

_____

11. What types of clients and situations in your agency are associated with high legal risk (i.e., cases most likely to result in a lawsuit alleging agency wrongdoing or professional malpractice)?

_____

_____

12. What agency policies apply in the following situations that raise legal questions?
    a. A client who appears to be a threat to self (e.g., possible suicide)

_____

_____

    b. A client who appears to be a threat to others (e.g., verbal threats, previous violent behavior)

_____

_____

    c. A client who may not be mentally competent to make legal, medical, or financial decisions

_____

_____

_____

d. A client who is a minor

_____

_____

e. A client who is injured while in your agency or while participating in an agency program

_____

_____

f. A client who insists on withdrawing from a treatment program or another agency service when doing so will place him or her at risk of harm

_____

_____

g. A client who threatens harm to a social worker or other staff member

_____

_____

h. A client who is suspected of or known to have committed a serious crime

_____

_____

i. A client who appears to need legal counsel or representation

_____

_____

j. A client who has been ordered by a court to receive certain services from your agency (e.g., assessment, treatment, intervention)

_____

_____

k. A client who has clearly lied, withheld information, or falsified an application in order to become eligible for the benefits or services provided by your agency

_____

_____

l. A client who states that he or she intends to bring a lawsuit against a social worker or the agency

_____

_____

13. What agency policies apply when you or others encounter the following situations and legal questions?

    a. How to proceed when a client requests the opportunity to read or copy the records in his or her case file

_____

_____

    b. How to obtain a client's permission to release his or her records to another agency or professional

_____

_____

    c. When and how to report suspected child or elder abuse and neglect

_____

_____

    d. How to obtain a client's informed consent to participate in certain programs and services

_____

_____

    e. How to handle and record the receipt of gifts from a client or donations to the agency

_____

_____

    f. How to respond when one receives a subpoena for client records or to be a witness in a trial or court action

_____

_____

SUGGESTED LEARNING ACTIVITIES

- Examine your agency's policy manual and identify policies that refer to the need for staff to conform to specific legal codes or requirements.

- Identify situations in which there might be a conflict between what is required by the NASW *Code of Ethics* and the requirements of a specific state or federal law.

- Observe court proceedings, especially ones in which your agency is involved.

- Determine whether your agency has a staff attorney. If so, familiarize yourself with the legal services provided by the attorney to staff social workers.

- In Sheafor and Horejsi (2008), read the sections entitled "Avoiding Malpractice Suits" (587–592) and "Testifying in Court" (592–594).

- Familiarize yourself with the 2003 privacy rule and standards for security of electronic health information of the Health Insurance Portability and Accountability Act (HIPAA) of 1996.

Succeed with **PEARSON mysocialworklab**

Log onto **www.mysocialworklab.com** and select the **Career Exploration** videos from the left-hand menu. Answer the questions below. (*If you did not receive an access code to MySocialWorkLab with this text and wish to purchase access online, please visit www.mysocialworklab.com.*)

1. **Watch question 15 (Continuing Education) in the interview with Christine Mitchell.** She spoke about the

continuing education requirements for her license as a clinical social worker. What are the continuing education requirements for social workers in your state?

2. **Watch question 7 (Testifying in Court) in the interview with Sue Dowling.** She refers to the numerous reasons she and other child protective services workers must testify in court. How can you prepare yourself for such professional responsibilities?

PRACTICE TEST

The following questions are similar in phrasing and content to those asked in social work licensing examinations. They should help you prepare to take the licensing examination in your state.

1. Social workers must inform themselves of the laws regulating their practice because
   a. malpractice can be proven easily
   b. ignorance of the laws is not considered a legal defense
   c. professional liability policies require it prior to covering social workers
   d. clinical practice is based on legal issues

Ethical Practice

2. Breaking confidentiality, dual relationships with clients, and use of ineffective treatment are examples of
   a. common reasons for professional liability lawsuits
   b. state laws regulating social work
   c. agency guidelines for practice
   d. moral codes

3. The obligation to notify authorities of a client's threat to harm others is
   a. a violation of client confidentiality
   b. an ethical dilemma
   c. the concept of duty to warn
   d. always a clear cut decision

Ethical Practice

4. Making sure that clients provide informed consent to intervention is important

   a. because it would be easy to manipulate clients
   b. because clients have the right to autonomy in decision making
   c. because outcomes will likely be more positive
   d. all of the above

5. Which is true?
   a. there are no limits to client rights to confidentiality
   b. client rights to confidentiality are limited when clients do not understand
   c. limits to client confidentiality may be based on legal or payment issues
   d. social workers can decide on client rights to confidentiality

Critical Thinking

6. In a malpractice suit, the plaintiff must prove that
   a. He/she suffered harm because of what the social worker did or did not do (proximate cause)
   b. The social worker violated the NASW Code of Ethics
   c. The agency was derelict in its duty
   d. The social work supervisor was negligent

7. Social workers may be found negligent
   a. for what they did
   b. for what they failed to do
   c. both
   d. neither

16

Social Work as Planned Change

LEARNING GOALS FOR THIS CHAPTER

- ▶ To become aware of the fundamental beliefs about change which guide your agency's services

- ▶ To become aware of perspectives and theories used to plan and guide intervention and agency programs

- ▶ To become aware of the data-gathering and assessment tools used in your agency

- ▶ To become aware of commonly used interventions in your agency

- ▶ To become aware of how the effectiveness of social work interventions is evaluated in your agency

CONNECTING CORE COMPETENCIES *in this chapter*

| Professional Identity | Ethical Practice | Critical Thinking | Diversity in Practice | Human Rights & Justice | Research Based Practice | Human Behavior | Policy Practice | Practice Contexts | Engage Assess Intervene Evaluate |

Fundamentally, the practice of social work is about the ***process of planned change***. The verb process means to advance, to progress, to move onward. In the practice of social work, the worker takes deliberate and specific steps to encourage and facilitate movement toward a certain goal. Your practicum offers an excellent opportunity to observe and critically examine the values, beliefs, ethical principles, and knowledge base that guide a social worker's efforts to bring about a desired change.

In this chapter, you will be encouraged to think about the nature of change. All social agencies are committed to and structured around deep-seated beliefs about how clients, communities, or broad social conditions change. Strive to identify the assumptions about change that are embedded in your agency's programs and policies as well as in its various approaches to practice. Identify your own beliefs about how, why, and under what circumstances desirable change by individuals, families, small groups, organizations, and communities is possible and probable.

BACKGROUND AND CONTEXT

Engage Assess Intervene Evaluate

At what levels of practice is your agency most active, and how can you make sure that you gain experience with individuals, families, groups, organizations, and communities?

As explained in Chapter 13, social work is often seen as the profession that supports and promotes the social functioning of individuals, groups, and communities and also works to establish societal structures and policies that support that social functioning. Planned change at all levels is the central focus of social work. Social workers assist clients, families, and communities to make changes that will improve their lives or change the conditions and social policies which impact their lives.

At the level of the individual, ***social functioning*** can be viewed as a person's motivation, capacity, and opportunity to meet his or her basic human needs (e.g., food, shelter, health care, education, meaningful work, protection, and self-worth) and carry out his or her social roles (e.g., parent, student, employee, citizen, neighbor). In order to create conditions favorable for effective social functioning, social workers also seek needed changes in social policy, programs, and services.

To accomplish the goals of their profession, social workers assume a wide variety of roles. ***Social work practice roles*** are many and varied, and include client advocate, broker of services, case manager, counselor or therapist, group leader or facilitator, community organizer, administrator, supervisor, social planner, evaluator, educator, program developer, researcher, policy analyst, teacher, and educator. Depending on their practice setting and usual role, social workers are sometimes people changers or sometimes system changers, and often they are both. This is often seen as the essence and uniqueness of generalist social work practice.

Human Behavior

How can clients effectively shape their social environments (e.g. family, neighborhood, community, societal attitudes) in ways that enhance their own social functioning?

Social workers see the connections between people and the social environments of which they are a part. In order to be truly effective, social workers need to be skilled in and committed to interventions that reflect the ways in which people's lives are influenced by societal conditions and social policies. They must believe in clients' abilities not only to address their own needs and goals but also to change and enhance their social environment.

The social worker and client may seek change and formulate interventions at one or more of three levels: micro, mezzo, and macro. The ***micro*** level of social work practice refers to interventions that focus on personal individual or family concerns such as relationships, communication problems, emotional or psychological problems, and issues related to individual social functioning.

The **mezzo** level of social work practice refers to improving social functioning at the level of the neighborhood, the group, or the organization. This may include interventions through the use of support groups, neighborhood development projects, and organizational growth and development. The **macro** level of social work practice refers to interventions aimed at changes in communities, societies, and social policies. These interventions focus on community capacity building, community organization, and large scale social change efforts.

Although these three levels of intervention may have different targets for change, they are all built on the same process of planned change. In addition, social workers often practice at multiple levels simultaneously, recognizing the connections between them and moving between levels as the situation requires. Social work at all of these levels, whether the client is an individual or a community, typically moves through the **phases of a planned change.** These are:

1. Identifying and defining the problem or concern
2. Gathering data, studying the problem, and identifying strengths
3. Assessing the problem (i.e., deciding what needs to change, what can be changed, how it might be changed, and what resources are available to the client)
4. Establishing goals, objectives, and tasks for change based on client goals and agency guidelines
5. Taking action based on the plan (i.e., intervention)
6. Monitoring of progress and determining if the intervention is achieving the desired outcomes and modifying the plan if necessary and trying again
7. Terminating the intervention once goals and objectives have been reached and evaluating the change process to learn for future practice

This list of phases gives the impression that the change process is quite orderly and linear, but that is seldom the case. Typically, the client and worker move back and forth between these phases several times during the intervention process. In addition, others involved in the intervention, such as extended family members, may not move through the intervention process at the same pace or with the same goals in mind. This can make the change process more complex and unpredictable, and needs to be taken into account.

Although the use of the problem-solving process is pervasive in social work and in many other professions, it has been criticized for being essentially a negative orientation that results in social workers giving too much attention to what is wrong and too little attention to client strengths and situational assets. Indeed, if social workers focused only on problems and deficits, they would lose sight of the strengths and assets of clients and the social systems surrounding them. Although most social work interventions are based on addressing problems or concerns, they must always build these interventions on identified strengths.

When considering the various phases of the problem-solving process, it is helpful to make a distinction between data collection and assessment. **Data collection** refers to the gathering of facts and information about the client and/or the situation targeted for change. **Assessment** refers to the worker's understanding, interpretation, or explanation of these data in a way that lays a conceptual foundation for a plan of action or intervention. Needless to say, several different meanings can be drawn from the same set of facts. The client may

Engage Assess Intervene Evaluate

What is the importance of each phase of the planned change process?

or may not see the situation in the same ways as the social worker, even when viewing the same assessment data. The meaning assigned to data is often shaped by the practice perspectives, theories, and models used by the social worker and his or her agency. Social workers need to be cautious not to overlook or underemphasize the intensely personal meanings that clients attach to their situations. Social workers who do not at least partially understand the situation from their clients' perspectives will be less successful than those who try to build interventions that start where their clients start.

Social workers use what are called conceptual frameworks to guide practice. A ***conceptual framework*** is a way of organizing ideas about social work practice, and includes practice perspectives, orienting theories, practice theories, and practice models. A ***practice perspective*** is an intentional viewing of a practice situation using a certain professional lens, which helps to clarify and magnify a particular facet of the person-in-environment. Using these lenses helps us to examine and draw attention to what needs attention in any given situation. A situation may require a generalist perspective because it needs to be addressed at multiple levels, using a variety of theories and models. All practice situations require a strengths perspective in order to highlight strengths and resources upon which to build an intervention. An ecological perspective prompts us to consider the impact of the social environment on our clients, as well as the interaction between our clients and their social environments. A diversity perspective ensures that we consider the ways in which diversity of all kinds impacts a client's experience and view of that experience. Depending on the situation, a social worker may use one perspective more than another to understand the unique features of that situation.

Orienting theories are those that contribute to a social worker's body of knowledge about how individuals, families, groups, communities, and societies develop and change over time. They often build on and synthesize the social and behavioral sciences such as psychology, sociology, economics, and political science. Such theories attempt to explain human behavior, human development, social forces that shape human experiences, and political and economic systems which impact individuals, families, and communities. Although necessary to good practice because they help us understand what might be happening and why, these theories are limited because they do not provide guidance on how to facilitate planned change. Examples of orienting theories include social systems theory, human development theory, group dynamics theory, organizational theory, and community development theory.

Practice theories are those that offer explanations of behaviors or circumstances and general guidelines about how to intervene at various levels of practice. They form the basis for practice models, and suggest that certain situations call for certain practice theories. Examples of practice theories used with individuals and families include behavioral learning theory, psychodynamic theory, and crisis theory. Drawing on both orienting theories and practice theories, social workers use a variety of ***practice models.*** They are the actual approaches and techniques chosen to use in real interventions. Examples of practice models include task-centered casework, crisis intervention, empowerment model, cognitive behavioral model, case management model, mutual aid model, structural model, community organization, social planning, organizational development models, and social change models.

Generalist social workers, even when involved at one level of practice, must be cognizant of the implications of their work at other levels. Practice

Which orienting theories have you studied that attempt to explain why clients served by your agency are experiencing struggles or problems?

Which practice theories have you studied that attempt to explain why clients served by your agency are experiencing struggles or problems?

perspectives, theories, and models are to be used at all levels. Hopefully when you are working with individuals and families, you will always remember that practice needs at times to change societal systems and institutional structures. Social workers who are true generalists take on large-scale social change efforts at times, even if their job description may not include this responsibility.

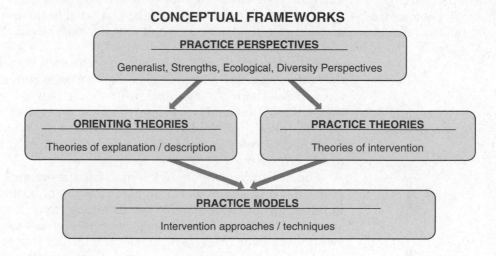

CONCEPTUAL FRAMEWORKS

PRACTICE PERSPECTIVES

Generalist, Strengths, Ecological, Diversity Perspectives

ORIENTING THEORIES

Theories of explanation / description

PRACTICE THEORIES

Theories of intervention

PRACTICE MODELS

Intervention approaches / techniques

GUIDANCE AND DIRECTION

Research Based Practice

What recommendations do you have for improving your agency's methods for measuring the effectiveness of its work?

It is important to identify the practice frameworks (perspectives, orienting theories, practice theories, and models) used in your agency. Whether implicit or explicit, these frameworks influence how your agency designs its programs and services and how it works with clients. Determine why these particular practice frameworks are seen to be appropriate and most effective for the clients served by your agency. Consider what your agency's choice of practice frameworks reveals about the agency's beliefs and assumptions concerning the causes of personal and social problems, how and why clients and client systems change, and actions most likely to facilitate change. Learn about how success is measured and ask about the importance placed on identifying and using client strengths.

Your practicum agency will expect you to use the regularly selected forms of intervention used by other social workers, and will train you in these approaches. Do your best to learn the skills required to implement these interventions, remembering that many of these skills can be transferred to another setting even if that organization takes a different approach to intervention. Over time you will see how interventions, even though they may seem similar for several clients, are customized based on different needs and goals. You will begin to see how your own interventions will be tailored for those reasons as well. As you grow in experience and confidence, your ability to craft appropriate interventions will increase as well.

Because social workers, like all people, are unique with regard to their core values, personality, and style of interaction, individual workers usually find some practice perspectives, theories, and models more attractive than others. Carefully examine the possible reasons you are drawn to certain ones and reluctant to use others. Usually, one's choice of a practice framework is

Ethical Practice

What ethical principles do you believe to be most central to the choice of an intervention?

the result of a combination of factors, including beliefs about the causes of human problems, beliefs about what can be changed and what cannot, beliefs about personal and social responsibility, beliefs about how much people should be involved in defining and assessing their own problems, and beliefs about the role and responsibility of the professional in facilitating change.

Examine your preferences for certain practice frameworks, and decide how much they are based on your personal beliefs, values, and attitudes; on effectiveness research and empirical data reported in the professional literature; or on what your field instructor and school faculty have told you about what does and does not work.

Recognize that your practicum experience is limited to one setting and that other agencies and programs may be quite different from the one you know best. There are significant differences between programs, even when they have similar goals and serve the same types of clients. Try to learn how and why other agencies have adopted forms of intervention, practice perspectives, and theories and models that are different from the ones used in your practicum setting.

Social workers are often drawn to certain practice roles, and sometimes prefer to avoid others. For example, some might be attracted to roles related to advocacy and social action because they want to see changes in societal structures that can benefit large numbers of people, while others might avoid these same roles because they are uncomfortable with conflict and the use of power and influence. Some might be attracted to the clinician or counselor role because they like face-to-face contact with individual clients

---

Food for Thought

Social work practice from a strengths perspective recognizes that resources can be tapped in both the social worker and the client, as well as the community. Therefore, the relationship is approached as collaborative and avoids hierarchy; the intent is to empower the client to actively collaborate in the change process. A strengths perspective acknowledges that the client possesses knowledge, abilities, resilience, coping, and problem-solving skills that are there to be employed. . . . It is important to identify and amplify strengths so that the client can go back and rediscover what has already worked for him or her in the past. Therefore, the role of the social worker is to facilitate the process, serve as a bridge to the client's own resources, move ahead, and seek solutions (Roberts, 2009, 217).

• • •

Accentuating the problems of clients creates a wave of pessimistic expectations of, and predictions about, the client, the client's environment, and the client's capacity to cope with that environment. Furthermore, these

labels have the insidious potential, repeated over time, to alter how individuals see themselves and how others see them (Saleeby, 2006, 4).

• • •

Initiating and implementing assessment and intervention procedures that are not supported by research is no longer considered acceptable (O'Hare, 2005, 9).

• • •

Very often, clients are in a "one-down" position. They need something they cannot get for themselves. It could be something tangible, such as food or shelter, or something less concrete, such as control over a substance abuse problem or help in understanding some bureaucratic procedure. You and your agency have what they need; you are holding the cards. . . . Your clients will bring their fears about past experiences with authority to their relationship with you, and those factors will shape how they respond (Sweitzer, H. Fredrick, and Mary King 2009, 180).

Professional Identity

Although you may not be equally drawn to all levels of practice, how can you make sure that you develop the skills of a generalist expected to practice at various levels and move between levels as needed?

and want to make a difference in individual lives, whereas others might be uncomfortable with the discussion of painful personal problems. Still others might either be attracted to or wish to avoid the tasks of budgeting, grant proposal writing, personnel selection, and public relations that are associated with the roles of administration and program planning. Make sure that you broaden your experience to all areas in which a social worker is expected to function.

During your practicum, gain experience in as many practice roles as possible in order to understand the nature of these roles and better understand your own abilities. Do not limit yourself to the performance of only a few practice roles. Most likely your career in social work will require that you assume many different practice roles and perform a wide range of tasks and activities. This variety of roles is also one of the most attractive aspects of the social work profession because social workers can move between roles, creatively addressing needs in a variety of ways and at a variety of levels.

Observe how the professionals in your agency go about their work of helping clients and providing services. Identify the practice frameworks, approaches, methods, and techniques used during the various phases of their work with clients. Consider the following questions in your analysis:

Engagement and Relationship Building

- What are the major reasons that clients seek services from your agency?
- Are most clients voluntary or involuntary?
- How does this impact the engagement process?
- How do the experiences of clients or those pressuring clients to seek services impact the engagement process?
- What specific techniques are used to facilitate building an effective helping relationship?
- What approaches are used to make the client feel more at ease and less fearful about entering a professional relationship?
- What approaches are used to address the client's possible questions and concerns about utilizing the services offered by the agency?

Clarification of Client's Concern, Problem, or Request

- What approaches are used to help the client specify, elaborate, and clarify the concerns that brought them to the agency?
- Are clients actively involved in the process of identifying and defining their problems, concerns, and strengths?

Data Gathering

- What information is routinely gathered about clients and their problems, concerns, and strengths?
- What tools or instruments are used to aid the gathering of this data (e.g., interview schedules, checklists, needs assessment instruments, questionnaires, and observation)?
- What issues of diversity and power need to be addressed in the data gathering process?

Assessment

- How are available data and information organized, combined, and analyzed in order to arrive at a clear picture of the client's situation and a possible plan of action?

- Are clients actively involved in deciding what needs to change and how it might be changed?
- If clients and workers disagree on what needs to change, how is this difference resolved?

Formulation of an Intervention Plan

- When several issues are identified, how are they prioritized?
- How are client goals and preferences incorporated into the plan? How is potential resistance addressed?
- What issues of diversity and power need to be addressed in the plan?
- Is a formal contract developed?
- Are ethical and legal issues related to the plan addressed?
- Is the plan based on sound theoretical models and perspectives?
- Is the plan based on empirically supported evidence?
- Are the plan's outcomes reasonable and measurable?

Intervention and Monitoring

- What system (e.g., client, family, community) is typically targeted for change by your agency's programs and professional staff? Why?
- What other agencies or organizations often become involved in the client's intervention plan?
- What conceptual frameworks (perspectives, theories, and models) guide the change process?
- What specific methods, techniques, or procedures are used to facilitate change?
- What specific methods are used to measure the effectiveness of the change process?

Termination and Evaluation

- In what ways does the agency determine if its interventions, programs, and services are effective?
- To what extent are clients involved in determining if interventions, programs, and services are effective?
- What additional forms of evaluation do you suggest?
- Under what conditions are interventions terminated by social workers or clients?
- What specific procedures and techniques are used to bring the professional relationship to a close and terminate the helping process?

Remember that although the process of planned change as outlined previously looks linear and suggests sequential steps in the intervention process, in reality intervention is more circular, with each step of the process being informed by the others with new information and evolving relationships being incorporated into the intervention over time. Expanding on this view of intervention, Finn and Jacobson (2008) suggest seven core processes that move social workers and clients or participants forward through a mutual process and series of steps resembling waves washing over each other.

1. ***Engagement*** is the process of relationship building, listening, acknowledging power and position, appreciating difference, and acknowledging the partiality of knowledge.

Diversity in Practice

What NASW cultural competence standards should be met when developing intervention plans?

2. *Teaching/learning* involves collaboration between worker and participant in the process of discovery and assessment, allowing both parties to teach and learn.

3. *Action* is the process of implementing plans, encouraging reflection, awakening possibilities, and paying attention to social justice.

4. *Accompaniment* refers to the partnerships that are used to advance action, and pays attention to power in the helping relationship as well as the worker's commitment to long-term participation.

5. *Evaluation* is the process of examining both process and outcomes of joint efforts, learning from each other and using this knowledge to enhance these efforts.

6. *Critical reflection* leads to learning from the shared experience, interpreting it from individual and collective perspectives, and perhaps reframing initial inquiries.

7. *Celebration* refers to the process of finding joy, honor, and play in the work and with those involved in it.

As you engage in the **assessment** phase of planned change, whether you are assessing a client, a community's capacity to serve its citizens, an organization's ability to provide services, or a social policy's ability to address the needs of a group of people, there are general guidelines that can help you do a thorough and effective assessment. When assessing client situations, make sure that you assess for strengths as well as problems and use assessment tools that are effective and appropriate. Include the client in the assessment process. Prioritize the identified needs in order to maximize your effectiveness. Consider the impact of diversity on your interventions. Pay attention to any ethical and legal issues related to assessment. Ask yourself what value judgments you might be making. Consider the sociohistorical context of your client or client system. Continually ask yourself what else you might need to know in order to have a comprehensive assessment upon which an effective intervention can be built.

As you design **interventions** from the micro level to the macro level, follow these guidelines for effective interventions. The intervention plan must address both strengths and needs, be built on as comprehensive an assessment as possible, and be feasible and reasonable for both the client and social worker. The plan should be mutually developed by the client and social worker, be based on a theory of change that matches the client's needs, and be within your knowledge base and skill level. Remember that your intervention may need to be modified at some point. Make sure that the plan has incremental steps and reasonable goals. Do what you can to minimize negative effects on clients, avoid being overly intrusive into the clients' lives, address important issues of diversity, and include a timeline and termination plan.

The profession of social work is rightfully being asked to hold itself accountable and to demonstrate its ability to address social issues in effective and efficient ways. Social workers are being asked to use what is commonly called **evidence-based practice,** which means that they need to base their interventions on some form of empirical evidence whenever possible and engage in proactive program evaluation to determine effectiveness of services provided. Such research on practice often leads to what is termed **best practices.** This refers to what the profession considers to be ideal approaches based on the values of the profession, research on what is effective, what is in the best interests of clients, and what clients wish for themselves. Learn to research the best practices in your field so that you can pattern your work after them.

Engage Assess
Intervene Evaluate

How do these steps compare with planned change steps you have learned about, and how might you incorporate them into your work?

Research Based Practice

What evidence based practice and best practices guide the work of your agency, and how could more of these be incorporated?

Social Work as Planned Change: A Workbook Activity

This workbook activity asks that you examine the conceptual frameworks (perspectives, theories, and models) used in your practicum agency. In order to analyze these frameworks, consider these questions.

1. What types of problems, needs, or concerns are typically addressed by your agency?

_____

_____

_____

2. What conceptual frameworks (perspectives, theories, or models) are typically used to guide assessment and interventions?

_____

_____

_____

3. At what level of practice (micro, mezzo, or macro) are interventions typically implemented?

_____

_____

_____

4. How is a particular practice model chosen for a specific client?

_____

_____

_____

5. Are social workers in your agency regularly trained in new intervention approaches?

_____

_____

_____

6. Are interventions tailored to diverse clients (i.e., culture, age, gender)?

_____

_____

_____

_____

7. What evaluation tools does your agency use to evaluate the effectiveness of its interventions?

_____

_____

_____

8. Does your agency adapt its strategies based on the result of its self-evaluation?

_____

_____

_____

9. What recommendations do you have for improved effectiveness in your agency?

_____

_____

_____

SUGGESTED LEARNING ACTIVITIES

- Examine the data-gathering and assessment tools and instruments used in your agency.

- Ask social workers or other professionals in your agency to identify the perspectives and theories that guide their practice. Ask why those frameworks are preferred over other possibilities.

- Identify the beliefs, values, and assumptions implicit in the perspectives, theories, and models used in your agency.

- Ask social workers or other professionals in your agency to describe how they and the agency determine whether they are being effective in their work with clients.

- In Sheafor and Horejsi (2008), read the chapter on the process of change.

- In the *Encyclopedia of Social Work* (Mizrahi, 2008), read chapters on the various practice frameworks used in your agency and by social work professionals.

- In Payne (2005), read descriptions of social work theories and models.

- Refer to the *Social Work Desk Reference* to see what interventions are recommended in certain situations.

Log onto **www.mysocialworklab.com** and select the **Interactive Skill Module** videos from the left-hand menu. Answer the questions below. (*If you did not receive an access code to* **MySocialWorkLab** *with this text and wish to purchase access online, please visit* www.mysocialworklab.com.)

1. **Watch page 20 (Engaging Clients in Problem-Solving) in the school social work module.**

Explain the reasons that clients should be involved in the development of an intervention plan. What might be the challenges associated with doing this?

2. **Watch page 22 (Reinforcing Mutual Support) in the group work module.** How is group work similar to and different from work with individuals? When is it preferable to individual work?

PRACTICE TEST

The following questions are similar in phrasing and content to those asked in social work licensing examinations. They should help you prepare to take the licensing examination in your state.

Engage Assess Intervene Evaluate

1. Each step of the planned change process
   a. is distinct and unrelated to the others
   b. is related to and builds upon the others
   c. legally requires social work supervision
   d. should utilize valid instruments

2. The portion of the planned change process which is the opportunity for the social worker to develop a positive working relationship with the client is
   a. the assessment stage
   b. the evaluation stage
   c. the termination stage
   d. the engagement stage

3. The conceptual frameworks that offer a professional lens through which to view clients are:
   a. professional ethics
   b. practice theories
   c. professional perspectives
   d. methodology

Human Behavior

4. The theories which attempt to explain social problems and human behavior are

a. practice theories
b. orientating or explanatory theories
c. professional theories
d. social functioning theories

5. The theories which are used to guide practice interventions are
   a. orientating or explanatory theories
   b. social systems theories
   c. practice theories
   d. psycho-social theories

6. Social work intervention methods that have been shown to be effective are considered examples of
   a. evidence based practice
   b. social work body of knowledge
   c. social work theory
   d. pilot programs

7. The evaluation phase of planned change efforts is vital because
   a. social workers are accountable for their work
   b. it is important to know whether interventions were effective or not
   c. evaluation results can be used to inform future practice
   d. all of the above

Answers

1) b 2) d 3) c 4) b 5) c 6) a 7) d

17

Evaluating the Practicum

CHAPTER OUTLINE

LEARNING GOALS FOR THIS CHAPTER

- To understand the importance of evaluating social work practice
- To understand the process of evaluating student performance in your practicum
- To understand the criteria commonly used to evaluate student performance
- To conduct a self-evaluation of performance in order to measure learning and to identify areas for continued learning or remediation

CONNECTING CORE COMPETENCIES *in this chapter*

Professional Identity | Ethical Practice | Critical Thinking | Diversity in Practice | Human Rights & Justice | Research Based Practice | Human Behavior | Policy Practice | Practice Contexts | Engage Assess Intervene Evaluate

A successful practicum prepares you for competent and responsible practice. This competence, developed over time, is seen when acquired skills and knowledge are compared with student learning goals set early in the practicum. A successful practicum is one that achieves that goal. Ongoing monitoring and frequent evaluations of your performance are necessary to determine whether you are making progress, to document learning, to identify strengths, and to identify areas of performance that may need special attention and remediation. It is important that you become familiar with the procedure and instruments that will be used to evaluate your performance in the practicum, as well as the criteria against which your performance will be measured.

This chapter will provide basic information on the process of student evaluation used by programs of social work education and encourage you to examine and evaluate your own performance so you can make the best possible use of the practicum as a learning opportunity.

BACKGROUND AND CONTEXT

Research Based Practice

Could the evaluation of student practicum performance be considered research based practice?

Ongoing evaluation of student performance is very important in a social work practicum. The practicum evaluation focuses on the student's behaviors and actions related to the role and obligations of a professional social worker. The primary question addressed is whether the student's performance is meeting the specified standards expected of the entry-level social work practitioner.

Every school of social work education uses some type of rating scale or evaluation tool to monitor and evaluate student progress. The evaluation process compares the student's performance to standards and criteria established by schools and required by the Council on Social Work Education's Educational Policy and Accreditation Standards, and also to the learning goals, objectives, and activities outlined in the student's learning contract (see Chapter 3).

Evaluations of student performance are of two types: formal and informal. An ***informal evaluation*** consists of the ongoing feedback and suggestions offered by the field instructor. This type of evaluation takes place on a weekly or even a daily basis. A ***formal evaluation*** is a detailed review and comparison of the student's performance with agreed-upon evaluation criteria, standards, and learning objectives for the practicum. It occurs at the end of each academic term or more often, depending on school policy or special circumstances.

Formal evaluations are based on a school's specific evaluation criteria and placed in a written report. This report typically consists of the ratings assigned to the various items on the school's evaluation tool and a few paragraphs of narrative that describe special strengths and abilities and/or special problems and deficiencies in performance. The report may also describe how needed learning experiences will be secured or deficiencies corrected prior to the next formal evaluation.

Some practicum programs and field instructors may ask the student to prepare for this evaluation by compiling a portfolio that includes various reports and documents that describe the student's practicum activities and achievements and serves to illustrate his or her level of performance. Students may be asked to evaluate their own performance using the evaluation instrument provided by their university and then compare their self ratings with those of their supervisor.

A variety of agency staff members may be asked to comment on student learning and performance based on their observations of student professional growth. The faculty supervisor will also participate in the formal evaluation. In some cases, other agency staff may be asked to join in the evaluation if they have worked closely with the student and observed the student's performance.

The areas addressed in the practicum evaluation are similar to those addressed in the performance evaluation of the social workers employed by an agency. In order to ensure high-quality performance and reduce their exposure to lawsuits and employee grievances, agencies strive to make their expectations of employees and students as clear as possible and to use personnel evaluation tools (i.e., rating scales) that are as objective as possible. These same forces have prompted programs of social work education to develop evaluation tools that are as valid and reliable as possible.

It is difficult to develop an evaluation tool that is both clear and specific in its descriptions of standards and criteria, and also flexible enough to accurately and fairly evaluate the practice of social work, which is complex and difficult to observe directly. An evaluation should be objective to the degree possible, but even a well-designed procedure will require judgments by the field instructor, and some of these may be open to charges of subjectivity. For example, ratings of a student's level of cooperation, motivation, adaptability, and use of supervision are difficult to assess except when in an extreme form (i.e., very high or very low motivation). Consequently, there will be times when the field instructor and practicum student disagree on the actual ratings given on a formal evaluation.

An evaluation can be considered fair and relevant when:

- The evaluation criteria, standards, and the agency's preferred practices and outcomes are made known to the student at the beginning of the practicum or at the beginning of the time period to be evaluated.
- It addresses the areas of performance or competency that are truly important to professional social work and carrying out the agency's mission and goals.
- The criteria used to evaluate the student are clear and objective.
- The student's performance is compared to written standards rather than to unstated or implied standards.
- The student has been given adequate orientation and training.
- The student has been given ongoing feedback on professional growth.
- The student has been given ongoing feedback and warnings of unsatisfactory performance prior to the formal evaluation.
- The performance criteria and standards are realistic given the student's level (e.g., first semester versus second semester, BSW versus MSW).
- The evaluation can cite examples of performance that form the basis of the ratings.
- The evaluation gives consideration to extenuating circumstances that may influence the evaluation (e.g., the student had limited opportunity to learn or demonstrate certain skills and the supervisor had limited time to observe the student's performance).
- The evaluation takes into consideration the nature and complexity of the assignments given to the student.
- The evaluation recognizes student growth and good performance as well as student problems or need for continued learning.

An inaccurate or unfair evaluation exists when:

- The student did not understand what was expected of him or her, or did not understand the criteria to be used for evaluation.

Critical Thinking

Using these characteristics of a good evaluation process, what can you do to make sure that you and your agency field instructor use them to build your professional competencies?

▶ The rules, standards, and criteria used to evaluate the student are changed without the student's knowledge.

▶ The student receives low ratings without being given a description and explanation of the poor performance that resulted in the low ratings.

▶ The criteria or standards are unrealistically high or not relevant to the student's performance as a social worker.

▶ Several students receive essentially the same ratings when there were clear differences in their performances.

▶ The student was not given ongoing feedback, guidance, and suggestions prior to the evaluation.

▶ Interpersonal factors such as personality conflicts between the student and field instructor influence student performance.

▶ Student performance has not been observed and evaluations are not based on actual knowledge of student abilities.

Both the field instructor and the student must be alert to certain pitfalls that exist whenever one person attempts to rate another person's performance. These are:

▶ The **halo effect**—the tendency to rate a person the same on all items based on the observed performance in only a few areas.

▶ The **attraction of the average**—the tendency to evaluate every student or employee about the same or about average regardless of real differences in their performance.

▶ The **leniency bias**—the tendency to evaluate all students or employees as outstanding or to assign inflated ratings so as to avoid arguments or conflict or to avoid hurting their feelings.

▶ The **strictness bias**—the tendency to evaluate and rate all students or employees on the low side because the evaluator has unrealistically high expectations or holds the belief that low ratings will motivate them toward even higher levels of performance.

In some instances the field instructor or the practicum coordinator may conclude that the practicum arrangement is unworkable and unsatisfactory for the student, the field instructor, or both. This may happen when it becomes apparent that the setting cannot meet the student's learning needs or because the student's performance is irresponsible, unethical, or falls far short of expectations. Examples of student behaviors or performance problems that may prompt the field instructor or the school to consider terminating the practicum include the following:

▶ The student's behavior is harmful to clients, agency staff, or the agency's reputation.

▶ The student's behavior is irresponsible and unprofessional (e.g., late for work, missing scheduled appointments, unable to spend the required hours in the practicum setting).

▶ The student is unable to communicate adequately, either verbally or in writing.

▶ The student is hostile toward supervision and resistant to learning.

▶ The student displays symptoms of an emotional disturbance that interfere with work (e.g., bizarre behavior, inability to concentrate, aggressiveness, withdrawal, inappropriate emotional expression).

▶ The student inappropriately shares personal views, experiences, and problems with clients after being made aware of this unacceptable behavior.

▶ The student enters into dual relationships with a client (e.g., dates a client, sells a product to a client).

Ethical Practice

What are the potential negative impacts on clients or agencies when social workers engage in the above behaviors?

Food for Thought

For students, there tends to be an implicit assumption that learning about a subject has a start and an end-point at the conclusion of class. . . . For a professional, learning is ongoing, never stops, and the standard cannot be the minimum needed to pass a course. . . . There is no room for "just good enough to pass," and there is no room for kidding ourselves into thinking we know or can do something when in fact this is not so. The demand for meeting high standards will be ongoing throughout your professional work, and it can be very challenging, but it is also rewarding and is part of what you sign up for when you enter a profession (Baird, 2008, 19).

• • •

It is . . . encouraging that social workers are developing the skills of program evaluation and research.

Inquiry is vital, and evaluation makes it possible to represent what happens as a result of therapeutic or helping relationships. Rarely, however, does outcome evaluation represent the full story or the dynamics that are essential to understanding both the problem and the help given (Roberts 2009, 6).

• • •

. . .[S]ocial service evaluation is a process of systematically collecting and analyzing information to improve practice (Brun, 2005, 5).

• • •

In work with individuals, averages mean very little.
—*Mary Richmond*

Some behaviors by the student are considered so serious that they may result in the student's immediate dismissal from the practicum. These include:

- Clear and serious violations of the NASW *Code of Ethics*
- Clear and repeated insubordination
- Theft or the clear misuse of agency money, equipment, or property
- Concealing, consuming, or selling drugs on agency premises
- Being intoxicated or under the influence of drugs or alcohol when at work
- Reckless or threatening actions that place clients and staff at risk of serious harm
- Deliberately withholding information from a supervisor or from agency personnel that they need to know in order to properly serve clients and maintain the integrity and reputation of the agency and its programs
- Falsifying agency records and reports
- Soliciting or accepting gifts or favors from clients in exchange for preferential treatment
- Sexual or romantic relationships with clients
- Clear violations of strict agency policy
- Failure to correct or improve inadequate performance
- Inability to deal with the emotional and stressful aspects of practice

GUIDANCE AND DIRECTION

In all phases of your practicum, you will be observed, guided, encouraged, assigned tasks, given feedback, and evaluated. Your field instructor should provide an informal and ongoing critique so that you know how you are doing from week to week. You will be evaluated in a more formal and systematic manner at the end of each academic term.

When conducting the formal evaluation, your field instructor will most likely use an evaluation tool provided by your school. This tool will rate you on the specific values, attitudes, knowledge, and skills your school defines as important to your professional development. Obtain a copy of this evaluation tool early in your practicum and construct your learning agreement so that you will have opportunities to learn and grow in each of the areas of performance to be evaluated.

You may also be evaluated on the completion of the tasks, projects, and activities you planned at the beginning of your practicum. Review your learning goals for the practicum regularly to determine if you are making satisfactory progress (see Chapter 3).

Your field instructor and your faculty supervisor will ask you how the practicum is proceeding, as well as hear any suggestions or questions you might have. You may be asked the following:

> ▶ Are the tasks and activities that you are performing different from what you were expecting?
> ▶ What aspects of your practicum do you consider to be of highest priority? Lowest priority?
> ▶ Are the demands on your time reasonable?
> ▶ What do you hope to learn and accomplish in the next month? By the time you complete your practicum?
> ▶ Do you get enough supervision?
> ▶ Is this the right type of social work practice and practicum setting for you?
> ▶ What aspects of practice in this agency are most and least appealing?
> ▶ What new or additional learning experiences do you want or need?
> ▶ How well do you get along with agency staff?
> ▶ Which practicum tasks have you completed most and least successfully?
> ▶ Have you been able to strike a workable balance between the demands of the practicum, your other academic work, and your personal life and responsibilities?
> ▶ Do you have other comments, complaints, observations, or questions?
> ▶ What can be done to improve the learning experience for the next practicum student?

How is learning during the practicum comparable to the continuing education responsibilities of the professional social worker?

When reviewing and thinking about your performance in the practicum, your field instructor may ask him- or herself questions such as:

> ▶ Has this student demonstrated dependability and professionally responsible behavior?
> ▶ Can this individual be counted on in a stressful and demanding situation?
> ▶ Would this student be able to handle a social work position in this agency?
> ▶ Would I hire this person for a social work job?
> ▶ Would I want this person to be a social worker for my mother? My child? For a good friend of mine?
> ▶ Would I be willing to write a strong letter of recommendation for this student?

Behaviors and personal qualities that impress a field instructor include the following: initiative, dependability, honesty, punctuality, capacity to meet deadlines, perseverance, ability to handle conflict in interpersonal relations, sensitivity to others, ability to achieve goals and objectives, ability to plan and organize work, clear writing, motivation and willingness to work hard, receptivity to new learning, self-awareness and openness to examining personal values and attitudes, capacity to work under pressure, personal maturity, emotional stability, respect for clients and other students, fairness in decision making, and professionalism.

Behaviors and qualities that cause a field instructor to doubt a student's ability to perform as a social worker include the opposite of the above listed behaviors, especially dishonesty, missing deadlines, disrespect for others, manipulation and efforts to bend rules and requirements, attempts to secure special concessions or privileges, not informing supervisors of problems, and the inability to keep personal problems from interfering with professional tasks and activities.

In order to prepare for a formal evaluation, review your learning agreement and its stated goals and activities, as well as the practicum evaluation tool used by your school. Give careful thought to the question of how well you have managed to carry out your various responsibilities and completed assigned tasks. Prepare a list of your assigned tasks and responsibilities and assemble documentation of your work and accomplishments so it can easily be reviewed by your field instructor. Prior to meeting with your field instructor for the formal evaluation, you may be asked to complete a self-evaluation using your school's evaluation tool. You can also prepare for your evaluation by completing the workbook activity of this chapter.

Think of the evaluation as a learning experience that can help you become more self-aware, insightful, and skilled. Become aware of any feelings of inadequacy or any emotional triggers that might be activated during the process of evaluation. If you know what they are, you are more likely to benefit from supervision and suggestions for improvement than if you lack this level of self-awareness.

Prepare yourself emotionally for the formal evaluation session so that you will be open to hearing feedback about your performance. When receiving feedback on your performance, strive to maintain an openness toward what you are hearing. Although it may be difficult to hear a frank appraisal of your work, avoid being defensive. Consider this feedback carefully and work to improve in the areas noted, knowing that feedback is actually a gift to you that will make you a better practitioner.

Should you feel uncomfortable receiving feedback on your performance, consider your reaction to be similar to what clients may feel when you give them feedback on their social functioning or their performance on an intervention plan. Being evaluated yourself will hopefully make you more empathetic and humble, and will remind you of the importance of identifying both strengths and areas for growth.

In addition to constructive criticism, you will receive positive feedback related to areas in which you are doing well. Take note of what your field instructor sees as your skills and gifts. If you want more specific feedback about what you have done well so that you know what your skills or abilities are, ask for it. Review the workbook section of Chapter 1, and determine if the strengths you identified there have been demonstrated in your performance and if the ones you did not identify earlier have been demonstrated over time. Complete once more the checklist called "Strengths for a Successful Practicum" as a post-test and compare your view of your strengths as a social worker with your view of yourself at the beginning of practicum. It will be helpful to see your professional growth to this point in practicum. This will underscore the fact that throughout your career you will continue to develop the strengths needed for professional practice. Build on your strengths because they will form the basis of your professional knowledge and abilities.

Strive to understand what your field instructor observed in your performance that led him or her to draw a particular conclusion concerning your performance. Seek descriptions and examples of any poor performance and ask for

Human Rights & Justice

As you move closer to becoming a professional, what do you see as your responsibility in terms of promoting social justice by advancing and improving the social work profession?

specific suggestions on how it can be improved. Request descriptions of performances that were rated higher than most others. Reflect on these descriptions and determine why you perform some tasks and activities better than others. If you and your field instructor disagree on the adequacy of your performance, prepare factual documentation supporting your point of view. However, if you agree that your performance is deficient, it is best to acknowledge the problem rather than entering into a pointless argument that can only leave you looking dishonest or lacking in self-awareness.

A common problem experienced by social work practicum students in direct services agencies is for the student to have an unusually strong or unexpected emotional reaction to specific client problems or situations. This is usually rooted in the student's own history of personal or family problems. If this happens to you, discuss these reactions with your field instructor. In some cases it will be necessary for students to undergo counseling as a way of better understanding these reactions and finding ways to keep them from interfering with social work performance.

Finally, remember that although you are just beginning your practice as a social worker, you have much to offer. Build on those gifts, attributes, values, and skills over time, knowing that professional growth is your responsibility. Continue to evaluate your own growth, expecting yourself to continuously acquire new learning, exhibit new skills, and advance practice.

Professional Identity

What is your plan to continue the professional growth that will increase your level of competency over time?

A Self-Evaluation of Your Practicum Performance: A Workbook Activity

Every school of social work education uses some type of evaluation instrument or tool for evaluating student performance in the practicum. Before beginning this workbook activity, carefully examine the instrument that will be used in the evaluation of your performance.

In this activity you are asked to reflect on and evaluate your own performance in relation to eleven broad categories and fifty-five dimensions or specific areas of social work knowledge and skills. These dimensions are fairly typical of those used in various practicum evaluation instruments.[*] Evaluate your performance in relation to each of the fifty-five statements below. Describe your performance using the following descriptors: **excellent, above average, average, below average.**

Category A: Social Work as a Profession

A1. Understands the social work role and purpose as distinct from the role and purpose of other professions.

Excellent	Above Average	Average	Below Average

A2. Demonstrates competence in a variety of social work practice roles (e.g., case manager, advocate, planner, counselor, broker).

Excellent	Above Average	Average	Below Average

A3. Understands social work ethics and conducts self in accordance with the NASW *Code of Ethics* and its underlying values (e.g., client self-determination, confidentiality, human dignity, social justice).

Excellent	Above Average	Average	Below Average

A4. Demonstrates competence in the various levels of social work interventions from micro- to macro-level practice (e.g., from direct practice with individuals to social change efforts).

Excellent	Above Average	Average	Below Average

[*]The author has adapted The University of Montana BSW Practicum Evaluation with permission of Tondy Baumgartner, MSW, Practicum Coordinator at The University of Montana School of Social Work.

A5. Conducts self in a professional manner (e.g., punctual, reliable, efficient, organized, completed assigned tasks, dresses appropriately).

Excellent	Above Average	Average	Below Average

Category B: Organizational Context of Practice

B1. Understands agency's purpose, mission, history, funding, and structure.

Excellent	Above Average	Average	Below Average

B2. Understands and facilitates the flow of work in the agency and follows established agency policies, procedures.

Excellent	Above Average	Average	Below Average

B3. Works creatively and collaboratively within agency guidelines.

Excellent	Above Average	Average	Below Average

B4. Understands the relationship of the agency to other agencies in the community.

Excellent	Above Average	Average	Below Average

B5. Analyzes agency evaluation tools and suggests additional evaluation procedures if needed.

Excellent	Above Average	Average	Below Average

Category C: Community Context of Practice

C1. Is aware of various services, programs, and resources in the community relevant to the client population served by agency.

Excellent	Above Average	Average	Below Average

C2. Uses those community resources most appropriate for specific clients.

Excellent	Above Average	Average	Below Average

C3. Uses advocacy, when appropriate, to obtain resources needed by clients and/or empowers clients to advocate for themselves.

Excellent	Above Average	Average	Below Average

C4. Is able to identify gaps in services within the community.

Excellent	Above Average	Average	Below Average

C5. Understands the effect of community factors on clients and services (e.g., rural/urban, demographics, funding priorities, attitudes, and economics).

Excellent	Above Average	Average	Below Average

Category D: Data Gathering and Assessment

D1. Purposefully and selectively gathers relevant data needed for assessments and interventions.

Excellent	Above Average	Average	Below Average

D2. Sorts, categorizes, and analyzes data in order to understand the nature of client concerns, needs, or problems.

Excellent	Above Average	Average	Below Average

D3. Engages and involves the client in the process of data collection.

Excellent	Above Average	Average	Below Average

D4. Addresses client strengths, including client's capacity for change.

Excellent	Above Average	Average	Below Average

D5. Identifies the major systems related to the problem or concern being addressed.

Excellent	Above Average	Average	Below Average

Category E: Planning and Intervention

E1. Sets priorities and identifies clear and measurable objectives for intervention.

Excellent	Above Average	Average	Below Average

E2. Involves the client in setting goals and choosing interventions and develops a contract or working agreement.

Excellent	Above Average	Average	Below Average

E3. Understands various perspectives, theories, and models that guide interventions.

Excellent	Above Average	Average	Below Average

E4. Is able to determine the most feasible and effective level of intervention (micro, mezzo, or macro).

Excellent	Above Average	Average	Below Average

E5. Selects specific interventions matched to the client's situation, needs, available resources, and agency purpose.

Excellent	Above Average	Average	Below Average

Category F: Termination and Evaluation

F1. Helps clients evaluate movement toward agreed-upon goals and objectives.

Excellent	Above Average	Average	Below Average

F2. Terminates helping relationship appropriately and constructively.

Excellent	Above Average	Average	Below Average

F3. Seeks out and utilizes tools and instruments that can be used to measure client progress.

Excellent	Above Average	Average	Below Average

F4. Seeks out and uses tools and instruments that can measure and evaluate own practice.

Excellent	Above Average	Average	Below Average

F5. Is able to examine own performance in an objective and nondefensive manner.

Excellent	Above Average	Average	Below Average

Category G: Understanding Social Problems

G1. Identifies and describes the social problems or conditions that agency addresses.

Excellent	Above Average	Average	Below Average

G2. Identifies and describes the social problems or conditions faced by clients of the agency.

Excellent	Above Average	Average	Below Average

G3. Understands how social problems develop as a result of the interaction between individuals, social systems, and the larger social environment.

Excellent	Above Average	Average	Below Average

G4. Is aware of the major social problems facing the community.

Excellent	Above Average	Average	Below Average

G5. Uses an ecosystems perspective and social systems theory to analyze social problems.

Excellent	Above Average	Average	Below Average

Category H: Social Policy and Social Change

H1. Identifies and analyzes social policies affecting clients of the agency.

Excellent	Above Average	Average	Below Average

H2. Recognizes the positive and negative impacts of social policy on clients.

Excellent	Above Average	Average	Below Average

H3. Understands how social policies develop and are modified over time.

Excellent	Above Average	Average	Below Average

H4. Identifies needed changes in social policy.

Excellent	Above Average	Average	Below Average

H5. Is able to participate in social change or social justice efforts.

Excellent	Above Average	Average	Below Average

Category I: Diversity

I1. Is aware of and sensitive to client issues related to diversity (e.g., culture, ethnicity, gender, age, socioeconomic status, disability, sexual orientation).

Excellent	Above Average	Average	Below Average

I2. Treats all people with respect regardless of their behavior, characteristics, and background.

Excellent	Above Average	Average	Below Average

I3. Understands the effects of stereotypes, prejudice, discrimination, and oppression on individuals, families, and communities and on the formation of social policy.

Excellent	Above Average	Average	Below Average

I4. Is effective in communicating with persons of differing backgrounds and life experiences.

Excellent	Above Average	Average	Below Average

I5. Is able to individualize procedures for assessment, planning, intervention, and evaluation for diverse clients.

Excellent	Above Average	Average	Below Average

Category J: Communication Skills

J1. Effectively uses nonverbal communication and verbal helping skills (e.g., empathic responding, active listening, mediating, counseling, interviewing).

Excellent	Above Average	Average	Below Average

J2. Effectively uses written communication (e.g., correspondence, reports, records).

Excellent	Above Average	Average	Below Average

J3. Is able to engage and work with nonvoluntary, resistant, or hard-to-reach clients.

Excellent	Above Average	Average	Below Average

J4. Recognizes the underlying meaning and significance of clients' concerns and situation.

Excellent	Above Average	Average	Below Average

J5. Handles questions and disagreements with other staff and agency policies and procedures with understanding, tact, and diplomacy.

Excellent	Above Average	Average	Below Average

Category K: Knowledge and Use of Self

K1. Takes initiative in developing and implementing own learning activities.

Excellent	Above Average	Average	Below Average

K2. Uses supervision for guidance, learning, and professional growth.

Excellent	Above Average	Average	Below Average

K3. Understands how personal values, beliefs, and ethics enhance or interfere with social work practice.

Excellent	Above Average	Average	Below Average

K4. Is aware of own biases and deals with them appropriately.

Excellent	Above Average	Average	Below Average

K5. Recognizes personal changes needed in order to function more effectively as a social worker.

Excellent	Above Average	Average	Below Average

SUGGESTED LEARNING ACTIVITIES

- Compare the practicum evaluation instrument used by your school with the evaluation tool used to evaluate the performance of social workers in your agency. This will help you see what is expected of social workers that is not expected of practicum students.

- Evaluate yourself using both your school's evaluation instrument and the sample tool in this chapter.

- Identify fears you may have about being evaluated and discuss them with your supervisor.

- Talk with other practicum students about their experiences with the evaluation process.

- In Sheafor and Horejsi (2008), read the sections entitled "Developing Self-Awareness" (576–680) and "Worker Performance Evaluation" (481–484).

Succeed with

Log onto **www.mysocialworklab.com** and select the **Career Exploration** videos from the left-hand menu. Answer the questions below. (*If you did not receive an access code to* **MySocialWorkLab** *with this text and wish to purchase access online, please visit* www.mysocialworklab.com.)

1. **Watch question 21 of the interview with Karen Cowan.** Karen describes the measures by which she

gauges her success. Are they qualitative or quantitative? What is an optimal balance of these two types of evaluation?

2. **Watch question 15 with Beth Harmon.** Most social workers are motivated by making a difference in the lives of others. What difference do you believe generalist social workers can make?

PRACTICE TEST

The following questions are similar in phrasing and content to those asked in social work licensing examinations. They should help you prepare to take the licensing examination in your state.

**Engage
Assess
Intervene
Evaluate**

1. The most important perspective on whether an intervention is successful is
   a. that of the social worker
   b. that of the agency
   c. that of the client
   d. that of the funding source

2. The reason that intervention evaluations are often not done well is that
   e. Social workers are not trained to do evaluations
   f. It is impossible to measure the outcomes of most interventions.
   g. Time is limited and agencies do not value them enough.
   h. Clients do not insist upon them.

3. Although it is important to evaluate the process of interventions, it is also important to
   a. evaluate client input
   b. evaluate outcomes
   c. evaluate expenditures
   d. evaluate agency policies

**Research
Based
Practice**

4. Which is true?
   a. quantitative research is preferable to qualitative research
   b. qualitative research is preferable to quantitative research

   c. both are important and useful
   d. clients prefer quantitative research

5. The NASW Code of Ethics:
   a. does not speak to the process of evaluation of interventions
   b. provides detailed guidelines for evaluation
   c. is often in conflict with agency evaluation guidelines
   d. provides support for the process of evaluation

6. Client involvement in evaluation of interventions
   a. is only necessary in client centered casework
   b. is important in all interventions
   c. is optional and at the discretion of the social worker
   d. is ethical only if clients agree

7. Social workers whose performance is evaluated as substandard
   a. may face legal sanctions
   b. may face licensing sanctions
   c. may face agency sanctions
   d. all of the above

**Engage
Assess
Intervene
Evaluate**

18

Merging Self and Profession

LEARNING GOALS FOR THIS CHAPTER

- ▶ To identify important considerations in preparing for a social work career

- ▶ To identify factors important to your selection of a particular type of social work practice and practice setting

- ▶ To learn the importance of balancing personal and professional aspects of one's life

- ▶ To develop personal and professional self-awareness

CONNECTING CORE COMPETENCIES *in this chapter*

| Professional Identity | Ethical Practice | Critical Thinking | Diversity in Practice | Human Rights & Justice | Research Based Practice | Human Behavior | Policy Practice | Practice Contexts | Engage Assess Intervene Evaluate |

Human Rights & Justice

As you move closer to becoming a professional, what do you see as your responsibility in terms of promoting social justice by advancing and improving the social work profession?

When you chose social work as a profession, it was no doubt because of your commitment to helping others, facilitating social change, and contributing to social justice. Your family and friends, while certainly commending you for your commitment, may have raised the following questions: What is social work? Why do you want to be a social worker? Why do you need a degree in social work? Will you be able to get a job and earn a living? How will you keep from burning out in a stressful profession such as social work? These are good questions, and you should be able to answer them and be comfortable with your answers. It is likely that your responses to these questions will be rooted in your commitment to the welfare of others, making a significant difference in the world, and promoting social justice. Hopefully your practicum will serve to cement your decision to pursue social work as a career because you will be able to enhance your knowledge and skills and see how you are suited for this work.

Each of us is an individual with a unique personality and set of abilities and interests. In addition, each profession and occupation has a discrete set of demands and required skills. For you to be satisfied and effective as a social worker, there must be a good match between you and the profession. Selecting a career or occupation is one of the most important decisions you will ever make. That decision will have far-reaching implications for your basic contentment in life, the level of satisfaction you find in work, and your economic situation. A good match between your choice of occupation and your interests, abilities, and values will bring you personal satisfaction, challenge, and stimulation. A mismatch can give rise to general discontent and stress-related health problems.

The practicum provides an invaluable opportunity to examine and test the match between who you really are, your values, beliefs, temperament, abilities, and skills and the demands, requirements, and rewards of social work practice. This chapter is designed to help you examine and celebrate that match.

BACKGROUND AND CONTEXT

Most social workers feel a calling to the profession of social work because they are committed to and passionate about helping others and they find the profession's values compatible with their own. They want to make a positive contribution to their community and world and they see that the practice of social work is a way of doing that. Some also feel drawn to the profession because events and experiences in their lives have opened their eyes to certain problems and to the needs of other people. Others are attracted to social work because they have the natural skills and abilities necessary to the profession and see social work education as a formal way of acquiring the ability to make even more impact in terms of social justice. Most are drawn to social work by virtue of the way they think the world should be, the responsibility they feel to act on behalf of others, and the belief that they must become involved in social justice efforts.

It is important for those preparing for such a rewarding and challenging career to become familiar with the types of jobs that are available and the demands of the work. They must have a high level of self-awareness so they can make good choices in relation to the type of job they seek, practice self-care and stress management, and balance personal and professional responsibilities. Social workers must be aware of their unique gifts, their values, and their biases. Such self-awareness is also critical to becoming a professional who is effective in his or her use of self in relating to clients. Social workers must understand how their particular style and manner of interacting is perceived by others, especially clients. Those planning to enter social work must be emotionally healthy, skilled in communication, able to build and maintain relationships, able to manage stress, and willing to continually learn and grow, both personally and professionally.

Choosing a helping profession as one's life's work usually means that you care deeply about those you serve. This commitment to others may take a toll on your personal life unless you learn to find a healthy balance between work and personal life. It is not possible to make a complete separation between our personal and professional lives. Our work affects our personal lives and our personal lives affect our work. Sheafor and Horejsi (2006, 17) observe that the social worker's "own beliefs, values, physical and emotional well-being, spirituality, family relationships, friendships, and all other facets of living will both influence and be influenced by the day-to-day experiences of social work practice." Knowing this, it is vital to find a workable balance between your personal life and your professional life.

It is important to find this balance because it is easy to allow your concern for clients to overtake you. You may worry about them or take more responsibility for them than is healthy for you. It is important to learn to set clear boundaries between your personal and professional selves early in your career because this will help you retain your energy, enthusiasm, and optimism while also preventing discouragement and burnout. Ask your field instructor for suggestions on how to do this.

Employers are looking for certain traits when they screen job applicants for social work positions. Knowing what employers seek and value in a social worker will help you to anticipate the requirements for certain jobs and work to develop the ability to meet these requirements. Typically, they are especially interested in these qualities, which you should aspire to:

- Skills related to the job to be performed
- Character traits and experiences that reflect creativity, flexibility, and enthusiasm for solving problems
- The ability to work cooperatively with others
- The ability to work creatively and collaboratively within an organizational structure
- A genuine interest in and an enjoyment of the type of work to be performed
- Written and verbal communication skills
- A commitment to professional competence and excellence

Practice Contexts

What organizational characteristics listed below will be most important to you as a professional, and how will you maximize the number of them available in your first professional position?

The relationship between career satisfaction and one's overall satisfaction with oneself and life is a close one. Those who are satisfied with their careers tend to have high self-esteem, are able to manage stress, and believe that they have influence and control over the outcome of their work. Other factors also contribute to job and career satisfaction. Among them are the following:

- ***Overall workload***—Most people prefer jobs that are stimulating, challenging, and that keep them busy, but are not overwhelming or exhausting.
- ***Variety***—Most people prefer work that provides some variety. Most people do not care for jobs that are highly repetitive.
- ***Opportunity***—Most people desire jobs that will provide opportunities for promotion, advancement, ongoing learning, and professional development.
- ***Social interaction***—Most people prefer jobs that allow friendly, pleasant, and informal interactions with co-workers.

Keep these in mind as you begin the search for a professional position in the field of social work. The work itself will be rewarding, so the work environment should contribute to your overall well-being as a professional.

GUIDANCE AND DIRECTION

Critical Thinking

How can you continue to engage in self-reflection and professional growth when you assume the responsibility for a full time professional position?

Research Based Practice

How can you integrate what you are learning into your practice, and what research questions do you have as a result of your practicum?

Social work requires an integration of professional knowledge and ethics with a high level of self-awareness. It is not enough to know "about" people, to have skills, to know theories, or to understand models and techniques. You as a "person" must merge with the you as a "professional." Remember that all the skills and knowledge in the world are not enough to make you an effective social worker. You also need to bring your personal gifts, strengths, creativity, passion, and commitment to the social work profession. It is in the unique blending of your personal qualities and your professional education that you will become a truly skilled and qualified social worker.

Who you are as a person is just as important as what you know or can do. View your practicum as an opportunity to grow both personally and professionally, and to blend your unique personality and professional style with the requirements of your chosen profession. Over time the two parts of you will blend so that you will bring everything that is unique about you to your personal way of being a social worker.

Seek opportunities to continually enhance your professional growth. For example, read books and journals, attend workshops and in-service training, try out new skills and techniques, think critically about intervention strategies, carefully observe the behavior and practice of social workers in your agency, and spend time talking with knowledgeable and skilled practitioners. Engage in critical self-reflection, asking yourself and trusted colleagues what you can do to continue growing. Open yourself to feedback so that you see yourself as others do. You will certainly see your own growth over time, and this will not only reinforce your choice of social work as a profession, but will also remind you of the importance of self-awareness as a tool for helping others.

Ask for feedback from coworkers, your field instructor, and clients. Use this information to better understand who you are, what you have to offer, and what you may need to change in order to become a skilled and effective social worker. You are certain to see that you have grown over time, that your questions have become more probing, and your reflections more sophisticated. This will reinforce the fact that you are growing as a professional.

Continue to think about how well your professional and personal lives fit together. Do you have the temperament to be a social worker? Are you able to handle the demands and the stress of the job? What demands of the job make you most uncomfortable? What tasks and activities make you anxious? Do you like to do what social workers do? Can you put your knowledge into practice? What additional knowledge do you need to more effectively enhance your personal skills? Which of the profession's values do you feel most strongly about?

Your practicum is truly job-related experience. It is relevant preparation for practice and the job market. Do your best and remember that the skills you develop now, combined with favorable evaluations and recommendations from your field instructor, can help you obtain employment in the profession.

Observe how the social workers in your agency deal with challenges such as high caseloads, potentially modest salaries, unmotivated and difficult clients, seemingly intractable social problems, funding cuts, and the stress of dealing with deeply emotional and painful situations on a daily basis. Begin

Food for Thought

Those who work to bring about changes are able to see even in darkest circumstances how improvements are possible if the right kind of effort is made. They can see beyond inconsistencies, human frailty, and fearsome injustice to the goal that beckons them. The constant presence of that goal carries them on and sets them apart from others who do not make a difference (Armstrong and Wakin, 1978, 82–89).

• • •

The moment of commitment cannot be deferred. It must become a lifelong process, one that links our lives to the lives of others, our souls to the souls of others, in a chain of being that reaches both backward and forward, connecting us with all that makes us human (Loeb, 1999, 349).

• • •

As a social worker, you cannot separate your personal self entirely from your professional self. Just as the client does, you bring your attitudes, beliefs, and life experiences to the relationship. Unlike the client, however, you are responsible for balancing the personal with the professional. Therefore, you must determine the amount and scope of integrating yourself into the client relationship (Birkenmaier and Berg-Weger, 2007, 148).

• • •

When our professional lives or volunteer services consume so much time and energy that we neglect relationships important to our own well-being, our priorities are out of alignment. When this happens, a measure of our own health is the capability we have to step back, assess the situation, and take appropriate action on behalf of ourselves. This is what we ask of our clients and therefore what we are willing to do for ourselves (Schmidt, 2002, 82).

• • •

Social work practice involves the blending or merging of a unique human being with a set of professional responsibilities. The social worker, like the client and all other people, has many dimensions, including the physical, emotional, intellectual, spiritual, and social. The social worker responds to his or her professional role and responsibilities as a whole person, and all these dimensions affect and are affected by the moment-by-moment activities of practice (Sheafer and Horejsi, 2008, 33).

now to develop stress management skills and habits that will help you avoid excessive job-related stress or burnout. Learn how to set limits, define personal boundaries, make time for your family and yourself, and maintain a positive outlook on clients and the work you do.

Begin to develop the habit of monitoring your own personal growth. Ask yourself these questions regularly:

▶ What is my vision for myself as a social worker?
▶ How can I maintain this vision?
▶ What social work values are most important to me as I embark on this career?
▶ Am I growing as a person and a professional?
▶ Do I know myself better than I did last month? Last year?
▶ Am I satisfied with who I am and what I am doing?
▶ If I am not satisfied, what can I do about it? What will I do about it?
▶ How can I continue to grow and change in a positive way?
▶ Do I continue to see the potential, possibility, and strengths of clients?
▶ Do I continue to believe in the goals and ethics of the profession?
▶ Am I optimistic about social change?

Engage Assess
Intervene Evaluate

When social workers use themselves as a tool for helping others, what professional attributes are most needed at each phase of the planned change process?

Remember one of the basic guidelines your professors probably gave you at the outset of your social work education—the concept of using yourself as a tool for practice. We use ourselves in relationship with individuals, families, groups, and communities to effect the social change so important to us. This then requires that we continually hone our knowledge, skills, and self-awareness if we wish to be effective.

Merging Self and Profession: A Workbook Activity

The questions presented below are intended to encourage careful thought about how your choice of social work as a career will enhance and affect your whole being and influence your many other roles and responsibilities.

1. What strongly held values led you to pursue social work as a profession?

   _____

   _____

   _____

2. Do you feel a calling to social work? If so, on what is this calling based?

   _____

   _____

   _____

3. What is it about a career in social work that you find most positive and attractive? How can you make sure that you retain this view?

   _____

   _____

   _____

4. Is there anything about a career in social work that you find particularly negative or aversive? How can you minimize or cope with these aspects of social work?

   _____

   _____

   _____

5. What have you learned about yourself during the practicum that confirms your choice of social work as a profession?

   _____

   _____

   _____

6. What gifts and abilities have you discovered and developed in yourself that will make you a good social worker?

   _____

   _____

   _____

7. What specific self-care activities will you engage in to maintain your energy, passion, optimism, and commitment?

_____

_____

_____

8. After five years of experience and employment as a social worker, what type of work would you like to be doing? After fifteen years?

_____

_____

_____

9. What impact do you hope to make as a result of your work?

_____

_____

_____

10. What advice would you give to other social work students who are just beginning their practicum?

_____

_____

_____

SUGGESTED LEARNING ACTIVITIES

▶ Interview experienced social workers in your agency and in other agencies. Ask about their level of job satisfaction, as well as the pros and cons of a career in social work. Ask them whether, if they could do it all over, they would select a social work career.

▶ Speak with social workers who have obtained advanced degrees (MSW, Ph.D., or DSW) and ask them to help you consider the possibility of further education.

▶ Observe the self-care practices of those around you and develop your own self-care plan for practice.

▶ In Sheafor and Horejsi (2008), read the section entitled "Getting a Social Work Job" (574–576).

▶ Examine the social work–related job openings advertised in local and regional newspapers, public agency bulletins, and in NASW news. (The NASW web site is www.socialworkers.org.)

▶ Read "Taking Heart: Spiritual Exercises for Social Activists" in Macy (1991).

Succeed with  **PEARSON mysocialworklab**

Log onto **www.mysocialworklab.com** and select the **Career Exploration** videos from the left-hand menu. Answer the questions below. (*If you did not receive an access code to **MySocialWorkLab** with this text and wish to purchase access online, please visit* www.mysocialworklab.com.)

1. **Watch question 14 in the video interview with Beth Harmon.** What can you learn from Beth about balancing personal and professional issues, values, and responsibilities?

2. **Watch question 13 in the video interview with Karen Cowan.** She finds herself juggling many professional responsibilities. This is common for social workers, especially administrators. What are some ways to manage the multiple demands on time for administrators?

PRACTICE TEST

The following questions are similar in phrasing and content to those asked in social work licensing examinations. They should help you prepare to take the licensing examination in your state.

1. Social workers' personal values
   a. generally provide the motivation for their choice of profession
   b. are totally separate from their professional values
   c. should be secondary to those of the agency in which they work
   d. none of the above

Professional Identity

2. Self awareness is an important part of social work practice because
   a. social workers represent the profession to society
   b. social workers use themselves as professional tools
   c. it will help prevent professional burnout
   d. professional growth is required in the profession

3. Professional growth
   a. is expected of all social workers on an ongoing basis
   b. is synonymous with continuing education
   c. is regulated by state licensing boards
   d. is synonymous with personal growth

4. Social workers and their clients may have values conflicts, which should be resolved
   a. by having a mediator negotiate between them
   b. by the social worker ensuring that his/her values do not negatively impact clients
   c. by supervisors
   d. by client advocates

5. Professional boundaries are important to maintain because:
   a. social workers are vulnerable to client manipulation
   b. social workers tend to think they are unnecessary
   c. social workers need to protect themselves and clients
   d. agencies require them

6. The value of peer supervision is that
   a. it provides another perspective by a valued colleague
   b. it costs less than supervision by a trained supervisor
   c. it is less threatening
   d. it allows for colleagues to share information not shared with supervisors

7. Which term describes the vicarious victimization that can happen to social workers?
   a. burnout
   b. stress
   c. compassion fatigue
   d. secondary traumatic stress

19

Leadership and Social Justice

CONNECTING CORE COMPETENCIES *in this chapter*

| Professional Identity | Ethical Practice | Critical Thinking | Diversity in Practice | Human Rights & Justice | Research Based Practice | Human Behavior | Policy Practice | Practice Contexts | Engage Assess Intervene Evaluate |

Now that your practicum is nearing its completion, you have nearly fulfilled all of the requirements necessary to obtain your degree. You are, no doubt, excited about job possibilities and also thinking seriously about the personal ramifications of entering the world of social work. This is a time of transition. What lies ahead for you? Where will you work? What will be expected of you? What kind of social worker do you hope to become? Perhaps even more important, what kind of person do you want to become? This chapter invites you to reflect on these questions.

As a social worker, social work educator, and the author of this book, I desire three things for you:

1. That you become an effective and ethical social worker

2. That you become a leader within your profession and your community—one committed to the pursuit of social and economic justice

3. That you become the person you want to be and live a life filled with meaning and purpose

This final chapter offers suggestions on how you might achieve these three ends. Completing your practicum means that others have confidence that you will be able to reach your goals, contribute to the profession, and have a personally and professionally satisfying life.

BECOMING THE SOCIAL WORKER YOU WANT TO BE

Professional Identity

Referring to Table 13.2 (on page 138) which compares student and professional roles, identify the areas in which you have truly become a professional and those in which you still function at times like a student. What can you do to move into the professional category in all the dimensions listed?

It is both exciting and rather daunting to think about being a social worker. There are many problems to be addressed and numerous clients to be served. Injustices must be challenged and many programs need to be designed or redesigned. There is so much to be done and so few resources. There is also much more to learn as you move from the academic world of a practicum student to the real world of the professional social worker.

Because you have completed the requirements for a social work degree in a program accredited by the Council on Social Work Education, your professors have concluded that you are ready to begin the practice of social work. Although you may still feel anxious and ill prepared to assume the full responsibilities of a social worker, your professors and supervisors believe that you possess the knowledge and basic skills needed to move into a social agency and apply what you have learned. You have been educated in an academic setting, trained in a social agency, and exposed to many social problems and various ways of addressing them. Do not underestimate what you have learned and what you are capable of doing. You are now a professional social worker by virtue of all you have learned and the ways in which you have demonstrated your competence and commitment to ethical practice.

Reflect often on what you have learned about the unique mission of social work and its commitment to those in society considered most vulnerable and oppressed. Social work is a profession deeply committed, both by its history and current practice, to creating communities and a society that will nurture the well-being of individuals and families and to making sure that all people have access to the basic resources and opportunities necessary to live with dignity. You have entered a profession that is committed to challenging those systems and institutional structures that do not treat people in a fair and humane manner. If you, as a social worker, do not speak out against and seek to correct

Why don't all clients have access to these resources and opportunities, and what should be your response to this?

How would you describe to a new practicum student the relationship between the micro, mezzo and macro levels of social work practice?

Which ethical principles and research guidelines will you use to continue evaluating the effectiveness of your practice and that of your agency?

a social or economic injustice you are, in effect, giving your tacit approval to the current state of affairs.

View the practice of social work as being much more than the tasks and activities listed in your job description or suggested in your agency's mission statement. Work hard at whatever you are hired to do, but also assume the additional responsibility of becoming an advocate for those who are not able to speak for themselves. Social work, at its unique best, is about going beyond one's job description and acting on a commitment to social justice by weaving together the networks of people and resources that can bring about needed changes at the community, state, and national levels. In fact, a true leader sees what is possible and is not constrained by a job description or by limited resources. A leader develops a vision, knows what needs to be done, and makes things happen, building on acquired knowledge and skills, combined with the synergy generated by bringing committed people together.

You have been schooled in the person-in-environment perspective that is fundamental to the way social workers view people, assess human problems and concerns, and design interventions. Social workers, whether employed to work at the micro or macro level, must be cognizant of the wider societal context of the lives and problems of their clients and the context of the agencies, programs, and interventions that address these client concerns. For example, a social worker employed at the micro level as an advocate for those in poverty should question why poverty exists and take a macro-level leadership role in addressing the myriad of macro level contributors to poverty. Conversely, social workers working on the macro level to change social policies must never forget the very serious impact of any social policy changes on the lives of individual people struggling with poverty. This is a very broad and demanding mission, but a crucial one that a leader will embrace.

The realities and time pressures associated with employment in an agency that has a particular mission and program tend to set in motion a number of forces that tend to narrow a social worker's range of concerns, interests, and vision. You will feel very busy with all of the demands of your job, but it will be important that you find ways to remain involved in social issues beyond the scope of your work responsibilities. Doing so will help remind you that others care about their work as much as you and can serve as a source of inspiration for you. Strive to maintain a wide range of interests, involvements, and professional activities. Seek out new ideas, even when they are not immediately applicable in your everyday work.

As you enter into the work of a particular agency, you may discover that the agency uses an unfamiliar conceptual framework or rationale to guide its practice activities. As you are exposed to new practice frameworks, remember that each one needs to be examined in terms of its potential to enhance practice effectiveness, its appropriateness for use with particular types of clients in particular settings, evidence of its effectiveness, its stated or implied assumptions about clients and the process of change, and its compatibility with social work values.

Carefully consider why you might prefer one approach over other possibilities. Most likely, you prefer a particular practice framework because it is the one most compatible with your beliefs about human behavior and human problems, and because it instructs you as a professional to perform those tasks and activities to which you are especially attracted. Although it is natural to pursue your own interests, seek to broaden and deepen your understanding of the various perspectives, theories, and models used in social work practice and carefully examine the assumptions underlying each approach. Strive to understand the strengths and limitations of each one. Be open to gaining insights and guidance from several practice frameworks.

To know whether you are being effective over time, document your work and study the outcomes of your practice, both individually and in concert with other professionals and agencies. Be ready to change your approach if you are not being as effective as you had hoped or think is possible. Needless to say, much of what social workers do and much of what clients experience is difficult to measure, but resist the temptation to use this as an excuse for not making a genuine effort to evaluate your practice. You cannot improve your practice unless you are willing to look at it critically and allow others to offer constructive criticisms.

To the extent possible, build your knowledge base from empirical and scientific studies, but remember that there are many other sources of useful knowledge. Some are empirical and some are not. Balance the ***positivist view of knowledge building,*** which rests primarily on the scientific method of understanding, with contributions from ***practice wisdom,*** which refers to the collective professional experiences and observations of practitioners. Add to that insights derived from study of the humanities, religion, and classic and modern literature. Finally, learn from your clients as you listen to their stories and experiences, and add their wisdom to yours.

As you use new research findings and theories drawn from the social and behavioral sciences, consider the observation by sociologists that such knowledge is ***socially constructed.*** Our knowledge of a social or psychological phenomenon or a particular human problem is shaped and limited by the context in which it was studied, by our positionality in relation to the problem, and by the language used to describe it. It is very much tied to culture, history, economics, and politics. Our knowledge is, at best, incomplete and only temporarily true. The awareness that knowledge is a social construction helps us to put data and conclusions in perspective and realize that the concepts and theories used in practice, no matter how well-conceived and impressive, are purely human inventions. It is your prerogative and your responsibility to thoughtfully question all findings and claims, regardless of their source.

It is actually the job of critically reflective social workers to deconstruct their knowledge and what is being told to them. This means that you must examine what you know, question how you came to know it, ask yourself how this view might be inaccurate or limited, and become comfortable at times with not knowing everything you need to know. In a similar vein, recognize that the ***concept of client*** is a human invention or social construction that has arisen out of our cultural views and presumptions about who is in need of help, who is powerless to help himself or herself, and who is qualified to help another person. Always be sensitive to the possibility that agencies, social workers, and other professionals can misuse their power and authority to label a person, family, or group as troubled and in need of certain services or interventions. Remember also that the designation of one person as a client and another as a social worker does not mean that the social worker is more knowledgeable or more insightful than the client. Rather, the opposite could be true. The lines between social worker and client, although useful, are arbitrary and can limit our ability to relate to each other in significant and ways.

Become involved in those professional organizations that can support your work, challenge you intellectually, and remind you that others are also involved in the struggle to create a just society. Remember that you are expected to contribute to the ongoing development and shaping of the profession, and that social work educators need to hear your observations and suggestions as much as clients need your skills. Voice your opinions about directions you believe the profession should take based on your observations and your projections of future needs. Speak up when you see your profession becoming focused too heavily on one aspect of social work to the detriment of its overall mission.

Remain in the world of ideas and questions, and commit to lifelong learning. There are numerous approaches you can take to continue learning and growing, which will not only make you more effective, but will also make you a better, more informed, and capable person. These guidelines may be helpful to you:

- Continue to read professional literature and attend advanced training sessions.
- Join or form a group of professionals that takes seriously its commitment to continuing education and peer supervision.
- Look globally and internationally for possible solutions to nagging and serious social problems.
- Learn from your clients who experience on a daily basis what you may only observe, read about, or imagine.
- Identify the connections between social conditions and the social problems resulting from them.
- Stay connected to schools of social work through training, conferences, and by offering guest lectures
- Talk on a regular basis to those with whom you fundamentally disagree in order to retain an open mind and clarify your own beliefs and values.
- Find ways to come to know and understand yourself better over time.
- Ask yourself regularly what your vision for the world is and determine what you need to learn to bring yourself closer to your goals.
- When you have the opportunity, supervise practicum students, recalling what it was like to be a student.

Recognize your ability to be a *catalyst for change,* which means that you can bring individuals and groups together, contribute your skills and knowledge, and stimulate positive movement or changes that would not have occurred without your intervention. Remember that you are not alone in your efforts to help others. There are many social workers who will support and encourage you in your efforts. Seek them out, offer your support in return, and find avenues of renewal for yourself, both personally and professionally.

Take care of yourself, see the good in the world as well as the problems, celebrate large and small successes, learn to laugh, and cultivate the sources of your passion and strength. Use your family, friends, spiritual beliefs, and core values to guide you, and take pride in your chosen profession.

BECOMING A SOCIAL JUSTICE LEADER

As a social worker you will encounter many situations of oppression and social and economic injustice. You will also encounter situations in which agency policies, programs, and practices are in need of revision to make them fairer and more effective. You will want to change these situations but may quickly discover that bringing about needed and meaningful change can be a difficult and slow process. In order to bring about change you must be willing and able to assume the role, tasks, and responsibilities of leadership. Desirable changes do not happen by accident. Rather, they are set in motion by individuals who assert themselves, articulate their beliefs, and step forward to take on the hard work of leading.

Although it may be true that a few leaders are the so-called born leaders, most had to learn the skills of leadership much like they learned any other skill. Aspiring leaders must consciously and continually cultivate the development of those qualities, ways of thinking, attitudes, and interpersonal skills that are associated with effective leadership.

Leadership is much more than having good ideas. It is not enough to know what needs to be done. Leadership is the ability to make things happen and to inspire others to join in the effort. Leaders must have a clear vision of what they want to accomplish. Equally important, they must be able to articulate this vision and explain it in words that others understand. The vision must be one that can be translated into action steps and programs that are inspiring but also feasible and realistic.

It is the leader's vision that gives him or her the critically important sense of purpose, direction, and self-confidence to make difficult decisions. This sense of purpose must be evident in all that the leader does. Indecisiveness and the unwillingness to take action when action is clearly necessary can deeply undermine confidence in a leader's ability. It is better for a leader to occasionally make a bad decision than to avoid making a critically important decision, so learn to be decisive and bold when necessary as well as thoughtful and well prepared.

Effective leaders lead by example. Followers are inspired and motivated by the passion, resolve, courage, hard work, and sacrifices of their leaders. Leaders must model the behaviors they want to see in others. They should not ask others to do what they are unwilling to do themselves. Leaders must demonstrate respect and genuine concern for the wishes, values, and abilities of those they lead. They must be willing to curtail some of their own preferences and plans in order to avoid moving too far ahead of those they lead. Leaders cannot lead unless there are people who choose to follow them.

Effective leaders must maintain open and honest communication with those they lead. This communication must keep everyone focused on the goal while attending to the concerns, fears, and ambivalence they may have about investing their time, energy, and money in working toward this goal. Good leaders anticipate possible conflicts and disagreements among those they lead. They are proactive in taking steps to prevent or resolve these conflicts before they can distract from goal achievement and splinter the followers into competing factions.

Leaders must be skilled in the art of collaboration and building bridges between individuals and organizations. They must reward others for their cooperation and share the credit for success with others, even those with whom they may disagree. Leaders must be willing to compromise when this is a necessary step toward reaching the sought-after goal.

The exercise of leadership always occurs within a context of competing and conflicting forces. Leaders shape, guide, and redirect those forces, so they move in directions that produce the desired effect and move people toward the desired goal. Because leaders must function within environments

Critical Thinking

What critical thinking skills are necessary for the leader committed to social justice and effectively contributing to social change?

and situations that are unpredictable and always changing, they must be willing to take necessary risks and cope with ambiguity and uncertainty.

Effective leaders possess a high level of self-awareness. They understand their own strengths and limitations and constantly examine their own motives and behavior. Some leaders destroy their capacity to lead by allowing feelings of self-importance and a need for recognition to dominate their decisions or by becoming arrogant and overly confident because of past successes. Decide now that you will never let that happen to you.

In addition to the factors mentioned previously, the following personal qualities and characteristics are important to the exercise of effective leadership:

- ▶ Capacity to think critically and examine personal decisions and actions
- ▶ Capacity to speak and write clearly to articulate a vision and purpose in ways people can understand
- ▶ Perseverance when faced with difficulties and disappointments
- ▶ Ability to delegate responsibility and teach or empower others to perform as well as they can
- ▶ Ability to make difficult decisions in situations that are complex and fluid
- ▶ Willingness to assume personal responsibility for one's decisions and actions
- ▶ Personal flexibility, openness to new ideas, and the ability to work with people with various abilities and from diverse backgrounds
- ▶ Ability to create a sense of belonging and community among those working toward the same goals
- ▶ Ability to make effective use of available time and get things done
- ▶ Willingness to assess one's own effectiveness in a nondefensive manner and to adopt approaches that will be more effective

Ethical Practice

Which ethical competencies listed in chapter 14 are most closely related to the characteristics of an effective leader committed to social justice?

Work hard to become what is commonly referred to as a ***transformational leader***—someone who understands and embodies the interpersonal and moral aspects of leadership. Through their passion and vision, transformational leaders inspire others through their deeply held beliefs and strong moral values. They are able to get others to join with them because they are enthusiastic and energetic. Their integrity leads others to trust them. Their genuine desire to see others succeed makes others more enthusiastic. This form of leadership, which is motivated by the welfare of everyone involved in a common effort, is markedly different from the form of leadership that only pays attention to the tasks at hand. Try to become the sort of leader that balances the work to be done with the professional and personal support of those working together.

Clearly, it is a challenge to be an effective leader in one's agency or profession. It is an even more difficult undertaking when the leader's goal is to promote social and economic justice. However, this is at the heart of social work. At a fundamental level, justice can be defined as fairness in relationships. Although there are several categories or types of justice, matters of social and economic justice are of special concern to social workers.

Social justice refers to the basic fairness and moral rightness of the social arrangements and institutional structures that impact the people of a community or society. Although closely related to economic justice, social justice focuses more on how society is organized and whether governmental and corporate policies and powerful groups recognize basic human rights and the dignity and worth of all people.

What threats to human rights and social injustices do you see as most challenging to address and why?

Human
Behavior

As you read the following mechanisms for maintaining power and oppression, identify the beliefs about human behavior and the social environment inherent in each.

Economic justice (also called *distributive justice*) can be defined as that dimension of justice having to do with the material or the economic aspects of a community or society. Economic justice denotes the fair apportioning and the distribution of economic resources, opportunities, and burdens. Principles of economic justice relate to fairness in, for example, wages paid for work performed, access to jobs, access to credit, prices charged for essential goods and services, and taxes imposed.

Because social and economic injustices are, by definition, embedded in existing institutional arrangements and social policies, many political, economic, and cultural forces are at work maintaining the unjust conditions. Those who seek change will encounter many powerful individuals and groups who will want to maintain the status quo. In order to secure real change, a leader working for social justice must be willing to take substantial risks and make significant personal sacrifices.

As a seeker of social justice, you will need to find ways to combat oppression. This means you must recognize and oppose the ways in which those in power might oppress others. Goldenberg (1978, 4–13) identifies several mechanisms (presumptions, beliefs, and deliberate actions) used by those in power to rationalize and perpetuate the oppressive and unjust conditions from which they benefit, directly or indirectly. These include:

- **Containment.** Efforts to restrict the opportunities and resources available to others in order to retain power and control over them.
- **Expendability.** A belief that some people and groups are more valuable to society and, therefore, devalued persons can be discarded, displaced, or ignored for the benefit of the society as a whole.
- **Compartmentalization.** Limiting people's exposure to enriching and empowering ideas, roles, and images in order to lessen their discontent. Creating and maintaining conflict and division among those without power in order to prevent them from developing a sense of shared problems, solidarity, and unity.
- **Personal culpability.** A belief system that presumes all of the social and economic problems experienced by people are matters of personal choice and moral character. Thus, because these are individual problems, existing systems and structures need not be changed and those with power are excused from trying to improve social and economic conditions for the people of a society.
- **Individual remediation.** A belief system holding that self-improvement is the only real answer to the existence of social problems. Thus, those who want a better life or who desire political power should first "pull themselves up by their bootstraps." Only after they prove their worth should they expect to participate in the political and economic decisions affecting their lives.

If you work for justice, you must understand that the belief systems and attitudes that perpetuate social and economic injustice can also be found in the thinking of those who are members of the various helping professions. Among social workers, there is a range of attitudes toward and perspectives on the appropriate place of social and political change in social work practice and on how such change is best achieved. Goldenberg (1978, 21–27) describes four of these. Think about which one best describes you.

1. The *social technician* identifies with and supports society's dominant values and its institutional structures. A professional with this

orientation seeks to help individuals adjust to the existing system and sees little need for changing social systems.

2. The ***traditional social reformer*** believes that oppressive social systems can be changed over time and works methodically to make those changes. The emphasis is on helping those with power understand the problem and decide that it is desirable and reasonable to make changes. The reformer trusts the tools of negotiation and mediation to build bridges between those with power and those without.

3. The ***social interventionist*** believes that bringing about needed social change will require conflict, consciousness raising, and change from the bottom up. An individual holding to this orientation assumes that those in power will accept change only when their survival and self-interest depend on it.

4. The ***social revolutionary*** is basically at odds with and rejects existing social institutions and the usual avenues of seeking change. The revolutionary believes that current systems and institutions are corrupt and cannot be salvaged. This individual is not satisfied with small steps or incremental change and believes that radical and revolutionary approaches are necessary to take power away from those who have it.

Alle-Corliss and Alle-Corliss (1999, 233) suggest that social workers can choose from a variety of professional stances as they take social action to effect change. The ***social prophet*** seeks to promote radical change not only by questioning the status quo, but by envisioning alternative perspectives, attitudes, and policies. The ***social visionary*** learns from the past and envisions a world in which social problems do not exist. The ***social reformer*** promotes change by directly confronting those who may be responsible for injustice and by influencing the structure of power through persuasion of actions of power. Whether you become a social prophet, a social visionary, or a social reformer, stay in touch with the values that underscore your views of social action and social justice. Regularly ask yourself how you think the world should be for those who inhabit it. Ask yourself what sorts of social institutions, policies, or programs will support that vision. Think about what sort of community nurtures its individuals and families. See what organizations do to help or hinder social functioning. Consider what you can do at each of these levels, sometimes simultaneously, to support individuals, families, and communities. Find others who share your vision, and make sure that your clients' visions for their lives become your visions also.

A good leader remembers the history of the movement in which he or she is involved, as well as the lessons of the past. Reflect in a critical and appreciative manner on the evolution of the social work profession and the many significant contributions of social workers to social justice and the building of a social welfare system. Educate yourself about the contributions of the social work profession in such areas as Social Security, civil rights, child labor laws, Medicaid, unemployment insurance, minimum wage, the peace movement, and many others. Consider the contributions made by those who developed theories of practice, assumed leadership in the academic preparation of professional social workers, and the countless clients whose lives and stories have provided the motivation and inspiration for such service.

Best practices guide the work of leaders. They are the accumulated wisdom of many practitioners, often compiled in written form, describing what social workers consider to be the standards of care and intervention by which we all measure our work. Identify best practices for your chosen field, and remember that your own work may define future best practices as you make your own contributions to the profession.

While appreciating the progress made by a profession only a century old, look to the future and the continuing evolution of the social work profession. Claim your history, be proud of it, and become part of the development of new knowledge, improved skills, and deeply felt values. Find ways to build a world that will be a better place because you have challenged injustices and held fast to the vision of a world in which opportunity and possibility are the possessions of all.

BECOMING THE PERSON YOU WANT TO BE

Many social workers say that social work is not what they do, but it is who they are. Their professional lives are guided by their personal beliefs, values, and spirituality, and they believe that being a social worker allows them to live out the beliefs and values they hold dear and feel passionate about. That notion indicates a compatible merger between person and the profession (see Chapter 18). However, always remember that you are now and will always be more than your profession and your job. If your whole identity is tied up in being a social worker, broaden your horizons and life experiences. You need to be healthy for your clients, but also for yourself, friends, and family.

Because very ordinary and small choices are very powerful in shaping our lives, strive as Gandhi urges to "be the change you want to see in the world." If you desire others to have more compassion and understanding, strive each day to become more compassionate and more understanding of others. If you desire others to be more generous and more involved in bringing about needed change, strive each day to be more generous with your time and money and involve yourself more deeply in social action and social change. If you desire others to be honest and responsible, strive to be honest and responsible in all of your own choices and actions, both the big ones and the small ones. Trust that those efforts will inspire and motivate others.

Your practicum will soon come to an end, and your professors and field instructors will tell you that you are ready for professional social work practice. You will have earned the designation of a professional social worker by virtue of your academic preparation, your practicum experience, your commitment to the National Association of Social Workers *Code of Ethics,* and your sense of calling to promote social justice. You have all of the tools needed to be a social worker, whether you are working with individual clients or whether your efforts are focused on large-scale social change. Those tools, including your knowledge, your commitment to helping others, and your helping skills, will all come together in a unique way as you become a professional social worker. In fact, you yourself are the tool by which clients will be served and social justice will be furthered. Welcome to the proactive, progressive, and visionary profession of social work.

Professional Identity

What vision of the world do you have, that if achieved by you and others during your professional careers, would allow you to consider yourself successful in your career of helping others?

Food for Thought

Social justice work is about building capacity and sharing leadership. Reaching back to the participatory democracy exemplified in the work of Jane Addams and other social reformers at the turn of the 20th century, a pattern emerges and weaves its way through social work history. This pattern is one of having faith in the capacity of humans, even under the most severe conditions, to challenge the conditions of their lives and participate in its transformation. Thinking of our practice, at least partially, as a way to create opportunities for participation and leadership development, provides us with a clear goal upon which to set our sights. It forces us to pose the following questions: How do I do my work in such a way that I build and support new forms of leadership? What forms and shapes might practice take should I strive to build the leadership capacity of those with whom I work? (Finn and Jacobson, 2008, 428).

• • •

Politics is simply social work with power.
—*Barbara Mikulski, social worker and Senator from Maryland*

• • •

The debate must focus on human rights for all, and we must believe that such a world is possible (Wronka, 2008, 12).

• • •

. . . [S]ocial workers are encouraged to see the empowerment process as beginning with the smallest of individual actions. When joined with others, these efforts create a chain reaction that releases human energy. Over time, this energy can build to become a critical mass that results in social change (Lum, 2006, 94).

• • •

If you think you're not political, guess again (Reisch, 1995, 1).

• • •

As we, as a profession, actively engage in the debate and invite others to participate, we would do well to remember that our ethical responsibility as social workers encompasses both efforts in harmony with the system and in opposition to the system (Lieberman and Lester, 2004, 416).

• • •

Learning is never finished, so resist the temptation to feel as if you must tie up all the loose ends. Instead, create an inventory for future work. Make a note in your journal of skills and behavior you still need to work on and experiences that repeating for consolidation. Acknowledging your strengths and evolving concerns is more helpful. It is not unusual to feel as if you are not ready to move on. Students often feel that they need more time in an internship. In fact, your supervisor will likely think you could benefit from more time in the internship. This is normal, and it is not to take away from what you know. Practice does make you more nearly perfect, but there will be plenty of time for that in the next phase of your learning (Thomlison and Corcoran, 2008, 374).

SUGGESTED LEARNING ACTIVITIES

- Subscribe to electronic listservs offered by professional organizations and advocacy groups to stay abreast of issues of importance to you, as well as legislative and social justice implications of their work.

- Search out web sites that will expand your understanding of social work's responsibility to maintain global standards of practice. For example, read the United Nations Universal Declaration of Human Rights.

- Read Pablo Freire's works, which describe the relationship between education and political struggles.

Succeed with **mysocialworklab**

Log onto **www.mysocialworklab.com** and select the **Interactive Skill Module** videos from the left-hand menu. Answer the following questions. (*If you did not receive an access code to* **MySocialWorkLab** *with this text and wish to purchase access online, please visit* www.mysocialworklab.com.)

1. **Now that you have watched all the Interactive Skill Modules,** what social justice efforts need to be undertaken in the fields of child welfare, domestic violence, or child welfare?

2. What leadership qualities are most important for those working toward social justice in the same fields listed above?

PRACTICE TEST

The following questions are similar in phrasing and content to those asked in social work licensing examinations. They should help you prepare to take the licensing examination in your state.

1. The NASW Code of Ethics preamble
   a. focuses on clinical social work
   b. focuses on human and societal well-being
   c. focuses on social change
   d. focuses on leadership

2. Social workers in leadership positions should promote social justice by
   a. earning a masters degree in social work
   b. supervising and mentoring social work students
   c. critically challenging societal assumptions and creating a vision for social justice
   d. focusing primarily on macro level practice

Human Rights & Justice

3. The professional knowledge obtained over time by social workers in practice is:
   a. continuing education
   b. practice wisdom
   c. self-awareness
   d. theory building

Critical Thinking

4. The process used by critically reflective social workers to examine their assumptions and examine new possibilities for practice is called:
   a. deconstruction
   b. self-evaluation
   c. peer supervision
   d. evidence based practice

5. Social workers wishing to become catalysts for social change can do so
   a. at any level of practice
   b. only at the macro level of practice
   c. through strategic planning in agency settings
   d. by engaging in counseling themselves

Human Rights & Justice

6. Empowerment in social work leadership refers to
   a. utilizing majority votes in client advocacy groups
   b. sharing power between social workers
   c. teaching clients to become peer counselors
   d. helping clients recognize and use the power they have

7. Which is true?
   a. social and economic justice are the same
   b. economic justice is one form of social justice
   c. social and economic justice are mutually exclusive
   d. none of the above

Appendix

SAMPLE LEARNING AGREEMENT

The following sample learning agreement used by The University of Montana School of Social Work BSW program presents goals for learning that can be reasonably expected of a typical social work practicum. Spaces are provided for you to devise your own learning objectives, including tasks and activities, to help you attain each set of goals, as well as your own criteria for monitoring progress and evaluating performance. This form can be used to structure the practicum experience and maximize learning. Note that some of the goals may need to be modified to fit the requirements of a particular school of social work and the unique characteristics of a particular practicum setting.

Practicum Learning Agreement

Student _____ Faculty Supervisor _____

Agency _____ Agency Field Instructor _____

INSTRUCTIONS: Student learning goals have been outlined in the left hand column. Students (in consultation with their agency field instructors), are to select activities that will help them reach these goals. Students are also to describe how their learning and performance will be evaluated. At the end of each semester, students will be evaluated by the agency supervisor on their learning and performance.

Learning Goals	Learning Objectives (Tasks & Activities to Reach Goals)	Monitoring/Evaluation Criteria
1. Social Work as a Profession a. Develop understanding of generalist social work practice b. Perform a variety of social work roles (e.g., broker, counselor, networker, case manager, educator, advocate, program planner, facilitator, policy analyst, researcher) c. Gain experience at various levels of practice (e.g., micro, mezzo, macro) and understand the implications of actions from different levels of practice for clients/client systems across the life span		

Learning Goals	Learning Objectives (Tasks & Activities to Reach Goals)	Monitoring/Evaluation Criteria
d. Apply the National Association of Social Workers' *Code of Ethics* in a practice setting		
2. Organizational Context of Practice a. Apply organizational analysis techniques to practicum agency b. Understand practicum agency's history, mission, purpose and function c. Understand practicum agency's structure and funding d. Understand practicum agency's methods for evaluating its effectiveness		
3. Community Context of Practice a. Understand the features of the community which impact clients: e.g., population, unemployment rates, cost of living, attitudes toward diverse populations, available recreation b. Identify both the strengths and problems of the community and issues relating to client populations c. Become aware of the range of community resources available, including gaps in services d. Utilize community resources		
4. Assessment a. Develop assessment skills for individuals, families, groups, organizations, and communities b. Develop skills in problem and strength identification c. Identify the major social systems involved with the problem or concern being addressed and their relationship to age groups d. Become familiar with the ongoing nature of assessment		

Learning Goals	Learning Objectives (Tasks & Activities to Reach Goals)	Monitoring/Evaluation Criteria
5. Planning and Intervention a. Acquire skills in goal setting, identifying measurable objectives, and planning of interventions b. Select appropriate level of intervention for individual client/client system needs (micro to macro) c. Develop intervention plans matched to client/client system needs, including client in selection of intervention d. Develop intervention skills based on theoretical understanding of client need and of interventions selected		
6. Termination and Evaluation a. Develop skills in appropriate termination and empowerment of clients b. Utilize tools and instruments to evaluate client progress c. Utilize tools and instruments to evaluate own professional performance d. Utilize tools and instruments to evaluate agency effectiveness		
7. Understanding Social Problems a. Understand one or more social problems from an ecosystems perspective b. Understand the major social problems addressed by practicum agency (e.g., etiology, incidence, causal factors, impact, consequences, multigenerational issues, prevention) c. Understand how social problems develop as a result of the interaction between individuals, social systems, and the larger social environment d. Identify the major social problems facing the community		
8. Social Policy and Social Change a. Analyze the development of social policies b. Analyze the effectiveness of social policies c. Assess the impact of social policies on clients and client systems across the life span d. Participate in social policy and social justice efforts		

Learning Goals	Learning Objectives (Tasks & Activities to Reach Goals)	Monitoring/Evaluation Criteria
9. Diversity a. Recognize the impact of diversity (e.g., culture, gender, age, disability, class, sexual orientation, religion) on clients b. Understand the impact of oppression, discrimination, prejudice, and stereotyping on clients c. Analyze practicum agency's ability to effectively and sensitively address the needs of diverse clients/client systems d. Communicate effectively and sensitively with members of diverse groups, individualizing interventions for diverse clients		
10. Communication Skills a. Communicate clearly and effectively in written form b. Communicate clearly and effectively in verbal form with clients, including nonvoluntary or hard-to-reach clients c. Communicate clearly and effectively in verbal form with co-workers and other professionals d. Demonstrate awareness of underlying client concerns		
11. Knowledge and Use of Self a. Recognize the impact of own personal issues/biases/values/attitudes on clients and make needed changes b. Establish effective and purposeful relationships with clients and co-workers c. Seek professional growth by taking initiative in designing and implementing learning activities d. Utilize professional supervision and training for guidance and learning		

Source: The University of Montana School of Social Work. Sample learning agreement used with permission of Tondy Baumgartner, MSW, Practicum Coordinator.

Selected Bibliography

Chapter 1

Alle-Corliss, Lupe, and Randy Alle-Corliss. *Advanced Practice in Human Service Agencies*. Boston: Brooks/ Cole, 1999.

Barker, Robert. *The Social Work Dictionary*. 5th ed. Washington, DC: NASW Press, 2003.

Berg-Weger, Marla, and Julie Birkenmaier. *The Practicum Companion for Social Work: Integrating Class and Field Work*. 2nd ed. Boston: Allyn and Bacon, 2007.

Brew, Leah and Jeffrey A. Kottler. *Applied Helping Skills: Transforming Lives*. Thousand Oaks, CA, 2008.

Chiaferi, Rosemary, and Michael Griffin. *Developing Fieldwork Skills*. Pacific Grove, CA: Brooks/Cole, 1997.

Cochrane, Susan F., and Marla Martin Hanley. *Learning through Field: A Developmental Approach*. Boston: Allyn and Bacon, 1999.

Commission on Accreditation. *Handbook of Accreditation Standards and Procedures, Educational Policies and Accreditation Standards*. Alexandria, VA: Council on Social Work Education, 2008.

Edwards, Richard L., ed. *Encyclopedia of Social Work*. 20th ed. Washington, DC: NASW Press, 2008.

Grobman, Linda May, ed. *The Field Placement Survival Guide: What You Need to Know to Get the Most from Your Social Work Practicum*. Harrisburg, PA: White Hat Communications, 2002.

Rogers, Gayla, Donald Collins, Constance Barlow, and Richard Grinnell. *Guide to the Social Work Practicum*. Itasca, IL: Brooks/Cole, 2000.

Rothman, Juliet. *The Self-Awareness Workbook for Social Workers*. Boston: Allyn and Bacon, 1999.

Rothman, Juliet. *Stepping Out into the Field: A Field Work Manual for Social Work Students*. Boston: Allyn and Bacon, 2000.

Royse, David, Surjit Singh Dhooper, and Elizabeth Rompf. *Field Instruction*. 5th ed. White Plains, NY: Longman, 2007.

Schneck, Dean, Bart Grossman, and Urania Glassman. *Field Education in Social Work*. Dubuque, IA: Kendall and Hunt, 1991.

Sheafor, Bradford, and Charles Horejsi. *Techniques and Guidelines for Social Work Practice*. 8th ed. Boston: Allyn and Bacon, 2008.

Sweitzer, H. Frederick, and Mary A. King. *The Successful Internship: Transformation and Empowerment in Experiential Learning*. 3rd ed. Florence, KY: Cengage Learning, 2008.

Chapter 2

Baird, Brian. *The Internship, Practicum, and Field Placement Handbook: A Guide for the Helping Professions*. 5th ed. Upper Saddle River, NJ: Prentice Hall, 2008.

Birkenmaier, Julie A. and Marla Berg-Weger. *The Practicum Companion for Social work: Integrating Class and Field Work*. 2nd ed. Boston: Allyn and Bacon, 2007.

Bogo, Marion, and Elaine Vayda. *The Practice of Field Instruction in Social Work*. 2nd ed. New York: Columbia University Press, 1998.

Commission on Accreditation. *Educational Policies and Accreditation Standards*. Alexandria, VA: Council on Social Work Education, 2008.

Grobman, Linda May, ed. *More Days in the Lives of Social Workers: 35 "Real-Life" Stories of Advocacy, Outrach, and Other Intriguing Roles in Social Work Practice*. Harrisburg, PA: White Hat Communications, 2005.

National Association of Social Workers. *Code of Ethics*. Washington, DC: NASW Press, 1999.

Sheafor, Bradford, and Charles Horejsi. *Techniques and Guidelines for Social Work Practice*. 7th ed. Boston: Allyn and Bacon, 2006.

Chapter 3

Baird, Brian. *The Internship, Practicum, and Field Placement Handbook: A Guide for the Helping Professions*. 4th ed. Upper Saddle River, NJ: Prentice Hall, 2008.

Commission on Accreditation. *Educational Policy and Accreditation Standards*. Alexandria, VA: Council on Social Work Education, 2008.

hooks, bell. *Teaching to Transgress: Education as the Practice of Freedom*. New York: Routledge, 1994.

Kolb, David. *Learning-Style Inventory*. Boston: McBer and Company Training Resources Group, 1981.

Kolb, David. *Experiential Learning: Experience as the Source of Learning and Development*. Upper Saddle River, NJ: Prentice Hall, 1984.

Sheafor, Bradford, and Charles Horejsi. *Techniques and Guidelines for Social Work Practice*. 7th ed. Boston: Allyn and Bacon, 2008.

University of Montana School of Social Work. *BSW Competency Catalogue*, 2008.

Chapter 4

Baird, Brian. *The Internship, Practicum, and Field Placement Handbook: A Guide for the Helping Professions*. 5th ed. Upper Saddle River, NJ: Prentice Hall, 2008.

Dolgoff, Ralph. *An Introduction to Supervisory Practice in Human Services*. Boston: Allyn and Bacon, 2005.

Healy, Karen. *Social Work Theories in Context: Creating Frameworks for Practice*. New York: Palgrave Macmillan, 2005.

Rothman, Juliet. *Stepping Out into the Field: A Field Work Manual for Social Work Students*. Boston: Allyn and Bacon, 2000.

Royse, David, Surjit Singh Dhooper and Elizabeth Lewis Rompf. *Field Instruction: A Guide for Social Work Students*. 5th ed. Boston: Allyn and Bacon, 2007.

Sweitzer, Frederic H. and Mary A. King. *The Successful Internship: Transformation and Empowerment in Experiential Learning*. 3rd ed. Pacific Grove, CA: Brooks Cole, 2009.

Walsh, Joseph. *Theories for Direct Social Work Practice*. Belmont, CA: Thomson Brooks/Cole, 2006.

Chapter 5

Baird, Brian N. *The Internship, Practicum, and Field Placement Handbook: A Guide for the Helping Professions.* 5th ed. Upper Saddle River, NJ: Prentice Hall, 2008.

Cohen, Robert. *Clinical Supervision: What to Do and How to Do It.* Pacific Grove, CA: Brooks/Cole, 2004.

Coulshed, Veronica, Audrey Mullender, David N. Jones, and Neil Thompson. *Management in Social Work.* 3rd ed. New York: Palgrave Macmillan, 2006.

Dolgoff, Ralph. *An Introduction to Supervisory Practice in Human Services.* Boston: Allyn and Bacon, 2005.

Ellison, Martha L. "Critical Field Instructor Behaviors: Student and Field Instructor Views." *Arete, Journal of the College of Social Work at the University of South Carolina* 18.2 (Winter 1994): 12–21.

Hayes, Robert, Gerald Corey, and Patricia Mouton. *Clinical Supervision in the Helping Professions: A Practical Guide.* Pacific Grove, CA: Brooks/Cole, 2003.

Kadushin, Alfred, and Daniel Harkness. *Supervision in Social Work.* 4th ed. New York: Columbia University Press, 2002.

Kaiser, Tamara. *Supervision as Collaboration in the Human Services: Building a Learning Culture.* Thousand Oaks, CA: Sage, 1997.

National Association of Social Workers. *Code of Ethics.* Washington, DC: NASW Press, 1999.

Rothman, Juliet Cassuto. *Stepping Out into the Field: A Field Work Manual for Social Work Students.* Boston: Allyn and Bacon, 2000.

Sheafor, Bradford, and Charles Horejsi, *Techniques and Guidelines in Social Work Practice.* 8th ed. Boston: Allyn and Bacon, 2008.

Shohet, Robin. *Supervision in the Helping Profesisons.* 3rd ed. Columbus, OH: Mayfield Publishing, 2007.

Shulman, Lawrence. *Interactional Supervision.* Washington, DC: NASW Press, 1992.

Tropman, John. *Supervision and Management in Nonprofits and Human Services: How Not to Become the Administrator You Always Hated.* Peosta, IA: Eddie Bowers Publishing, 2006.

Tsue, Ming-Sum. *Social Work Supervision: Context and Concepts.* Thousand Oaks, CA: Sage Publishing, 2004.

Weinbach, Robert. *The Social Worker as Manager: A Practical Guide to Success.* 5th ed. Boston: Allyn and Bacon, 2008.

Chapter 6

Birkenmaier, Julie and Marla Berg-Weger. *The Practicum Companion for Social Work: Integrating Class and Field Work.* 2nd ed. Boston: Allyn and Bacon, 2007.

Farestad, Karen. "Worker Safety: Agencies Should Recognize the Issue." *Protecting Children* 13.1 (1997): 2.

Harman, Patricia, and Molly Davis. "Personal Safety for Human Service Professionals: A Law Enforcement Perspective." *Protecting Children* 13.1 (1997): 15–17.

Horejsi, Charles, Cindy Garthwait, and Jim Rolando. "A Survey of Threats and Violence Directed against Child Protection Workers in a Rural State." *Child Welfare* (March, 1994): 173–179.

Irwin, Diane. "Safety Training for Human Services Professionals." *Protecting Children* 13.1 (1997): 8–10.

Newhill, Christina E. *Client Violence in Social Work Practice: Prevention, Intervention, and Research.* New York: Guilford Press, 2003.

Rey, Lucy. "What Social Workers Need to Know about Client Violence." *Families in Society* 77 (January, 1996): 33–39.

Sheafor, Bradford, and Charles Horejsi. *Techniques and Guidelines for Social Work Practice.* 8th ed. Boston: Allyn and Bacon, 2008.

Tully, Carol, Nancy Kropf, and Janet Price. "Is the Field a Hard Hat Area? A Study of Violence in Field Placements." *Journal of Social Work Education* 29.2 (Spring, 1993): 191–199.

Weinger, Susan. *Security Risk: Preventing Client Violence Against Social Workers.* Washington DC: NASW Press, 2001.

Chapter 7

Baird, Brian. *The Internship, Practicum, and Field Placement Handbook: A Guide for the Helping Profesions.* 4th ed. Upper Saddle River, NJ, 2008.

Baird, Brian. *The Internship, Practicum, and Field Placement Handbook: A Guide for the Helping Professions.* 5th ed. Upper Saddle River, NJ, 2008.

Beck, Andrew and Roger Smith. *Communication Skills and Social Work.* Columbus, OH: Mayfield Publishing, 2009.

Evans, William J., Daniel H. Honemann, Henry M. Robert, and Thomas J. Balch. *Robert's Rules of Order Newly Revised in Brief.* Boulder, CO: Perseus Books, 2004.

Kantz, Mary Kay and Kathryn Mercer. "Writing Effectively: A Kay Task for Managers" in *Skills for Effective Nonprofit Management.* Edwards, Richard L., John A. Yankey and Mary A. Altpeter. Washington DC: NASW Press, 1998.

Payne, Malcom. *What Is Professional Social Work?* 2nd ed. Chicago: Lyceum Books, 2007.

Sheafor, Bradford, and Charles Horejsi. *Techniques and Guidelines for Social Work Practice.* 8th ed. Boston: Allyn and Bacon, 2008.

Sidell, Nancy and Denise Smiley. *Professional Communication Skills in Social Work.* Boston: Allyn and Bacon, 2008.

Chapter 8

Austin, Michael J., Ralph P. Brody, and Thomas Packard. *Managing the Challenges in Human Services Organizations.* Thousand Oaks, CA: Sage Publishing, 2008.

Cooperider, David, and Suresh Srivasta. *Appreciative Management and Leadership.* San Francisco: Jossey-Bass, 1990.

Coulshed, Veronica, Audrey Mullender, David N. Jones, and Neil Thompson. *Management in Social Work.* New York: Palgrave Macmillan, 2006.

Dudley, James R. *Social Work Evaluaiton: Enhancing What We Do.* Chicago: Lyceum, 2009.

Haas, Richard N. *The Power to Persuade: How to Be Effective in Government, the Public Sector, or Any Unruly Organization.* Boston: Houghton-Mifflin, 1994.

Morales, Armando, and Bradford Sheafor. *Social Work: A Profession of Many Faces.* 11th ed. Boston: Allyn and Bacon, 2007.

O'Connor, Mary Catherine and F. Ellen Netting. *Organization Practice: A Guide to Understanding Human Services Organizations.* 2nd ed. Hoboken, NJ: John Wiley and Sons, 2009.

Rae, Ann, and Wanda Nicholas-Wolosuk. *Changing Agency Policy: An Incremental Approach.* Boston: Allyn and Bacon, 2003.

Sheafor, Bradford and Charles Horejsi. *Techniques and Guidelines for Social Work Practice.* 8th ed. Boston: Allyn and Bacon, 2008.

Unrau, Yvonne a., Peter A. Gabor, and Richard M. Grinnell. *Evaluation in Social Work: The Art and Science of Practice.* New York: Oxford University Press, 2007.

Weinbach, Robert. *The Social Worker as Manager: A Practical Guide to Success.* 5th ed. Boston: Allyn and Bacon, 2008.

Chapter 9

DiNitto, Diane and Aaron McNeece. *Social Work Issues and Opportunities in a Challenging Profession.* 3rd ed. Chicago: Lyceum Books, 2008.

Hardcastle, David, Stanley Wenocur, and Patricia Powers. *Community Practice: Theories and Skills for Social Workers.* 2nd ed. New York: Oxford University Press, 2004.

Hardina, Donna. *Analytical Skills for Community Organization and Practice.* New York: Columbia University Press, 2002.

Homan, Mark. *Promoting Community Change.* 2nd ed. Pacific Grove, CA: Brooks/Cole, 1999.

Homan, Mark. *Promoting Community Change: Making It Happen in the Real World.* 3rd ed. Belmont, CA: Brooks/Cole, 2004.

Lohmann, Nancy. *Rural Social Work Practice.* New York: Columbia University Press, 2005.

Netting, F. Ellen. *Social Work Macro Practice.* 4th ed. Boston: Allyn and Bacon, 2008.

Rubin, Herbert J. and Irene S. Rubin. *Community Organizing and Development.* 4th ed. Boston: Allyn and Bacon, 2008.

Sheafor, Bradford, and Charles Horejsi. *Techniques and Guidelines in Social Work Practice.* 7th ed. Boston: Allyn and Bacon, 2006.

Tropman, John E. *Strategies of Community Intervention.* 7th ed. Peosta, IA: Eddie Bowers Publishing, 2008.

Twelvetrees, Alan. *Community Work.* 4th ed. New York: Palgrave MacMillan, 2008.

Weil, Maria. *The Handbook of Community Practice.* Thousand Oaks, CA: Sage Publications, 2005.

Chapter 10

Becker, Dana. *The Myth of Empowerment: Women and the Therapeutic Culture in America.* New York: New York University Press, 2005.

Berlaget, Gai, and William Egelman. *Understanding Social Issues: Critical Analysis and Thinking.* 6th ed. Boston: Allyn and Bacon, 2003.

Edwards, Richard L., ed. *Encyclopedia of Social Work.* 20th ed. Washington, DC: Oxford University Press, 2007.

Eitzen, D. Stanley and George H. Sage. *Solutions to Social Problems: Lessons from State and Local Government.* Boston: Allyn and Bacon, 2009.

Eitzen, D. Stanley, Maxine Baca Zinn and Kelly E. Eitzen Smith. *Social Problems.* 10th ed. Boston: Allyn and Bacon, 2008.

Ginsberg, Leon. *Social Work Almanac.* Washington, DC: NASW Press, 1995.

Hardcastle, David A., Patricia R. Powers and Stanley Wenocur. *Community Practice: Theories and Skills for Social Workers.* 2nd ed. New York: Oxford University Press, 2004.

Hoefer, Richard. *Advocacy Practice for Social Justice.* Chicago: Lyceum Books, 2006.

Jansson, Bruce. *Becoming an Effective Policy Advocate: From Policy Practice to Social Justice.* 5th ed. Belmont, CA: Brooks/Cole, 2008.

Kettner, Peter M., Robert M. Moroney, and Lawrence L. Martin. *Designing and Managing Programs: An Effectiveness-Based Approach.* 3rd ed. Thousand Oaks, CA: Sage, 2008.

Leon-Guerrero, Anna. *Social Problems: Ccommunity, Policy, and Social Action.* 2nd ed. Thousand Oaks, CA: Pine Forge Press, 2009.

Lieberman, Alice. *The Social Workout Book: Strength-Building Exercises for the Pre-Professional.* Thousand Oaks, CA: Pine Forge Press, 1998.

Sullivan, Thomas. *Social Problems.* 8th ed. Boston: Allyn and Bacon, 2009.

Unrau, Yvonne A., Peter A. Gabor, and Richard M. Grinnell. *Evaluation in Social Work: The Art and Science of Practice.* 4th ed. New York: Oxford University Press, 2007.

Zastrow, Charles. *Social Problems.* 5th ed. Belmont, CA: Wadsworth, 2000.

Chapter 11

Barusch, Amanda S. *Foundations of Social Policy: Social Justice in Human Perspective.* 3rd ed. Florence, KY: Brooks/Cole, 2009.

Blau, Joel and Mimi Abramovitz. *The Dynamics of Social Welfare.* 2nd ed. New York: Oxford University Press, 2007.

Bochel, Hugh, Catherine Bochel, Robert Page, and Robert Sykes. *Social Policy: Themes, Issues and Debates.* 2nd ed. Boson: Longman, 2009.

Chambers, Donald and Kenneth Wedel. *Social Policy and Social Programs: A Method for The Practical Public Policy Analysis.* 5th ed. Boston: Allyn and Bacon, 2009.

DiNitto, Diana, and Linda Cummins. *Social Welfare: Politics and Public Policy.* 6th ed. Boston: Allyn and Bacon, 2007.

Dolgoff, Ralph and Donald Feldstein, *Understanding Social Welfare: A Search for Social Justice.* 8th ed. Boston: Allyn and Bacon, 2009.

Gilbert, Neil, and Paul Terrell. *Dimensions of Social Welfare Policy.* 6th ed. Boston: Allyn and Bacon, 2005.

Jansson, Bruce. *Becoming an Effective Policy Advocate.* 5th ed. Pacific Grove, CA: Brooks/Cole, 2008.

Long, Dennis D., Carolyn J. Tice, and John D. Morrison. *Macro Social Work Practice: A Strengths Perspective.* Belmont, CA: Thomson Brooks/Cole, 2006.

Lowy, Louis. *Social Work with the Aging.* 2nd ed. Prospect Heights, IL: Waveland, 1991.

Midgely, James. *The Handbook of Social Policy.* 2nd ed. Thousand Oaks, CA: Sage Publishing, 2009.

Mkandawire, Thandika. *Social Policy in a Developmental Context.* New York: Palgrave Macmillan, 2004.

National Association of Social Workers. *Social Work Speaks: NASW Policy Statements 2006–2009.* 7th ed. Washington, DC: NASW Press, 2006.

Perez-Koenig, Rosa, and Barry Rock, eds. *Social Work in the Era of Devolution: Toward a Just Practice.* New York: Fordham University, 2001.

Popple, Philip R., and Leslie Leighninger. *The Policy-Based Profession: An Introduction to Social Welfare Policy Analysis for Social Workers.* 4th ed. Boston: Allyn and Bacon, 2008.

Rocha, Cynthia. *Essentials of Social Policy Practice.* Thousand Oaks, CA: Sage Publishing, 2007.

Segal, Elizabeth. *Social Welfare Policy and Social Programs: A Values Perspective.* Florence, KY: Brooks Cole, 2007.

van Wormer, Katherine. *Confronting Oppression, Restoring Justice: From Policy Analysis to Social Action.* Alexandria, VA: CSWE Press, 2004.

Chapter 12

Anderson, Joseph, and Robin Wiggins Carter, eds. *Diversity Perspectives for Social Work Practice.* Boston: Allyn and Bacon, 2003.

Appleby, George A., Edgar Colon, and Julia Hamilton. *Diversity, Oppression, and Social Functioning: Person-in-Environment Assessment and Intervention.* 2nd ed. Boston: Allyn and Bacon, 2007.

Child Welfare League of America. *Cultural Competence Self-Assessment Instrument.* Washington, DC: Child Welfare League of America, 2002.

Cross, Terry. "Services to Minority Populations: Cultural Competence Continuum." *Focal Point* 3.1 (Fall 1988): 1–4.

Dhooper, Sirjit Singh, and Sharon S. Moore. *Social Work Practice with Culturally Diverse People.* Thousand Oaks, CA: Sage Publications, 2001.

Dominelli, Lena. *Anti-Racist Social Work.* 3rd ed. New York: Palgrave MacMillan, 2008.

Egan, Gerald. *Skilled Helping around the World: Addressing Diversity and Multiculturalism.* Belmont, CA: Thomson Brooks/Cole, 2006.

Laskowski, Timothy. *Every Good Boy Does Fine.* Dallas: Southern Methodist University, 2003.

Lum, Doman. *Culturally Competent Practice: A Framework for Understanding Diverse Groups and Justice Issues.* 3rd ed. Florence, KY: Brooks/Cole, 2007.

Lum, Doman. *Social Work Practice with People of Color: A Process-Stage Approach.* 5th ed. Pacific Grove, CA: Thomson Brooks/Cole, 2004.

National Association of Social Workers. *NASW Standards for Cultural Competence in Social Work Practice.* Washington DC: NASW Press, 2007.

Rothman, Julie C. *Cultural Competence in Process and Practice: Building Bridges.* Boston: Allyn and Bacon, 2007.

Shaefer, Richard. *Racial and Ethnic Groups.* 10th ed. Upper Saddle River, NJ: Prentice-Hall, 2006.

Sheafor, Bradford, and Charles Horejsi. *Techniques and Guidelines for Social Work Practice.* 8th ed. Boston: Allyn and Bacon, 2008.

Sisneros, Jose, Catherine Stakeman, Mildred C. Joyner, and Catheryne L. Schmitz. *Critical Multicultural Social Work.* Chicago: Lyceum, 2008.

Sue, Donald, and David Sue. *Counseling the Culturally Diverse: Theory and Practice.* 5th ed. New York: John Wiley and Sons, Inc., 2008.

Weaver, Hilary. *Explorations in Cultural Competence: Journeys to the Four Directions.* Florence, KY: Brooks/Cole, 2005.

Whittaker, James, and Elizabeth Tracy. *Social Treatment.* 2nd ed. New York: Aldine De Gruyter, 1989.

Wronka, James. *Human Rights and Social Justice: Social Action and Service for the Helping and Health Professions.* Thousand Oaks, CA: Sage Publishing, 2007.

Chapter 13

Barker, Robert L. *The Social Work Dictionary.* 5th. Washington, DC: NASW Press, 2003.

Commission on Accreditation. *Educational Policy and Accreditation Standards.* Alexandria, VA: CSWE, 2008.

DuBois, Brenda, and Karla Miley. *Social Work: An Empowering Profession.* 5th ed. Boston: Allyn and Bacon, 2008.

Finn, Janet L., and Maxine Jacobson. *Just Practice: A Social Justice Approach to Social Work.* 2nd ed. Peosta, IA: Eddie Bowers Publishing, 2008.

Gambrill, Eileen. *Social Work Practice. A Critical Thinker's Guide.* 2nd ed. New York: Oxford University Press, 2006.

Haynes, Karen and Mickelson, James. *Affecting Change: Social Workers in the Political Arena.* 4th ed. Boston: Allyn and Bacon, 2000.

Hokenstad, M. C., and James Midgley. *Lessons from Abroad: Adapting International Social Welfare Innovations.* Washington, DC: NASW Press, 2004.

National Association of Social Workers. *Code of Ethics.* Washington, DC: NASW Press, 1999.

Payne, Malcolm. *Modern Social Work Theory.* 3rd ed. Chicago: Lyceum, 2005.

Reid, P. Nelson, and Philip R. Popple. *The Moral Purposes of Social Work: The Character and Intentions of a Profession.* Chicago: Nelson-Hall Publishers, 1992.

Sheafor, Bradford, and Charles Horejsi. *Techniques and Guidelines for Social Work Practice.* 8th ed. Boston: Allyn and Bacon, 2008.

Sheppard, Michael. *Social Work and Social Exclusion: the Idea of Practice.* Burlington, VT: Ashgate Publishing, 2006.

Specht, Harry, and Mark Courtney. *Unfaithful Angels: How Social Work Has Abandoned Its Mission.* New York: Free Press, 1995.

Thompson, Neil. *Anti-Discriminatory Practice.* 3rd ed. Palgrave, 2001.

Chapter 14

Baird, Brian N. *The Internship, Practicum, and Field Placement Handbook: A Guide for the Helping Professions.* 4th ed. Upper Saddle River, NJ: Prentice Hall, 2005.

Banks, Sarah. *Ethics and Values in Social Work.* 3rd ed. New York: Palgrave Macmillan, 2008.

Corey, Gerald, Marianne Schneider, and Patrick Callahan. *Issues and Ethics in the Helping Professions.* 6th ed. Florence, KY: Brooks/Cole, 2003.

Dolgoff, Ralph, Frank Loewenberg, and Donna Harrington. *Ethical Decisions for Social Work Practice.* 8th ed. Florence, KY: Brooks/Cole, 2009.

Galper, Jeffrey. "Code of Ethics for Radical Social Service." In *The Politics of Social Services.* Englewood Cliffs, NJ: Prentice Hall, 1975.

Hartsell, Thomas L. and Barton E. Bernstein. *The Portable Ethicist for Mental Health Porfessionals: An A-Z Guide to Responsible Practice.* New York: John Wiley and Sons, 2000.

National Association of Social Workers. *Code of Ethics.* Washington, DC: NASW Press, 1999.

Payne, Malcolm. *What Is Professional Social Work?* 2nd ed. Chicago: Lyceum Books, 2007.

Pilseker, C. "Values: A Problem for Everyone." *Social Work* 23 (1978): 54–57.

Reamer, Frederick. *Ethical Standards in Social Work: A Review of the NASW Code of Ethics.* 2nd ed. Washington DC: NASW Press, 2006.

Ruggiero, Vincent. *Thinking Critically about Ethical Issues.* 7th ed. Boston: McGraw Hill, 2008.

Sheafor, Bradford, and Charles Horejsi. *Techniques and Guidelines for Social Work Practice.* 8ed. Boston: Allyn and Bacon, 2008.

Somers Flanagan, Rita and John Somers Flanagan. *Becoming an Ethical Helping Professional: Cultural and Philosophical Foundations.* Thousand Oaks, CA: Sage Publishing, 2007.

Strom-Gottfried. *Straight Talk about Professional Ethics.* Chicago: Lyceum Books, 2007.

Thomlison, Barbara and Kevin Corcoran, ed. *The Evidence-Based Internship: A Field Manual.* New York: Oxford University Press, 2008.

Chapter 15

Albert, Raymond. *Law and Social Work Practice: A Legal Systems Approach.* 2nd ed. New York: Springer Publishing Company, 2000.

Baird, Brian N. *The Internship, Practicum, and Field Placement Handbook: A Guide for the Helping Professions.* 5th ed. Upper Saddle River, NJ: Prentice Hall, 2008.

Barker, Robert, and Douglas Branson. *Forensic Social Work: Legal Aspects of Professional Practice.* 2nd ed. New York: Haworth, 2000.

Bernstein, Barton E., and Thomas L. Hartsell, Jr. *The Portable Guide to Testifying in Court for Mental Health Professionals: An A–Z Guide to Being an Effective Witness.* Hoboken, NJ: John Wiley and Sons, 2005.

Birkenmaier, Julie and Marla Berg-Weger. *The Practicum Companion for Social Work: Integrating Class and Field Work.* 2nd ed. Boston: Allyn and Bacon, 2007.

Bullis, Ronald. *Clinical Social Worker Misconduct: Law, Ethics, and Interpersonal Dynamics.* Chicago: Nelson-Hall, 1995.

Edwards, Richard L., John A. Yankey, and Mary A. Altpeter, eds. *Effective Management of Non-Profit Organizations.* Washington, DC: NASW Press, 1998.

Houston-Vega, Mary K., Elane M. Nuehring, and Elizabeth R. Daguio. *Prudent Practice: A Guide for Managing Malpractice Risk.* Washington, DC: NASW Press, 1997.

Kurzman, Paul A. "Managing Risk in Nonprofit Settings." In *Skills for Effective Management of Nonprofit Organizations.* Washington, DC: NASW Press, 1998.

National Association of Social Workers. *Code of Ethics.* Washington, DC: NASW Press, 1997.

Pollack, Daniel. *Social Work and the Courts.* 2nd ed. New York: Garland, 2003.

Reamer, Frederic. *Social Work Malpractice and Liability.* New York: Columbia University Press, 1994.

Reamer, Frederic. *Social Work Malpractice and Liability.* 2nd ed. New York: Columbia University Press, 2003.

Schroeder, Leila. *The Legal Environment of Social Work.* Washington, DC: NASW Press, 1995.

Sheafor, Bradford, and Charles Horejsi. *Techniques and Guidelines for Social Work Practice.* 8th ed. Boston: Allyn and Bacon, 2008.

Chapter 16

Alle-Corliss, Lupe, and Randy Alle-Corliss. *Advanced Practice in Human Service Agencies: Issues, Trends and Treatment Perspectives.* Belmont, CA: Wadsworth, 1999.

Brill, Naomi, and Joanne Levine. *Working with People: The Helping Process.* 8th ed. Boston: Allyn and Bacon, 2005.

Cournoyer, Barry R. *The Evidence-Based Social Work Skills Book.* Boston: Pearson Education, 2005.

Finn, Janet L., and Maxine Jacobson. *Just Practice: A Social Justice Approach to Social Work.* 2nd ed. Peosta, IA: Eddie Bowers Publishing, 2007.

Hull, Grafton. *Understanding Generalist Practice with Families.* Pacific Grove, CA: Brooks/Cole, 2006.

Jordan, Catheleen and Cynthia Franklin. *Clinical Assessment for Social Workers: Qualitative and Quantitative Methods.* 2nd ed. Chicago: Lyceum Books, 2003.

Karls, James M. and Maura O'Keefe. *Persno-in-Environment System Manual.* 2nd ed. Washington DC: NASW Press, 2008.

Miller, William R., Stephen Rollnick, and Kelly Conforti. *Motivational Interviewing: Preparing People for Change.* 2nd ed. New York: Guilford Press, 2002.

Mizrahi, Terry, ed. *Encyclopedia of Social Work.* 20th ed. New York: Oxford University Press, 2008.

Netting, F. Ellen, Peter McKettner, and Steven L. McMurty. *Social Work Macro Practice.* Boston: Allyn and Bacon, 2004.

O'Hare, Thomas. *Evidence-based Practices for Social Workers: An Interdisciplianry Approach.* Chicago: Lyceum Books, 2005.

Payne, Malcolm. *Modern Social Work Theory.* 3rd ed. Chicago: Lyceum, 2005.

Plionis, Elizabeth Moore. *Competency in Generalist Practice: A Guide to Theory and Evidence-Based Decision Making.* New York: Columbia University Press, 2006.

Roberts, Albert R. *Social Workers' Desk Reference.* 2nd ed. New York: Oxford University Press, 2009.

Saleeby, Dennis, ed. *The Strengths Perspective in Social Work Practice.* 4th ed. Boston: Allyn and Bacon, 2006.

Sheafor, Bradford, and Charles Horejsi. *Techniques and Guidelines for Social Work Practice.* 8th ed. Boston: Allyn and Bacon, 2008.

Schweitzer, H. Fredrick and Mary King. *The Successful Internship: Personal, Professional, and Civic Development.* Florence, KY: Brooks/Cole, 2009.

Chapter 17

Baird, Brian N. *The Internship, Practicum, and Field Placement Handbook.* 5th ed. Upper Saddle River, NJ: Prentice Hall, 2008.

Brun, Carl F. *A Practical Guide to Social Service Evaluation.* Chicago: Lyceum Books, 2005.

Courneyer, Barry R., and Mary J. Stanley. *The Social Work Portfolio: Planning, Assessing and Documenting Lifelong Learning in a Dynamic Profession.* Pacific Grove, CA: Brooks/Cole, 2002.

Drake, Robert E., Matthew R. Merrens, and David W. Lynde, eds. *Evidence-Based Mental Health Practice: A Textbook.* New York: W. W. Norton, 2005.

Ellis, Rodney A., Kimberly Crane, Misty Y. Gould, and Suzanne Shatila. *The Macro Practitioner's Workbook: A Step-by-Step Guide to Effectiveness of Organizations and Communities.* Florence, KY: Brooks Cole, 2008.

National Association of Social Workers. *Code of Ethics.* Washington, DC: NASW Press, 1999.

Roberts, Albert R. *Social Workers' Desk Reference.* 2nd ed. New York: Oxford University Press, 2009.

Rothman, Juliet Cassuto. *The Self-Awareness Workbook for Social Workers.* Boston: Allyn and Bacon, 1999.

Sheafor, Bradford, and Charles Horejsi. *Techniques and Guidelines for Social Work Practice.* 8th ed. Boston: Allyn and Bacon, 2008.

Chapter 18

Armstrong, Richard, and Edward Wakin. *You Can Still Change the World.* New York: Harper and Row, 1978.

Birkenmaier, Julie and Marla Berg-Weger. *The Practicum Companion for Social work: Integrating Class and Field Work.* 2nd ed. Boston: Allyn and Bacon, 2007.

Gibelman, Margaret. *What Social Workers Do.* 2nd ed. Washington, DC: NASW Press, 1995.

Loeb, Paul Rogat. *Soul of a Citizen: Living with Conviction in a Cynical Time*. New York: St. Martin's Griffin, 1999.

Macy, Joanna. *World as Lover, World as Self*. Berkeley, CA: Parallax Press, 1991.

Rothman, Juliet Cassuto. *The Self-Awareness Workbook for Social Workers*. Boston: Allyn and Bacon, 1999.

Schmidt, Jona J. *Intentional Helping: Philosophy for Proficient Caring Relationships*. Upper Saddle River, NJ: Prentice Hall, 2002.

Schon, Donald A., and Aleksandr Romanovich Luria. *The Reflective Practitioner: How Professionals Think in Action*. New York: Basic Books, 1990.

Sheafor, Bradford, and Charles Horejsi. *Techniques and Guidelines for Social Work Practice*. 8th ed. Boston: Allyn and Bacon, 2008.

Chapter 19

Alle-Corliss, Lupe, and Randy Alle-Corliss. *Advanced Practice in Human Service Agencies: Issues, Trends, and Treatment Perspectives*. Florence, KY: Brooks/ Cole, 1999.

Bloom, Sandra. *Creating Sanctuary: Toward the Evolution of Sane Societies*. New York: Routledge, 1997.

Chambon, Adrienne, S., Allan Irving, and Laura Epstein, eds. *Reading Foucault for Social Work*. New York: Columbia University Press, 1999.

Figueira-McConough, Josefina. *The Welfare State and Social Work: Pursuing Social Justice*. Thousand Oaks, CA: Sage Publishing, 2007.

Finn, Janet L., and Maxine Jacobson. *Just Practice: A Social Justice Approach to Social Work*. 2nd ed. Peosta, IA: Eddie Bowers Publishing, 2008.

Freire, Pablo. *Pedagogy of the Oppressed*. New York: Seabury, 1973.

Freire, Pablo. *Pedagogy of the Heart*. New York: Continuum, 1997.

Gil, David. *Confronting Oppression and Injustice: Concepts and Strategies for Social Workers*. New York: Columbia Press, 1998.

Goldenberg, Ira. *Oppression and Social Intervention*. Chicago: Nelson-Hall, 1978.

Haynes, Karen S., and James S. Mickelson. *Affecting Change: Social Workers in the Political Arena*. 6th ed. Boston: Allyn and Bacon, 2006.

Hoefer, Richard. *Advocacy Practice for Social Justice*. Chicago: Lyceum Books, 2006.

Lieberman, Alice A., and Cheryl B. Lester. *Social Work Practice with a Difference: Stories, Essays, Cases, and Commentaries*. Boston: McGraw Hill, 2004.

Lum, Doman. *Culturally Competent Practice: A Framework for Understanding Diverse Groups and Justice Issues*. 3rd ed. Florence, KY: Wadsworth Publishing, 2006.

Payne, Malcolm. *Modern Social Work Theory*. 3rd ed. Chicago: Lyceum Books, 2005.

Reisch, M. "If You Think You're Not Political, Guess Again." *NASW Network* 21.13 (1995): 1.

Specht, Harry, and Mark E. Courtney. *Unfaithful Angels: How Social Work Has Abandoned Its Mission*. New York: Free Press, 1994.

Thomlison, Barbara and Kevin Corcoran, eds. *The Evidence-Based Internship: A Field Manual*. New York: Oxford University Press, 2008.

Wronka, Joseph. *Human Rights and Social Justice: Social Action and Service for the Helping and Health Professions*. Thousand Oaks, CA: Sage Publishing, 2008.

Photo credits: